AS TO ROGER WILLIAMS,

AND HIS

'Banishment' from the Massachusetts Plantation;

WITH A FEW FURTHER WORDS

CONCERNING

THE BAPTISTS, THE QUAKERS, AND RELIGIOUS LIBERTY:

A Monograph,

BY

HENRY MARTYN DEXTER, D.D.,

Member of the Massachusetts Historical Society, the American Antiquarian Society, and the New England Historic-Genealogical Society; Corresponding Member of the Long Island Historical Society; Editor of THE CONGREGATIONALIST; *Author of "Congregationalism: Whence it is, What it is," etc.; "The Church Polity of the Pilgrims, the Polity of the New Testament;" "Pilgrim Memoranda," etc.; and Editor of Wiggin's Annotated Exact Reprint of "Mourt's Relation," "Church's Philip's War, and Eastern Expeditions," etc.*

Πάταξον μὲν ἔφη, ἄκουσον δέ.

BOSTON:
CONGREGATIONAL PUBLISHING SOCIETY,
1876.

ELECTROTYPED BY
THOMAS TODD,
CONGREGATIONAL HOUSE,
BOSTON.

FRANKLIN PRESS:
RAND, AVERY, AND COMPANY,
117 FRANKLIN STREET,
BOSTON.

TO THE

HONORABLE ROBERT C. WINTHROP, LL.D.,

President of the Massachusetts Historical Society.

My Dear Sir:

For a contemporary record of the greater portion of the events which illustrate the relation of Roger Williams to the Massachusetts men, posterity is indebted to the diligent and candid pen of your noble and illustrious ancestor, "ye Governour." This circumstance suggested the desire — which the sense of your eminent worthiness of such a lineage, and a large experience, these many years, of your marked personal kindness, have confirmed — to be permitted thus to associate your Name with this endeavor to throw additional light upon the life and character of the renowned, but unpretending, Founders of the Colony of the Bay.

I have the honor to be,

With great and grateful regard,

Faithfully yours,

HENRY M. DEXTER.

INTRODUCTORY NOTE.

A FEW excellent — if not erudite — people last winter petitioned our General Court to revoke "the sentence of banishment against Roger Williams," which was decreed in 1635. They urged such action, in the interest of "historical justice," on the ground that that decree was in the nature of punishment for the "offence" of his advocacy of "perfect religious liberty."

I have sought to take advantage of any possible public interest growing out of this remarkable procedure, to invite the intelligent, thinking and candid portion of the community, to re-examine the whole subject of the relation of the Massachusetts people of the seventeenth century to the case of the distinguished person whose memory this petition aimed to vindicate; and, later, to the case of the Baptists and Quakers, as well. I have been the more anxious to do this, because the limited acquaintance of some of our earliest historians with the facts — to say nothing of any misconceptions, or prejudices, which made it easier for them to see things in one light than in another — has introduced much erroneous conception, and consequent honest misrepresentation, to the pages of many modern histories having wide circulation, and giving tone to the public mind, but which have been written by scholars quite too content to take such writers as Hubbard, Backus and Bentley for their warrant, without the pains to go behind them to those underlying registers, treatises and documents, which are, in reality, the only "original" authorities.

The task — a very humble, if an arduous one — which I set for myself, was to go carefully through all accessible records, books and papers, which from their date, intent, or authorship, offer any coeval contribution of fact to the illustration of the subject in hand; and then collate and arrange the results. I cannot aver that my research has been exhaustive; only that I have sought to make it such. I cannot claim that I have succeeded perfectly, and without any coloring from prejudgment, in classifying and harmonizing the fruits of that research; only that I have conscientiously endeavored to do so. I cannot hope that, as the result of the new view which, in this contemporaneous light, is put upon many passages in the history, the world will be convicted of a great wrong hitherto largely done to the memory of the Puritans of Massachusetts; but I must be allowed to think that any historian who shall go on to reproduce the former slanders in the face of the demonstration of their true character herein offered, must — unless he refute it — fairly be condemned as paying better fealty to indolence, or prejudice, than to the truth.

For greater clearness, all dates of importance — as will be seen — have been given in both Old Style and New.

I have only to add that, as I have intended to make no statement, however comparatively unimportant, which does not rest upon valid evidence, and as I have desired in all cases to guide others to the sources of knowledge which I have found for myself; I have no apology to make for the notes with which, otherwise, so small a treatise might seem to be overburdened.

H. M. D.

Greystones, New Bedford, 15 Jan. 1876.

THE general subject of the character of Roger Williams, and of his relation to the early colonists of New England, has been called up to public attention afresh by a petition from sundry residents in the town of Sturbridge, Mass., addressed to the Massachusetts Legislature of 1874–5, asking them to revoke the order of banishment before which, in the winter of 1635–6, he retreated into what is now known as Rhode Island. It is not important here to refer to the various inaccuracies of statement found in that petition itself, or to discuss either the legal question how far the General Court of the Commonwealth, in these years of Grace, has power to annul action taken by the Court of the Colony two hundred and forty years ago; or the moral question, how much such action, if taken, could do in the way of securing any needed "justice" toward the remarkable man to whom reference is made, or to his memory. It does seem to be suitable, however, to avail of the occasion for making a clear, authentic and complete statement of the facts, as they actually occurred; to the end that slanders oft-repeated may be seen in their true character, and "justice" be done to *all* the noble memories involved.

It is astonishing how much the inherent difficulty of thoroughly comprehending a man who lived two or three hundred years ago is increased, if he were a somewhat pivotal and distinguished person; and, more especially, if he have been subsequently taken up and glorified, as their pet hero, by any large and enthusiastic body of believers. This seems to be particularly true of Roger Williams. The materials for his exact history are exceptionally abundant. Of few who shared with him the labors, and excitements, and controversies, of the first half-century of New England, will the close student discover so many and so amply revealing testimonies; from his own hand in letters and treatises, and from the hands of friends and enemies in letters, records, and anti-treatises. He, of all men, ought, by this time, to be as accurately as widely known. But the denomination of Christians known as Baptists, having canonized him — although never such a Baptist as they are, and for but a very short period of time a Baptist at all — have manifested great reluctance to give due consideration to a large portion of the evidence bearing upon the case; and seem to prefer, without regard to facts making fatally against their position, to re-utter the old encomiums and denunciations; as if an inadequate statement could, by persistent reiteration, be made a whole truth.

It has thus become a common representation of the case, that it was the Church-and-State controversy, and Mr. Williams's superior liberality on that subject, which led to his banishment; and it has even gone so far that leading journals[1] of that denomination scout the very idea of any other view, as something which to all the rest of the world but Massachusetts is special pleading, that is, on the face of it, absurd.

There is a very simple, albeit a laborious, way to settle this question. It is the only way in which it ever can be settled. It is to go straight to the original sources, and candidly, and in detail, to examine them, and make up a judgment upon them; without regard to the rhetoric of superficial biographers, or prejudiced historians, or the misapprehensions of a later public sentiment by them misled. This it is proposed now to attempt.

As is true of so many of those best known in connection with the settlement of New England, it is extremely difficult, if not impossible, to fix with absolute certainty the date, and place, of the birth of Roger Williams. All that can be positively *proved* concerning his early life is that, when a youth, he attracted the favorable attention of Sir Edward Coke, and, on his influence, was elected a scholar of Sutton's Hospital (now the Charter House) 25 June–5 July, 1621;[2] that he obtained an exhibition there 9–19 July, 1624;[3] and that he was matriculated a pensioner of Pembroke College, Cambridge, 7–17 July, 1625, and took the degree of Bachelor of Arts there in January, 1626–7.[4] It is *probable*

---

[1] The *Examiner and Chronicle* of 7 April, 1875, blandly reaffirms, without so much as an apology for the want of proof, the old notion that it was this controversy which led to the harsh action of the colony; with amusing conceit intimating that it is superfluous to thresh again the straw of this old controversy, because "all the world outside of Massachusetts [which happens to have in her archives the best material in the world for judgment; some of it in the shape of 'straw' that never yet was 'threshed'] has long since made up its verdict." And the *Watchman and Reflector* of 15 April—replying to an article in the *Christian Register*—says again: "the main ground of the action against Williams was his doctrine of soul-liberty." It goes on: "Toleration was [by the Massachusetts men] decreed as a fountain-head of heresy, even as original sin was the primal source of all sins. . . He proclaimed truth against the [this] mighty error of our fathers. That his views, if he had been let alone, would have wrecked the colony, is absurd. They would have saved it from a long dark night in its history, and made it the brightest spot on earth." It surely cannot be an error to assume that, so far as it takes representation in the columns of two of its principal journals, the historical scholarship of the Baptist denomination now stands pledged to this proposition: that Roger Williams was banished by the Massachusetts Colony specifically for asserting the doctrine of "soul-liberty," and for advocating universal toleration in religion.

[2] *Sadleir MSS.* in the Library of Trinity College, Cambridge.

[3] *Records of Charter House.* Elton's *Life of Roger Williams,* 10, 100.

[4] Arnold, in his, for the most part, excellent *History of Rhode Island,* [i: 47–50] discusses this subject with care and candor. He gives full weight to Prof. Elton's examination of the matter, and to all the evidence adduced by him in proof that *Rodericus* Williams, who entered at Jesus College, Oxford, from Conwyl Cayo in Wales, was our Roger; but is compelled — by various considerations — to decide that the weight of probability strongly favors the conclusion that *Rogerus* Williams, whose name appears upon the "subscription book" of Pembroke College, Cambridge, under date of 1626, was the man. There would seem to be no reasonable doubt that he is right.

that he was a native of Wales;[5] that he was born between 1599 and 1603;[6] that he had the inestimable advantage of pious parentage;[7] and that he was beneficed in Lincolnshire,[8] or its neighborhood, before coming to New England, and became a Nonconformist there. There is a story, which seems to rest purely upon tradition, that he studied law for a time after leaving the university.[9]

As to the steps along which the mind of Mr. Williams was led in his progress through Nonconformity to the principles of rigid Separation, we are not informed; but there is evidence of a severe mental struggle on his part.[10] When fully persuaded in his own mind, he embarked from Bristol with his wife Mary in the ship Lyon, Captain Pierce master, 1–11 Dec. 1630, and after a tedious and tempestuous voyage of sixty-six days, arrived off Nantasket 5–15 February following. Winthrop notes his arrival as that of "a godly minister."[11]

Two facts may wisely be remembered at this point, before entering upon the minute details of the transactions of the next five years. In the first place, Roger Williams was still very young. According to Prof. Elton, he would be scarcely more than twenty-five; by the chronology which seems more probable, he would not be over thirty-one, if more than twenty-eight. In the second

---

[5] All traditions agree as to this, and the family name there abounds.

[6] Benedict [*History of the Baptists*, i: 473,] quotes the records of the First Baptist Church in Providence as fixing his birth in 1598. But of course this is not a cotemporary record, and Knowles [*Memoir of Roger Williams*, 23] thinks 1599 the true year; as also do Gammell [*Life of Roger Williams*, 6] and Guild [*Pub. Narragansett Club*, i: 5]. Prof. Elton [*Life of Roger Williams*, 8, 9,] cites an entry of the admission of "*Rodericus* Williams, filius Gulielmi W. de Conwelgaio, Pleb. an. nat. 18," at Jesus College, Oxford, 30 April, 1624, in proof that Roger Williams was born in 1606 at Conwyl Cayo, in Carmarthen, South Wales. But that would be *Roderic* and not Roger; while Arnold seems to have proved that Roger studied at Cambridge and not Oxford—leading to the conclusion that Prof. Elton's "Rodericus" must have been another man. Williams himself has made three contributions toward the settlement of this date. In a document of 21 July, 1679, [Backus's *Hist. N. E.* i: 421] he speaks of himself as "being now near to four-score years of age;" in his address to the people called Quakers [*Geo. Fox Digged out of His Burrowes, etc.* vi:] dated 10 Mar. 1672–3, he says, "from my childhood, now above three-score years;" and in a letter to Jno. Winthrop, about 1632, [4 *Mass. Hist. Coll.* vi: 185,] he speaks of himself as "neerer vpwards of 30 then 25." The first would well suit either 1598 or 1599; the second might fit those years, but would better accord with a later birth-date; while the third, if construed literally (as not meaning that he was over 30, but was nearer that than 25) would make him then about 28; which would fix his birth not far from 1603.

[7] *Geo. Fox Digged, etc.*, vi.

[8] Hubbard [*Gen. Hist. New-England*, 206] says "in Essex, where he lived." But Williams himself incidentally alludes [*Bloudy Tenent yet more Bloudy, etc.* 12,] to a ride with Cotton and Hooker, "to, and from, Sempringham." Cotton was at Boston, and Boston and Sempringham are in Lincolnshire.

[9] *Benedict*, i: 474.

[10] "Truly it was as bitter as death to me when Bishop Laud pursued me out of this land, and my conscience was persuaded against the national church, and ceremonies, and bishops, beyond the conscience of your dear father [Sir Edward Coke.] I say it was as bitter as death to me, when I rode Windsor way, to take ship at Bristow [Bristol] and saw Stoke House [*Stoke Pogis, Buckinghamshire*], where the blessed man was; and I then durst not acquaint him with my conscience, and my flight." [*Letter to Mrs. Sadleir. Sadleir MSS. Elton*, 89.] "He [God] knows what gains and preferments I have refused in universities, city, country, and court, in Old England, and something in New England, &c., to keep my soul undefiled in this point, and not to act with a doubting conscience, etc." [*Letter to Rev. John Cotton, Jr.*, 25 March, 1671. *Proceedings Mass. Hist. Soc.* March, 1858, 316.]

[11] Winthrop's *Journal*, i: 41.

place, while never the most sedate, deliberate and conservative of men, he was now also — if we are to take the most kindly-phrased testimony of good and candid men who knew him at the time, and had much general regard for him; men like Elder William Brewster,[12] and Governor Bradford[13] — hasty to rashness, much given to extreme opinions, and very unsettled in the same.

John Wilson, pastor of the Boston church, was now on the point of revisiting England for some domestic reasons — in fact, sailed in the Lyon on her return voyage — and there is evidence that the church invited Mr. Williams to supply his place during this absence; and that he refused, on the ground of conscience, because they were "an unseparated people."[14] As Wilson left in less than sixty days after Williams landed, and as it is stated that when he did go he "commended them to the exercise of prophecy in his absence, and designated those whom he thought most fit for it, viz.: the Governor (Winthrop), Mr. Dudley, and Mr. Nowell the elder;"[15] it follows that the invitation given to Mr. Williams, with the reply made by him, must have taken place almost immediately after his arrival. It would seem to follow very naturally, also, that such a curt, off-hand, condemnation of this important church, and of the ablest and best men of the colony who were members of it, as he appears to have connected with his refusal, could hardly have failed to excite a feeling of prejudice against its utterer, mingled with solicitude lest the infant settlement might be in danger of trouble from him; nor would this feeling take much abatement from the consideration that it was a stripling stranger of scarcely a score and a half of years, who was thus assuming to sit in judgment upon his elders.[16]

This may well prepare us for the next intimation, on the 12–22 April following, to the effect that the Court, hearing that the church at Salem had invited Mr. Williams to be their teacher, caused a letter to be written to Mr. Endecott to say that they hoped the Salem people would act cautiously, and not proceed in this matter without due advisement; inasmuch as Mr. Williams had refused to fellowship the Boston church because it was not ready to proceed to the extreme of separation; and because he had broached novel opinions, "that the magistrate might not punish the breach of the Sabbath, nor any other offence,

---

12 Morton's *New-Englands Memoriall*, (first edition), 78.

13 Bradford's *History of Plimoth Plantation*, 310.

14 This rests wholly upon Mr. Williams's own testimony, no reference being made to it, so far as is known, in any record, by any other writer. In his letter to John Cotton, Jr., already cited, in 1671, he says: "being unanimously chosen teacher at Boston (before your dear father came, divers years) I conscientiously refused, and withdrew to Plymouth, because I durst not officiate to an unseparated people, as, upon examination and conference, I found them to be." [*Proceedings, etc.*, 316.] The only time when all this could have been true would seem to have been during the month immediately following his arrival in the country. Probably there was no formal call, and so no record.

15 Winthrop's *Journal*, i: 50.

16 Wilson must then have been about 43; Winthrop, 44; Pynchon, 42; Endecott, 41; Dudley, 55, and Elder Nowell perhaps something older than either.

as it was a breach of the first table."[17] The biographers of Mr. Williams have stigmatized the Court for this interference, and one most respectable writer has branded it as "persecution," as contrasted with "calm expostulation."[18] Calm expostulation, however, is precisely what it appears to have been. It has been assumed that here was a formal edict of the supreme tribunal, having all the force of law, interposing to come between the church of Salem and their chosen teacher. The fact seems to be, however, that there was no formal action whatever by the Governor and Council; certainly no evidence of any appears on the records. Our only knowledge of the circumstance is due to a minute in the private journal of the Governor; who speaks of it, not as a thing officially done, but in such a manner as would quite accord with an unofficial and expostulatory "letter written to Mr. Endecott," by the six gentlemen present, (Winthrop, Dudley, Ludlow, Nowell, Pynchon and Bradstreet,) in the friendly aim to forewarn their Salem friends against possible danger from some peculiarities of their proposed teacher, with which they might not have become as yet fully acquainted.

It is not absolutely certain whether the Salem church ordained Mr. Williams at this time, or not. Knowles,[19] Gammell[20] and Elton,[21] apparently relying upon Dr. Bentley,[22] say that he was settled over them on the 12–22 April — the very day on which the letter above-named was written. On the other hand, Hubbard — who wrote within fifty years of the event, and had important facilities for getting at the facts which are not now at hand — says that the church, "for the present, forbore proceeding with him[23]"; while Mr. Felt, whose patient accuracy is seldom at fault in such matters, says the "interference prevented the ordination of Mr. Williams, and he went to labor at Plymouth."[24] It is certain that he was in Plymouth in 1631, probably before the autumn,[25] where he taught as an assistant to the Rev. Ralph Smith. Here Winthrop and Wilson

---

[17] Winthrop's *Journal*, i: 52.

[18] Dr. Bentley, *Description of Salem.* [1 *Mass. Hist. Coll.* vi: 246.]

[19] *Memoir*, 49.

[20] *Life*, 19.

[21] *Life*, 15.

[22] *Description, etc.*, 246.

[23] *General History of New-England.* [2 *Mass. Hist. Coll.* v: 203.] Gov. Hutchinson, who acknowledges his special indebtedness to Hubbard's MSS., but who had many other original sources of knowledge, says: "The Governor and Council interposed with their advice, and prevented his settlement at that time." [*Hist. Mass.* i: 40.]

[24] *Annals of Salem*, ii: 569; see also his *Ecclesiastical History of New England* [i: 149] where he says of the letter to Endecott: "the communication suspends the ordination of Williams." Baylies [*Memoir of Plymouth Colony*, i: 266] represents Williams as leaving Salem in consequence of differing with Skelton; but gives no authority for the statement.

[25] Gammell [*Life*, 21] says, "probably in the month of August, 1631." Bentley [246] says, "before the close of summer." Hubbard [204] says Williams returned to Salem just before Skelton died, in August, 1634, while Morton [*New-Eng. Mem.* 78] says he had "lived about three years at Plimouth," which, if Hubbard were right, would render necessary the inference that Williams had gone to Plymouth about the time named by Mr. Gammell.

found him on their visit to the Pilgrim Colony in the latter part of October of the next year. And it will give us some hint of the manner of those times if we pause long enough to glance at the Massachusetts Governor's account of their public worship.[26]

On the Lord's Day there was a sacrament, which they did partake in; and, in the afternoon, Mr. Roger Williams (according to their custom) propounded a question, to which the pastor, Mr. Smith, spake briefly; then Mr. Williams prophesied; and after the governour of Plymouth [Bradford] spake to the question; after him the elder [Brewster]; then some two or three more of the congregation. Then the elder desired the governour of Massachusetts and Mr. Wilson to speak to it, which they did. When this was ended, the deacon, Mr. Fuller, put the congregation in mind of their duty of contribution; whereupon the governour and all the rest went down to the deacon's seat, and put into the box, and then returned.

A little incident seems to have occurred in connection with this visit (whether it had to do with the question propounded above, or not, is not certain) which will well illustrate on what painfully petty matters Mr. Williams's conscience was at this time laboring. Cotton Mather relates it, thus:[27]

There were at this time in Plymouth two Ministers [Smith and Williams], leavened so far with the Humours of the Rigid Separation, that they insisted vehemently upon the Unlawfulness of calling any *unregenerate* man by the Name of *Goodman Such an One;* until, by their indiscreet urging of this Whimsey, the place began to be disquieted. The wiser people being troubled at these trifles, they took the opportunity of Governour Winthrop's being there, to have the thing publickly propounded in the Congregation; who in answer thereunto, distinguished between a *Theological* and a *Moral* Goodness; adding that when Juries were first used in England, it was usual for the Crier, after the Names of Persons fit for that Service were called over, to bid them all: *Attend, Good Men and true;* whence it grew to be a Civil Custom in the English Nation, for Neighbours living by one another, to call one another *Goodman Such an One:* and it was pity now to make a stir about a Civil Custom, so innocently introduced. And that Speech of Mr. Winthrop's put a lasting stop to the Little, Idle, Whimsical Conceits, then beginning to grow Obstreperous.

During this residence in the Old Colony he seems to have entered upon a vigorous endeavor to familiarize himself with the aboriginal language and habits, and to gain some foundation for religious influence over the Indians; the result of which was seen in his *Key Into The Language of America, etc.*, which was published in 1643; and the good effects of which colored all his Rhode Island life.[28] He appears to have supported himself largely, if not

[26] Winthrop's *Journal,* i: 91.

[27] *Magnalia,* ii: 13.

[28] "My soul's desire was to do the natives good, and to that end to have their language." [*Answer to W. Harris, etc.*, cited by Arnold, *Hist. R. I.* i: 97]. So he says again: "And as to these Barbarians, the Holy God knows some pains I took uprightly in the Main Land and Islands of New England to dig into their Barbarous, Rockie Speech, and to speak something of God unto their souls, etc." [*Geo. Fox Digged out of His Burrowes, etc., Apendix,* 93]. So he says he had "a constant zealous desire to dive into the natives' language. God

mainly, by manual labor while there—as, in those days of poverty, was the common lot at Plymouth.[29] Although not engaged in trade as a business, he appears to have traded somewhat also, to help himself withal.[30] His oldest child, Mary, is reputed to have been born during this residence among the Pilgrims.[31]

Not finding at Plymouth such a concurrence as he expected in "divers of his own singular opinions" which he "sought to impose upon others" there; before the close of 1633,[32] Williams was back at Salem—practically assisting Mr. Skelton, "by way of prophecy," though "not in any office."[33] It will aid us toward the further comprehension of his character and life, if we pause here to consider the impressions which had been made by him upon the good men of Plymouth church during this residence; and especially upon persons of so sweet a charity, yet so sterling a discretion, as the two leading minds of that colony, Governor Bradford, and Elder Brewster.

Bradford says:[34]

Mr. Roger Williams (a man godly and zealous, having many precious parts, but very unsettled in judgmente) came over first to ye Massachusetts, but upon some discontente left yt

---

was pleased to give me a a painful, patient spirit to lodge with them in their filthy smoky holes (even while I lived at Plymouth and Salem) to gain their tongue. . . I was known by all the Wampanoags and the Narragansetts to be a public speaker at Plymouth and Salem, and therefore, with them, held as a sachem." [*Letter* cited in Knowles's *Memoir*, 108, 109.] So speaking, in 1661, of Ousamaquin [Massasoit] Mr. Williams said: "he and I had been great friends at Plymouth." [*Paper* of R.W. Backus's *Hist. N. Eng.* i: 73].

[29] "It is not unknown to many witnesses in Plymouth, etc., that the discusser's [*i. e.*, R. W.'s] time hath not been spent (though as much as any others whosoever) altogether in spiritual labours and publike exercise of the word; but, day and night, at home and abroad, on the land and water, at the How [hoe], at the Oare, for bread, etc." [*The Bloudy Tenent yet more Bloudy*, 38.] He afterwards speaks of "labours day and night in my field, etc.," at Salem. [*Mr. Cotton's Letter Examined, etc.* 13.]

[30] Six or seven years after we find him repeatedly writing to Winthrop about "his old and bad debtor, Mr. George Ludlow," [4 *Mass. Hist. Coll.* vi: 253, 256,] and this he elsewhere explains [*Ibid* 212] thus: "the debt was for mine owne and wiues better apparel put of to him at Plymmouth." Ludlow himself in a letter to Williams acknowledges further his indebtedness, for (1) a heifer; (2) upwards of 80 lbs. of tobacco; (3) some goats; (4) an "house watch;" (5) another new gown of Mrs. Williams's, that cost between 40*s* and 50*s*. [5 *Mass. Hist. Coll.* i: 250.] Such would seem to have been the custom of his life. In 1670, writing to Major Mason about his banishment, he names "the yearly losse of no small matter in my trading with English and natives, being debarred from Boston, the chiefe mart and port of New England, etc.;" as one of the injuries which it caused him. [1 *Mass. Hist. Coll.* i: 276.]

[31] Backus's *Hist. New Eng.* i: 57, 516, (who cites the Providence Records).

[32] Winthrop [*Journal* i: 117] in November, 1633, refers to his having returned from Plymouth to Salem. Mr. Cotton, who arrived at Boston 3–13 Sept. 1633, says Williams was "in the Bay not long before my coming." [*Reply to Mr. Williams his Exam., etc.*, 4.] Backus puts his return in 1633 [i: 57.] Elton says, "in August, 1633," [19.] On the other hand, Cotton Mather says [*Magnalia* vii: 7] he was only two years at Plymouth; and Bentley [1 *Mass. Hist. Coll.* vii: 247] without citing his authority, says he was back at Salem "before the close of 1632," and that his eldest child was born there. Savage [*Gen. Dict.* iv: 568] says he continued at Plymouth a "good part of two years." Morton [*N. Eng. Mem.* 78] who was himself there all the time—a young man perhaps twenty years of age—says he lived at Plymouth "about three years." The weight of evidence settles his being at Salem before the winter of 1633.

[33] Morton's *N. E. Mem.* 78; Winthrop's *Journal*, i: 117.

[34] *History of Plim. Plant.* 310.

place, and came hither, (wher he was friendly entertained, according to their poore abilitie,) and exercised his gifts amongst them, and after some time was admitted a member of ye church; and his teaching well approoved, for ye benefite whereof I still blese God, and am thankfull to him, even for his sharpest admonitions and reproufs, so farr as they agreed with truth. He this year [he is writing under date of 1633] begane to fall into some strang oppinions, and from opinion to practise, which caused some controversie betweene ye church and him, and in ye end some discontente on his parte, by occasion whereof he left them some thing abruptly. Yet after wards sued for his dismission to ye church of Salem, which was granted, with some caution to them concerning him, and what care they ought to have of him. But he soone fell into more things ther, both to their and ye goverments troble and disturbance. I shall not need to name perticulars, they are too well knowen now to all, though for a time ye church here wente under some hard censure by his occasion, from some that afterwards smarted them selves. But he is to be pited, and prayed for, and so I shall leave ye matter, and desire ye Lord to shew him his errors, and reduse him into ye way of truth, and give him a setled judgment and constancie in ye same; for I hope he belongs to ye Lord, and yt he will shew him mercie.

Elder Brewster's opinion of the eccentric young man, we gather from the record of it made by Nathaniel Morton, who says:[35]

In the year 1634,[36] Mr. Roger Williams removed from Plimouth to Salem: he had lived about three years at Plimouth, where he was well accepted as an assistant in the Ministry to Mr. Ralph Smith, then Pastor of the Church there, but by degrees venting of divers of his own singular opinions, and seeking to impose them upon others, he not finding such a concurrence as he expected, he desired his dismission to the Church of Salem, which though some were unwilling to, yet through the prudent counsel of Mr. Brewster [the ruling elder there] fearing that his continuance amongst them might cause divisions, and there being then many able men in the Bay, they would better deal with him then themselves could, and foreseeing (what he professed he feared concerning Mr. Williams, which afterwards came to pass) that he would run the same course of rigid Separation and Anabaptistry, which Mr. John Smith the Sebaptist at Amsterdam had done; the Church of Plimouth consented to his dismission, and such as did adhere to him were also dismissed, and removed with him, or not long after him, to Salem.

When Mr. Williams thus, in 1633, became an inhabitant of Salem, he appears to have been a resident of the country about two years and six months; to have been scarcely more than thirty years of age; and both to have deserved, and acquired, the reputation of being,—with all his sincerity of religious feeling, and all his fidelity of godly endeavor—a rash and headstrong man; lacking much of that consideration for the opinion of older and presumably wiser

---

[35] *New-Englands Memoriall*, 78. Mr. Cotton proves that this opinion was well known in New England, for in his *Reply to Mr. Williams his Exam. etc.* [4] published in London in 1647 (twenty-two years before the first issue of the *Memoriall* at Cambridge), he says: "Before my coming into New England, the godly-wise, and vigilant Ruling-Elder of Plymouth (aged Mr. Bruister) had warned the whole Church of the danger of his [Roger Williams's] spirit, which moved the better part of the Church to be glad of his removall from them into the Bay."

[36] See note 32 *ante*, for evidence that this should almost surely be 1633.

persons, which is ordinary and becoming on the part of youth;[37] and with an eye so single toward whatever reform for the moment absorbed and centered the devotion of his soul, as to be unable to see in their just relations, if at all, considerations which were leading others, with as good a conscience, if not a broader exercise of reason, to different, and very likely opposite conclusions.

Backus[38] says he was invited back to Salem. But he cites no authority for the statement, and I have observed none outside of his pages. However this may have been, it appears from Winthrop[39] that Mr. Williams soon began to act informally as an assistant to Mr. Skelton in his failing health; and it is agreed on all hands that after the death of that gentleman, which took place 2–12 Aug., 1634,[40] the church called him to be their pastor.

We have now reached a stage in this review at which it is absolutely necessary, if we desire anything like a full and just comprehension of the facts in their most important relations, that we should examine that contemporary history in the father-land, which had so much to do in shaping our entire colonial life; and without understanding which, it is impossible fairly to comprehend what took place on this side of the sea.

On the 3–13 Nov., 1620, a patent of land[41] "in the Parts of *America* between the Degrees of thirty-ffoure and ffourty-five," was granted by King James, on petition of Sir Ferdinando Gorges, to forty Associates; under a title, which, in its reduced form, is usually known as "The Council for New England." The success of this body in the disposition of its territory proved so indifferent as to lead its members to various extraordinary endeavors to further its ends; among which was the distribution of its lands by lot among them.[42] Cape Ann and its vicinity thus fell to Edmund, Lord Sheffield. He sold it, by indenture dated 1–11 Jan., 1623–4, to Robert Cushman, Edward Winslow, and their associates;[43] who conveyed it later to John White of Dorchester, Eng., and a joint-stock company which he had formed, with the view of establishing a settlement, as a point of supplies and a temporary haven for fishermen.[44] This company of "Dorchester Adventurers" was afterwards enlarged[45] and a new charter solicited and obtained for it of Charles I. on 4–14 Mar., 1628–9,

---

[37] His decided condemnation of the Boston Church, off-hand, almost immediately upon his landing, we have already seen (p. 4). We have also noted (p. 8), from Gov. Bradford's testimony, the evidence that Williams did not scruple at "sharp admonitions" and "reproofs"—some of which, at least, were not thought always to "agree with truth"—even of those who were in the highest office. Gov. Winthrop thought him guilty of "presumption." [*Journal*, i: 122.]

[38] *Hist. New-Eng.* i: 56.

[39] *Journal*, i: 117.

[40] *Ibid*, i: 138.

[41] Hazard's *Historical Collections*, i: 103.

[42] Thornton's *Landing at Cape Anne, etc.*, 13.

[43] *Ibid*, 31.

[44] Smith's *Generall Historie, etc.*, 247.

[45] "Our whole company, wch are much inlarged sence yr. departure out of England." [Cradock's *Letter to Endecott. Records of Gov. and Comp. of Mass.* i: 383.]

confirming and enlarging its powers — under the name of "The Governor and Company of the Massachusetts Bay in New England;" and it was under this instrument, thus obtained, that the affairs of the Colony of the Bay were conducted for five and fifty years — until, after long menace, in the autumn of 1684, the writ of *quo warranto* of the second Charles put an end, for a little time, to the very existence of Massachusetts as a body politic.

The reader will not fail to observe that this was, in the first instance, and essentially, a private trading corporation; composed of Sir Henry Rosewell, his twenty-five designated associates, and "such others as shall hereafter be admitted, and made free, of the Company and Society."[46] "To the ende," however, "that the affaires and buyssinesses which, from tyme to tyme, shall happen and arise concerning the said landes and the plantation of the same, maie be the better managed and ordered,"[47] the Company was made a "bodie politique," and empowered to choose officers and to make laws; to administer "the oathes of supremacie and allegiance, or either of them, to all and everie person and persons which shall at any tyme, or tymes, hereafter goe or passe to the landes and premisses hereby mentioned to be graunted, to inhabite in the same;" to punish crime, to repel force with force, and to expel and banish refractory and incompatible members. That is to say, some sort of public character, implying the power to institute a civil government for the safe management of the affairs of the enterprise considered as a trading corporation, was also included in the charter; being most clearly seen in the grant of the powers to pardon, and to make defensive war, without order from, or recourse to the crown.[48] In all this, however, was but half a truth.

The Separatists had long been harried out of England. But the growth of the feeling and conscience of dissent had been steady throughout the reign of that "learned fool" who had tried to fill Elizabeth's great throne; and there were multitudes, who, weary of waiting for better times, disheartened by the shutting down of the gloom of absolute monarchy upon the land, and disgusted and distressed with the profligacy of the court; looked toward expatriation as offering a sure relief, and a possibly bright future. Plymouth had been settled by the Scrooby-Leyden exiles just long enough to attract special Puritan attention toward New England, and there were many Puritans scattered up and down the land, all of them intelligent and stout-hearted men, and some of them per-

---

[46] Charter, *Mass. Col. Rec.* i: 10.

[47] *Ibid*, i: 9.

[48] *Ibid*, i: 16. For a statement of the want of distinction then existing between public and private corporations, and a clear, able and conclusive judgment on the question of the real quality of this Charter, the exact nature of the powers conferred by it, and the justice of colonial action under them, see the Lecture by Hon. Joel Parker, LL. D., on "The First Charter, and the Early Religious Legislation of Massachusetts," in *Lowell Institute Lectures, by Members of the Mass. Historical Society*, 1869. pp. 357-439.

sons of social consideration and financial ability, who were but waiting their opportunity to emigrate thither. And it was after conference with such men, and with the view of furthering their desires and designs, that John White took the steps which he did for the legalization and endowment of this Massachusetts company. It became, therefore, a trading corporation with colonial intentions, dedicated to the high purposes of religion, and made use of for their own relief by religious men, who had been aggrieved and oppressed under the hard and stupid policy of the reigning monarchs—for Charles had, now for four years, not only been making his father's bad matters worse, but had been adding new elements of discord, and introducing new expedients of oppression.

It is not important in this connection to dwell upon the details of the provisions of this Charter, further than to note: (1) that nothing whatever is said in it with reference to the subject of religious liberty (an omission which, under the circumstances, was taken as significant of the king's intent to pursue a liberal course on that subject);[49] (2) that it conferred on the company the function of self-government, so far as their laws should not be repugnant to those of England; (3) that it gave them the power to admit new associates on such terms as might seem good to them; (4) and to administer the oaths; (5) and, "for their speciall defence and safety, to incounter, expulse, repell, and resist by force of armes, aswell by sea as by lande, and by all fitting waies and meanes whatsoever, all such person and persons as shall at any tyme hereafter attempt or enterprise the destruccion, invasion, detriment, or annoyaunce to the said plantation or inhabitants."[50]

At first sight it is difficult to understand how Charles, consistently with his obvious feelings, and usual policy, could have signed a charter on the whole so liberal as this, and one so favorable to Puritan desires of emigration to New England. Dr. Palfrey, who was the first of our historians to develop fully the indispensableness of an accurate study of collateral events in England to any clear conception of the progress of affairs in the colonies, has acutely suggested that the King had, in this act, a purpose "to encourage the departure of Puritans from England, at the time when he was entering upon measures which might bring on a dangerous conflict with that party."[51] However this may

---

[49] There is plenty of evidence that private intimations were given of the intention of the government to allow the colonists to suit themselves in these matters. Winthrop [*Journal*, i: 103] sets down the assurance which came to them (in the spring of 1633) from the Privy Council, who had been pestered by Gardiner, and others, to control the matter of religion, in these words: "his majesty did not intend to impose the ceremonies of the Church of England upon us; *for that it was considered, that it was the freedom from such things that made people come over to us, etc.*"

[50] *Mass. Col. Rec.* i: 18.

[51] He adds to this, the following [*Hist. New Eng.* i: 392]: "The Charter of the Massachusetts Company had passed the seals almost simultaneously with the King's annunciation, after an exciting controversy with three

have been, the foundations on which the Massachusetts colony afterwards reared itself, were laid, in accordance with the provisions of this patent, under circumstances decidedly more favorable than had been enjoyed by their weaker Plymouth brethren ten years before.

Let me here repeat and emphasize, that it may be remembered by and by when it becomes essential to the fair interpretation of what was done to Roger Williams — that this "Dorchester Company," originally founded on the transfer of a portion of the patent of Gorges, and afterwards enlarged and reauthorized by the charter of Charles I. as the "Governor and Company of the Massachusetts Bay," was in its beginning, in point of fact, neither more nor less than a private corporation chartered by the government for purposes of fishing, real-estate improvement and general commerce; for which it was to pay the crown a fifth part of all precious metals which it might unearth.[52] It was then more than this only in much the same sense as the egg new-laid is the full-grown fowl, or the acorn the oak. It was not yet a State. It was not even, in the beginning, in the ordinary sense, a colony.[53] It was a plantation[54] with a strong religious idea behind it, on its way to be a colony, and a State. In the original intent, the Governor and General Court, and therefore, the government, were to be and abide, in England. When, in 1628, Endecott and his

---

Parliaments, of his purpose to govern without Parliaments in future. It might well appear to him, that, in the contests which perhaps were to follow, his task would be made easier if numbers of the patriots could be tempted to absent themselves from the kingdom; and when he should have succeeded, and the laws and liberties of England should be stricken down, there would be nothing in his past grants to embarrass him in his treatment of the exiles, and his arm would be long enough to reach, and strong enough to crush, them in their distant hiding-place. Or, if no scheme so definite as this was entertained, the grant of the charter, inviting attention to a distant object, might do something for his present relief, by breaking up the dangerous concentration of the thoughts of the Puritans on the state of affairs at home." Dr. Palfrey adds plausibility to this view, by appending a quotation from Thomas Carew, a dramatic poet who was on intimate relations with the King, and who remarked (in a masque, entitled *Cœlum Britannicum*, which was performed at Whitehall 18–28 Feb. 1633–4, at which performance the King himself took part): "Send them [the Vices] to the plantation in New-England, *which hath purged more virulent humors from the politic body*, than guaiacum, and all the West-Indian drugs have from the material bodies of this kingdom." [Chalmers's *English Poets*, v: 629.]

[52] *Mass. Col. Records*, i: 9.

[53] Blackstone designates three sorts of colonies, the third being: "Charter governments, in the nature of civil corporations, with the power of making by-laws for their own interior regulation, not contrary to the laws of England; and with such rights and authorities as are specially given them in their several charters of incorporation." [*Com. on Laws of Eng.* i. Introduc. sec. 4.] This accurately describes the kind of colony which Massachusetts eventually became. But there would seem to be, in all such enterprises, a nascent period during which the private trading corporation element strongly predominates over the colonial. I might illustrate by the Hudson's Bay Company, which existed into our time with its original charter — strongly resembling that of the Massachusetts Company — and which has always been rather a corporation for trade chartered by England, than a colony of England, on American soil.

[54] It was styled a "plantation" repeatedly by Winthrop at the time he was discussing the question of casting in his lot with it, and in the famous "agreement" which was signed 26 Aug.–5 Sept. 1629, by him and eleven others at Cambridge. [*Life and Letters of John Winthrop*, i: 327, 340, 344, *etc.*] It was so styled in the act of the General Court of the Company, which authorized Endecott and his companions to form a government at Salem, 30 Apr.–10 May, 1629. [*Collections of Amer. Antiq. Soc.* iii: 38.]

little party of pioneers had been sent over to Salem, his authority was expressly declared to be "in subordination to the Company heree [that is, in London]."[55] And it was only when Cradock found that so many practical difficulties threatened all procedure upon that basis, as to make it unlikely that Winthrop, and Saltonstall, and Johnson, and Dudley, and other men whose coöperation was greatly to be desired, would consent to become partners in the enterprise, unless a radical change were made in that respect; that he proposed and the Company consented, "for the Advancem^t of the Plantacon, the inducing & encouraging Persons of worth & qualitie to transplant themselues and famylyes thether, & for other weighty reasons therin contained, to transferr the Gou^vnm^t of the Plantacon to those that shall inhabite there, etc."[56] It was even a grave question of law whether, under the terms of the Charter, this transfer were possible; but as that instrument did not contain in express language any limitation of the residence of those who were to act under it; and on the general legal principle that a grant may be interpreted as favorably as possible to the grantees, reënforced by the special fact that the Charter contained in itself the warrant for putting the construction most favorable to the grantees upon its provisions;[57] they took the responsibility:—so quietly, however, that the home government seem to have remained in ignorance of the fact for more than four years thereafter.[58]

Such being this corporation styled "The Governor and Company of the Massachusetts Bay," let us carefully notice, step by step, the quality of its acts, after, by the coming over of Winthrop and his associates, it commenced its work on the ground over which its jurisdiction extended. By what it did, we shall gain important evidence as to what it considered itself authorized to do, not merely; but as to the pure and natural motives which governed some of its orders to which exception has not unfrequently been taken.

The first session of the Company for business on this side of the sea, of which we have record, was held ten weeks after the landing, at Charlestown, on the 23 Aug.–2 Sept. 1630. Among the votes passed at that session was one issuing a process against Thomas Morton of Mount Wollaston.[59] At the second

---

[55] *The Company's Records. Ibid,* iii: 47.

[56] *Ibid.*

[57] "And shalbe construed, reputed, and adiudged in all cases most favourablie on the behalf, and for the benefitt and behoofe, of the saide Governor and Company and their successors." [*Mass. Col. Rec.* i: 19.]

[58] Palfrey supposes that Cradock's answer to the Order of Council, 21 Feb.–3 Mar. 1633–4, first apprised the government of this. [*Hist. N. Eng.* 1: 371.]

[59] Thomas Morton, who describes himself as "of Cliffords Inne, Gent," and whom Dudley described as "an Atturney in the West Countryes, while he lived in England" [*Drake's Boston,* i: 115], who made himself a nuisance in New England from the beginning, and for his dangerous dealings with the Indians, and other things, had been sent home by the Plymouth men in the summer of 1628; but had returned, and commenced anew his reckless and perilous career at Quincy.

session, 7–17 Sept., that "process" bore fruit in an order to set this Morton "into the bilbowes," and then to ship him back to England. It would seem from Winthrop that this was done specially "for his many injuries offered to the Indians;"[60] while the Court order itself provided for payment to be made out of his goods "for a cannoe hee vniustly tooke away from them," and for the burning of his house "in the sight of the Indians, for their satisfaccion, for many wrongs hee hath done them, from tyme to tyme."[61]

At the very next Court, 28 Sept.–8 Oct., one Thomas Gray, who seems to have been an incorrigible rascal,[62] was ordered "to remoue himselfe out of the lymetts of this pattent before the end of March nexte."[63] Early in the ensuing spring, 1–11 March, 1630–1, six individuals were directed to leave the jurisdiction, as "persons vnmeete to inhabit here," besides "Sir Christopher Gardiner and Mr. Wright," who were sent as prisoners to England.[64] On the 3–13 May following, Thomas Walford of Charlestown and his wife were enjoined to "departe out of the lymits of this pattent before the 20th day of October nexte, vnder paine of confiscacion of his goods, for his contempt of authoritie & confrontinge officers, etc."[65] On the 14–24 June succeeding, Philip Ratcliffe was fined £40. and "banished out of yᵉ lymitts of this jurisdiccion, for vttering mallitious & scandulous speeches against the government & the church of Salem, etc., as appeareth by a particular thereof, proued upon oath."[66] At the Court of 6–16 September following, Henry Lynn was sentenced to be whipped and banished before the 6–16 October next, "for writinge into England falsely & mallitiously against the government & execution of justice here."[67]

Here, within a period less by one day than a single year, and within a period of only fourteen days more than a single year after the court of the corporation had first organized itself for business in New England, it passed sentences of exclusion from its territory upon fourteen persons. Endecott, in the summer of 1629, in like manner had not hesitated to take the responsibility of sending

---

[60] *Journal*, i: 34.

[61] *Mass. Col. Rec.* i: 75.

[62] Among other things laid to his charge, he was himself drunk, he kept a tippling house, he was profane, and drew his knife, in a ruffianly way, in presence of the Court. [*Ibid*, i: 92, 234, 268, 270, 297.]

[63] *Ibid*, i: 77.

[64] These were Messrs. Aleworth, Weaver, Plastowe, Shuter, Cobbett and Wormwood. [*Ibid*, i: 82.]

[65] *Ibid*, i: 86.

[66] *Ibid*, i: 88. This appears to have been a very aggravated case. The fellow [*Winthrop*, i: 56] was a servant of Mr. Cradock, and I am sorry to say, had his ears cropped, besides his fine and banishment; but those were days when such punishments were thought just and right. Within a few months of this time William Prynne, the famous Puritan lawyer, was sentenced by the Star Chamber to pay a fine of £5,000, to be expelled from Oxford, and Lincoln's Inn, to be disbarred and degraded, to lose both his ears, and to be close prisoner for life; all for having written the *Histrio-Mastix*, in which he had spoken sharply of "women-actors," which was supposed to be levelled at the Queen.

[67] *Ibid*, i: 91. Mr. Savage [note *Winthrop*, i: 61] thinks his sentence was remitted, though the records do not mention it, because he was fined ten shillings for absence from training, in Nov. 1632. But that may have been another person of the same name.

home John and Samuel Browne, although they were "amongst the number of the first Patentees, men of Estates, and men of Parts and port in the place,"[68] not because they insisted on worshiping with the aid of the Book of Common Prayer, but because they so conducted themselves in regard to the matter, as to endanger faction and mutiny; so that "the Governour told them 'That New England was no place for such as they.'"[69] In doing so, he had faithfully obeyed the spirit and the letter of the Company's instructions. They had foreseen the difficulty of getting on in a new plantation with opinionated and insubordinate men. They had written him especially as to Oldham: "Wee fynde him a Man soe affected to his owne opinion, as not to bee removed from it, nether by reason nor any prswasion; and vnlesse hee may beare sway, and haue all things Carryed to his good likinge, wee haue little hope of quiett or comfortable subsistance where he shall make his aboad;"[70] urging great forbearance, but counselling "a more severe course, when faire meanes will not prvaile." They had directed him also in regard to Rev. Ralph Smith: "That vnless hee wilbe conformable to our Gouernment, you suffer him not to remaine within the Limitts of our graunt."[71] And, in general, they had enjoined upon him to hold a strict and steady hand upon all who should prove to be disorderly: "Wee desire, (if it may bee) that Errors may bee reformed with lenitie or mylde Correccon; and if any prve incorrigable, & will not bee reclaimed by gentle correccon, ship such prsons home, rather then keep them there to infect, or to bee an occasion of Scandall vnto, others; wee being fully prswaded that if one or two bee soe reshipped back, and certificate sent home of their misdemeanor, it wilbe a Terror to the rest, and a meanes to reduce them to good conformitie."[72] It is noticeable also that in the same letter the company expressed themselves strongly as to the need of the prevention, if possible, of the "moving of needless questions to stirr vp strife . . from which small beginnings great mischiefs have followed;" and the special importance "that there be none in our precincts permitted to doe any iniurie (in the least kinde) to the heathen people; and if any offend in that way lett them receive due Correccon."[73] Their second General letter to Endecott and his associates, reiter-

---

[68] Morton's *N. E. Mem.*, 76.

[69] *Ibid*, 77.

[70] The Company's First General Letter of Instructions to Endecott and his Council. [*Trans. Amer. Antiq. Soc.* iii: 83.]

[71] *Ibid*, 85.

[72] *Ibid*, 89.

[73] "Yett, because it is often found that some busie prsons (led more by their will then any good warrant out of God's word) take opportunitie of moving needless questions to stirr vp strife, and by that meanes to begett a question, and bring men to declare some different Judgmt, (most comonly in things indifferent) from wch small beginnings great mischiefs haue followed, wee pray you, and the rest of the Councell, that if any such disputes shall happen among you, that you suppress them, and bee carefull to maintaine peace and vnitie." [*Ibid*, 90 and 89.]

ated their view of the importance of this general policy: "feare not to putt good lawes, made vpon good ground and warrant, in due execucon."[74]

Such having been the line of conduct adopted, after much consideration, in the earliest days of the settlement of Salem by the Dorchester Company, and subsequently endorsed by the enlarged body acting under the new Charter in their favorable review of Endecott's treatment of the Brownes,[75] it was the most natural thing in the world that it should be pursued by the "Governor and Company of the Massachusetts Bay," when they were brought in person face to face with the evils which it was intended to remedy. Apparently, Endecott on his arrival had found a few lawless men—like Thomas Morton and Thomas Walford—here and there settled upon the soil; whose evil conduct he could note, but, with the small company at his command, could not control. In the full conferences in regard to the state of things which would naturally follow Endecott's intercourse with, and report to, Winthrop and the Assistants on their arrival, it would be a matter of course that he should point out these nuisances which required abatement; and the large action of the first twelvemonth in this line may be thus accounted for; while it was to be expected that the vigor thus shown in the management of affairs would make such labor lighter for some time to come. More than a year, indeed, elapsed before it became needful to repeat this action, when at the Court of 3–13 Oct., 1632, Nicholas Frost, for sundry gross offences, among which theft from the Indians was included, was sentenced to "be fined, whipped, branded, & banished oute of this pattent, with penalty that if euer hee be found within the lymitts of the said pattent, hee shalbe putt to death."[76] This appended clause seems to have been the fruit of experience already had; some formerly sent away having availed themselves of the fact that no legal risk attended their return, to come back and repeat the offence of their presence. Almost another year went by, when one John Stone from the West Indies, captain of a small ship, behaving in a drunken and dissolute manner, blackguarding those who sought to restrain him, and exhibiting mutinous violence, the Court, 3–13 Sept., 1633, fined him heavily, and prohibited his again "comeing within this pattent without leaue from the Gouermt, vnder the penalty of death."[77] The next exercise of this power which I discover, was, twenty-five months and five days thereafter, when, on the same occasion, John Smyth and Roger Williams were ordered to "de-

---

[74] *Ibid*, 107.

[75] *Ibid*, 76.

[76] *Rec. Col. Mass.* i: 100.

[77] This fellow had had previous trouble with the Plymouth men, who had meditated sending him to England on a charge of piracy, and he was the next year killed by the Indians, on the Connecticut river. It seems, with his other iniquities, he was a punster, calling Mr. Justice Ludlow a "just-ass." [*Ibid*, i: 108; *Winthrop*, i: 104, 111, 148; Morton's *N. E. Mem.* 92; *Hubbard*, 156.]

parte out of this jurisdiccon within sixe weekes nowe nexte ensueing;"[78] which action will, by and by, be more particularly considered.

What was the precise nature of this Court action by which Roger Williams became, in his turn, not less than the twentieth person thus ordered beyond the limits of the Massachusetts plantation, within the first seven years of its life?

Banishment, in the usual sense of that term, clearly it was not. Both *Magna Charta*, and the *Habeas Corpus* act, forbid the sending of a freeman out of the realm without his consent, but by act of Parliament.[79] The king could not do that; although, by a writ of *ne exeat*, he could prohibit any subject from leaving his kingdom without license; and John Winthrop, and his associates, were much too shrewd, in the face of the fundamental condition of their Charter restraining them from all action "contrarie, or repugnant, to the lawes and statutes of England," to undertake what the king himself could not do. Moreover, banishment involved a State which could banish, and that the banished parties be members of it; conditions which could hardly be claimed here to exist. There is no evidence that this plantation had by this time come to regard itself as being strictly a civil government at all. It acted in this — as it was then acting in regard to all other matters — as a Company,[80] on those simple principles of natural justice which give to any association the right to decline to admit,[81] or to exclude, unsuitable and incompatible members. It acted, moreover, in exact accordance with that provision of its Charter which had been inserted to meet an exigency almost sure to arise, and which — if it could be met in any other way at all — could be met in no other way so well.[82] While the facts: that the plantation had a religious basis, which itself might

[78] *Mass. Col. Rec.* i: 159, 160. It is true, indeed, that in the winter of 1634–5 one Abigail Gifford, widow, who had been living upon the parish in Willesden, near London, but had been somehow smuggled over, "being found to be sometimes distracted, and a very burdensome woman," was sent back to the parish whence she came. [Winthrop's *Journal*, i: 153.]

[79] *Blackstone*, B. I. Chap. i: sec. 2. [*Personal Liberty of the Subject.*] He says that exile was first introduced into England as a punishment, in the 39th of Elizabeth [1596–7] when a statute enacted that "such rogues as were dangerous to the inferior people should be banished the realm." Whether in virtue of that act, just passed, or not, Francis Johnson, his brother George and others, were banished to Newfoundland in the summer of 1597. [Geo. Johnson's *Discourse of some Troubles and Excommunications in the Banished English Church at Amsterdam*, 106, 109.]

[80] "The right of the Governor and Company of Massachusetts Bay to exclude, at their pleasure, dangerous or disagreeable persons from their domain, they never regarded as questionable; any more than a householder doubts his right to determine who shall be the inmates of his home. No civilized man had a right to come, or to be, within their chartered limits, except themselves, and such others as they, in the exercise of an absolute discretion, saw fit to harbor." [Palfrey, *Hist. N. Eng.* i: 299.]

[81] This right to decline to admit was sometimes exercised. Winthrop says: "The master [of the ship Handmaid arrived at Plymouth] came to Boston [11–21 Nov. 1630] with Capt. Standish and two gentlemen passengers, who came to plant here, *but having no testimony, we would not receive them.*" [*Journal*, i: 38.]

[82] This clause gave them the right to "expulse" by "all fitting waies and meanes whatsoever," all persons who should "at any tyme hereafter attempt, or enterprise" any "detriment or annoyaunce to the said plantation, or inhabitants." [Charter, *Mass. Col. Rec.* i: 18.]

suggest exclusions possibly unsuggested by its commercial aspects, yet on that account rather the more, than the less, to be considered; that they were in the dangerous neighborhood of they knew not how many, nor how bloodthirsty, savages; and that certain threatening circumstances, which remain to be explained, were glooming the horizon at home, and exciting special solicitude as to the immediate future of the enterprise; urged them to exercise the extremest care to knit themselves, as soon as might be, strongly together—to make their company spiritually homogeneous, their policy humane and benevolent toward the Aborigines, and their entire life such as would triumphantly bear even hostile scrutiny.

A plantation like this—and all the more that it was at a remove from the mother country so considerable as three thousand miles of obscure ocean then necessitated—must have some method of effectually ridding itself of such rogues, vagabonds, visionary, pragmatical, incongenial and unmanageable characters as are apt to be thrown off like spray from the forefront of any advancing wave of immigration. Capital punishment would be open to many objections; would be generally extreme, even for those whose influence might be most intolerable. There were no prisons in which to submit them to long periods of confinement. So that by far the most available course of procedure clearly was to send such persons outside of the jurisdiction, and to hedge up the way against their return by such penalty as should make it for their safety, as well as for their interest, to relieve the Colony of the calamity of their presence.[83] Nor could such transportation outside of the lines of the plantation be, in itself, in the nature of an extreme hardship and barbarous punishment; for old England was always accessible to the outlaw, and, in the new world, besides unlimited wildwood range, where vastly more fertile and attractive shores invited inhabitation and tillage, there were the scattered settlements of Newfoundland

83 "The freemen of the Massachusetts Company had a right, in equity and in law, to expel from their territory all persons who should give them trouble. In their corporate capacity, they were owners of Massachusetts in fee, by a title to all intents as good as that by which any freeholder among them had held his English farm. As against all Europeans, whether English or Continental, they owned it by a grant from the crown of England, to which, by well-settled law, the disposal of it belonged, in consequence of its discovery by an English subject. In respect to any adverse claim on the part of the natives, they had either found the land unoccupied, or had become possessed of it with the consent of its earlier proprietors. For the purpose of being at liberty to follow their own judgment and inclination in respect to matters regarded by them with the profoundest interest, they had submitted to an abandonment of their homes, and to the extreme hardships incident to settlement in a distant wilderness. They thought they had acquired an absolute right to the unmolested enjoyment of what had cost them so dear. Having withdrawn across an ocean, to escape from the interference of others with their own management of their own affairs, they conceived that they were entitled to protect themselves from such interference for the future by the exclusion of disturbing intruders from their wild domain. . . In this, as in other respects, their charter was their Palladium." [Palfrey's *Hist. N. Eng.* i: 387.]

and what afterwards became Maine and New Hampshire; three preexistent regular colonies, with another just springing into life, which, together,

Gave ample room, and verge enough,

to the excused colonist. As John Cotton afterwards said in reference to Mr. Williams's own case, it may even be queried whether such "banishment" as this "be in proper speech a punishment at all, in such a Countrey as this is, where the Jurisdiction (whence a man is banished) is but small, and the Countrey round about it large, and fruitfull; where a man may make his choice of variety of more pleasant and profitable seats, then he leaveth behinde him. In which respect, Banishment in this Countrey is not counted so much a confinement, as an enlargement; where a man doth not so much loose civill comforts, as change them."[84]

So nearly as it is possible to judge from the meager records, there appear to have been four offences which seemed to the Governor and Company of the Massachusetts Bay to be, in the peculiar circumstances of its early, immature and precarious years, of moment enough to warrant and demand the expatriation of those guilty of them. These were: (1) incorrigible, unmanageable and intolerable wickedness, like that of the profane, drunken and ruffianly Gray; (2) dishonesty toward, and ill-treatment of, the Indians, like that of Morton and Frost;[85] (3) action and speech tending to overthrow the government of the plantation, and the order of its churches, when so violent and persistent as to break out into the beginnings of something like mutiny, as was the case with the two Brownes, Walford, Ratcliffe, and Stone; and (4) sending home to England malicious misrepresentations of the management of the affairs of the Colony, calculated to strengthen the hands of its enemies there, and so to endanger its prosperity, if not its very existence — as was the fact with Lynn.

I have intimated that there were circumstances taking place in England, of a nature to excite alarm in Massachusetts, and of a character to influence its policy and legislation. As will be remembered, the granting of the Patent seems to have been due less to any sincere good will toward the enterprise on the part of the king and his counsellors, than to the hope that it might at least temporarily play into his hands, by removing out of the kingdom numbers of a class of men who were too numerous and powerful there for the easy accomplishment

---

84 *Reply to Mr. Williams his Examination, etc.*, 8.

85 If "one Josias Plaistowe," whom Winthrop mentions [*Journal*, i: 62] and who figures in the court records of 27 Sept.–7 Oct. 1631, be the same as the "Mr. Plastowe" who had been ordered home to England in the previous March — but who, possibly, did not go — his sin was of the same description with Morton and Frost's; inasmuch as "for stealeing 4 basketts of corne from the Indians" he was ordered to "returne them 8 basketts againe, be ffined £5, & hereafter to be called by the name of Josias, & not Mr., as formerly hee vsed to be." [*Mass. Col. Rec.* i: 92.]

of his tyrannous ends. For the first three or four years of its existence the plantation was too feeble to call for special notice. But subsequently emigration from England grew larger, and included many men of substance and influence; and it became clear that the transplanted shoot had taken deep root, and would be reasonably sure of a vigorous life. The king had made considerable progress as an absolute monarch, reigning without the inconveniences of a parliament; the star chamber was as yet unopposed in its successful career of infamy; and to the royal eye all circumstances began to look favorably toward the execution of that real interior purpose of his heart, which involved the stamping out of dissent at home and abroad. So that he and his Privy Council were in a good frame of mind to listen kindly to any thing which might be made to afford pretext for a change of policy toward New England. Nor were there wanting individuals, some of them of social consideration and influential in position, who were in a state of chronic readiness to do all which it might come in their way to do, to work against the prosperity of Massachusetts. Sir Ferdinando Gorges, who had been for a quarter of a century vainly trying to secure a successful colony somewhere on the New England soil, and who held various chartered rights therein, had consented to the arrangement by which the Dorchester Company had undertaken a settlement at Cape Ann, "so far forth as it might not be prejudicial to my son Robert Gorges's interests."[86] But he was never a friend to the movement, and was at all times ready to use his, by no means inconsiderable, power to second every endeavor to its disadvantage. Capt. John Mason, who had been governor of "a plantation in the Newfoundland," and who had — with Gorges, and without him — grants of New England land, which led him to be sensitive to the growth of Winthrop's settlement; in 1632 became a member of the Great Council for New England, and soon after one of its officers; and stood ready with Gorges to endorse all murmurings of all malcontents. The Brownes were the first to complain. Morton was not long in following. Ratcliffe, and later arrivals home, furnished new exaggerations of facts. Chief of all was Sir Christopher Gardiner; one of whose duplicate English wives seems to have so prejudiced the New England men against him, that they doubted his nobility, doubted the nature of his connection with the ostensible female "cousin" with whom he traveled, and even went so far as to suspect him of being a Papist in disguise; and who returned their prejudice to the full.[87]

---

[86] Gorges's *Briefe Narration, etc.*, chap. xxvi, [3 *Mass. Hist. Coll.* vi: 80.] "Whereof," Sir Ferdinando adds, "he had a Patent, under the seal of the Council."

[87] *Winthrop*, i: 55; Morton's *N. E. Mem.* 85; Hubbard's *Gen. Hist. N. E.* i: 149, 153; *Letter of Thomas Wiggin*, [3 *Mass. Hist. Coll.* viii: 320.]

Early in 1633, while Roger Williams was in the last months of his ministry at Plymouth, these grumblings came to a head in an application to the Privy Council. Winthrop's own account of the matter is brief, and I will quote it, that we may see it exactly as he did:[88]

By these ships [the Mary and Jane which arrived in May, 1633] we understood, that Sir Christopher Gardiner, and Thomas Morton, and Philip Ratcliff (who had been punished here for their misdemeanours) had petitioned to the King and Council against us, (being set on by Sir Ferdinando Gorges and Capt. Mason, who had begun a plantation at Pascataquack, and aimed at the general government of New England for their agent there, Capt. Neal). The petition was of many sheets of paper, and contained many false accusations (and among some truths misrepeated), accusing us *to intend rebellion, to have cast off our allegiance, and to be wholly separate from the church and laws of England; that our ministers and people did continually rail against the State, church and bishops there, etc.*

Saltonstall, Humphrey and Cradock, members of the Company who remained in England, appeared before the Privy Council, and made answer to these charges so successfully that that body dismissed the accusations. It recognized that, were they true, they "would tend to the great dishonor of this kingdom, and utter ruin of that plantation," but, in virtue of the facts: that most of the charges were denied; that if true they could only be proved by witnesses summoned at great expense and waste of time; that it would work a serious harm to the adventurers if they "should have discouragement, or take suspicion that the State here had no good opinion of that plantation;" that the fault, if any existed, lay with a few men, rather than with those principally engaged; laying some of these things aside for future inquiry, it declared that "the appearances were so fair, and hopes so great," that his majesty would "not only maintain the liberties and privileges heretofore granted, but supply anything further that might tend to the good government, prosperity, and comfort of his people there of that place, etc."[89] And so this cloud blew over, and the sun again shone clear.

A year had hardly passed, however, when — the same injurious representations being pressed upon the attention of a not unwilling Court; and the precedent by which, in violation of the chartered rights of Virginia, its government had, by a writ of *quo warranto*, been usurped by the King in the summer of 1624, being pleaded — an Order in Council was obtained, in February, 1633–4, detaining certain ships loaded with emigrants for New England, and, among other things, demanding the production before the Board, by Mr. Cradock, *of the*

---

[88] *Journal*, i: 103.

[89] See a letter from Winthrop to Gov. Bradford, giving an account of the matter, and enclosing a copy of the Order of the Privy Council, of date 19–29 Jan. 1632–3, "exactly as wrote in Gov. Bradford's MSS.," in Prince's *New-England Chronology*, ii: 89–91.

Charter of the Massachusetts Company.[90] The ships were subsequently released on the ground of their favorable relation to fishing interests of value to the mother country, but Mr. Cradock was compelled to reply to the Council that the document which they demanded was not in his possession, having been transported to the territory which it covered. Whereupon he received a strict charge to procure and deliver it. He sent over accordingly to Boston; but the shrewd magistrates in July replied that they had no power to take such action without authority from the General Court, which would not meet for two months.[91]

A month had not passed, when (4–14 August, 1634), an old planter named Jeffery called upon Gov. Winthrop, and handed him a letter which he had just received out of England from Thomas Morton, in which, in an exultant tone, he informed him that "the King hath reassumed the whole Business into his owne Hands, appointed a Committee of the Board, and given order for a Generall Gouernour of the whole Territory to be sent ouer."[92] He cheerily added: "The Commission is past the Privy Seale; I did see it, and the same was 1 mo. of May sent to my Lord Keeper to have it pass the Greate Seale for Confirmation, and *I now staye to returne with the Gouernour, by whom all Complainants shall haue Relief.*" During the next month (18–28 September) the Griffin arrived with a copy of this commission, which had been granted (28 April–8 May), constituting the two Archbishops, and ten others of the Privy Council, a Board to regulate all plantations; with power to call in all patents, to make laws, to raise tithes and portions for ministers, to remove and punish governors, to hear and determine all causes, and inflict all punishments, even to death itself.[93]

The Governor and Company of Massachusetts seem to have had suspicion of what turned out to be the fact, that a storm was rising in England which, before long, might concentrate the thoughts of those in power upon domestic matters to that degree that the colonies should be for a time forgotten; and so they felt that their strength was to sit still. When the General Court did assemble in September, with the demand for their Charter, and the document establishing the High Commission, confronting them; it made no direct answer to either, but quietly took order for fortifying Castle Island, Charlestown and Dorchester Hights; for drilling and disciplining the train-bands, and for collecting arms and ammunition.[94] When the Court met again, in March,

[90] Winthrop's *Journal*, i: 135; Hazard's *Hist. Coll.* i: 341; Hubbard's *Hist. N. E.* 153.

[91] Winthrop's *Journal*, i: 137.

[92] See the letter, in Hazard's *Hist. Coll.* i: 342.

[93] Winthrop's *Journal*, i: 143. The commission itself is given at full length, in Hubbard's *Gen. Hist. N. E.* 264–268.

[94] *Mass. Col. Rec.* i: 123–125.

1634–5, these military preparations were still further pushed; bullets were made legal tender at a farthing apiece, and the circulation of farthings was forbidden; a beacon to be fired to alarm the country in case of invasion, was set up on what thence became named "Beacon Hill" in Boston; a strict military discipline was established; a military Commission was organized, "to do whatsoever may be further behoovefull for the good of this plantation in case of any warr that may befall vs," and entrusted with the power of the death-penalty; and a "Freeman's Oath" which should pledge fidelity to the powers that be, was required to be taken by every male resident within the jurisdiction, of the age of sixteen years, and over.[95]

During the month previous to this (19 Feb.–1 Mar. 1634–5,) all the "ministers" in the Colony had been convened by the Governor and Company, among other things, to answer the question: "What we ought to do, if a General Governour should be sent out of England?" All were present except the Rev. Nathaniel Ward of Ipswich, and all were agreed in replying to the question: "We ought not to accept him, but defend our lawful possessions (if we were able); otherwise to avoid, or protract."[96]

On the 16–26 June a ship arrived which brought the good news that the coming of the General Governor had been for the time frustrated, by the fact that a great new ship built to transport him and his attendant force, had fallen to pieces in the launching; and the bad tidings that the old Council for New England, worn out by ill success, had surrendered its charter to the king, and to the jurisdiction of a General Governor of his appointment; and that all its territory had been distributed by lot among twelve associates. As the Massachusetts men held originally by patent from this Council, of course this amounted to robbing them of their property, and redistributing it to others. In order that the forms of law might be respected, the Attorney General, in September, 1635, brought a writ of *quo warranto* in Westminster Hall against the Governor and Company of the Massachusetts; fourteen charges being trumped up — some of which simply alleged the due exercise of powers expressly granted by the charter! In the November following, judgment was given. Theophilus Eaton, and fourteen others of the original associates, came in and pleaded that they "wholly disclaymed" these franchises; and were "forever excluded from all use and claime of the same, and every of them." Matthew Cradock made default, and was convicted of the usurpation charged, and taken to answer to the king for the same. The remaining patentees "stood outlawed."[97]

---

[95] *Ibid*, 136–139.

[96] Winthrop's *Journal*, i: 154. Mr. Williams probably was not there, as he had not yet become pastor in Mr. Skelton's place, and so was not a "minister," in the close interpretation of those days.

[97] *Hutchinson Papers*, 101–104.

It looked as if all were over. In the eye of Westminster Hall the colonists of New England had no rights which anybody was bound to respect. It was left for those colonists to abdicate their sovereignty over the territory which at such cost they had legally acquired, and surrender their new homes; or to make the best terms which they might be able with their new masters, with no security that the fresh sanctions of law would prove more sacred or secure than the old; or wait until the new Governor made his appearance with his suite, and then try what virtue might be in the diligent use of the "ordnances"—"drakes," "sakers," "culverins," "musketts and bandaleroes"—which had been hastily gotten together for such an emergency.

The plot was well laid, but the pious Winthrop summarizes, in half a line, the issue thereof: "The Lord frustrated their design."[98] In what manner He wrought to this end, it does not fall within the necessities of this examination that I should take space to indicate; for the action by which Roger Williams was expatriated from Massachusetts was going on here, at the same time that this writ was on trial in London; and so all beyond this point would be *ex post facto* to his case.

Glancing back, now, at the condition of things thus revealed on both sides of the sea, several conclusions become inevitable:

1. This Massachusetts movement had powerful enemies to contend with, in England, from the beginning.

2. The Company had enemies as well, from the beginning, on its own soil—ready to play into the hands of those abroad. Some who have been named, were formidable enough to be sent out of the plantation; others less considerable remained, whose evil influence demanded unremitting watchfulness.[99]

3. The want of entire homogeneity here thus developed—as to which many additional facts might be cited—taken in connection with the obvious truth that, in the face of English hostility, the plantation not only had no strength to spare, but scarcely the reasonable assurance of success at the best, with almost the certainty of failure should it be further weakened by the rending influence of faction within; must obviously have pressed upon the minds of those occupying the chief places of responsibility, the indispensable necessity of taking

---

[98] *Journal*, i: 161.

[99] He who is curious to look into these minutiæ may find evidences of the truth of what I say in the Colony Records; such as the cases of Tho. Foxe, [*Mass. Col. Rec.* i: 84]; Tho. Knower, [*Ibid*, 94]; Ensigne Jennison, [*Ibid*, 132]; John Lee, [*Ibid*.] Even Israel Stoughton was "disinabled for beareing any public office in the Commonwealth, within this jurisdiccon, for the space of three yeares, for affirming the Assistants were noe magistrates" [*Ibid*, 136]; and Samuel Mavericke was ordered, under the penalty of £100, to "remove his habitacon for himselfe & his ffamily, to Boston," and meantime not to entertain strangers without leave—clearly because the Court was so distrustful of him as to desire, in those times of peril, to have him under its immediate eye. [*Ibid*, 140]

every reasonable precaution to avoid, if possible, further divisions of feeling, whether in matters of Church or State, among the settlers.

4. The right to restrain, punish, or "expulse," those whose spirit and influence threatened danger in this regard; who could not be convinced of their error, and the disservice they were doing to all concerned, and who would not be quiet; involved to the plantation, as it then was situated, the difference between a State and chaos.

5. Of various objectionable possibilities liable in this manner to threaten evil to the Colony, we may readily designate, as particularly to be dreaded, attacks upon the Charter, on the validity of which all their pecuniary rights, as well as their civil franchise, depended; on the justice and sacredness of the oaths by which they were seeking to cement the fragments of their immature commonwealth together; and on the moral and legal right of the magistrates to fill, and to fulfill, their office. While it is easy for us to see that for any person of influence in the Massachusetts of that day, to rail against the king; to speak violently and contemptuously of the Church of England, or to endeavor to introduce division and discord into the young churches which were still in the gristle of immaturity here; would be to work grievous mischief not only in the direct and immediate consequences of such action, but by indirectly endorsing the justice of the very claim set up by Gardiner, Morton and Ratcliffe before the Privy Council, that the New England "ministers and people did continually rail against the State, Church, and Bishops there, etc."[100]

6. Such was the exceptional prominence of the position of the elders of the churches of those days, that for a *minister* to be guilty of any of the ill conduct named above, would greatly exaggerate all probabilities of harm therefrom; and we find, accordingly, that the government was never slow to take action, —even in the case of men so excellent in spirit, and so high in position, as John Eliot and John Cotton—whenever such a danger menaced the plantation.[101]

---

[100] See p. 21, where the language is quoted from Winthrop's *Journal*, i: 103.

[101] As early as 21–31 July, 1631, a sort of Ecclesiastical Council was held at Watertown to consider the fact that Mr. Phillips and Mr. Brown, pastor and elder there, had publicly advocated the opinion that "the churches of Rome were true churches." [Winthrop's *Journal*, i: 58.] Another discussion followed on the 8–18 Dec. ensuing, when the matter was amicably settled [*Ibid*, 67.] There can be small question that the importance attached to this subject lay in its possible political significance; for if the churches of Rome were true churches, their members would be open to citizenship in Massachusetts under the law then existing; and in the not impossible event of England's becoming Roman Catholic, that question might become a practical, as it would be to them, a startling one. More trouble followed the next year, with the same men. A levy of £8 (out of a total of £60) had been laid upon Watertown, the payment of which Messrs. Phillips and Brown had advised their people to resist, as "it was not safe to pay moneys after that sort, for fear of bringing themselves and posterity into bondage." They were convented before the Court 17–27 Feb. 1631–2, and convinced that they had acted under a misapprehension as to the powers of the Company, when they "were fully satisfied; and so their submission was accepted and

I now return to Roger Williams, as we left him just established at Salem, after his removal from Plymouth, in the summer of 1633; that, in the light of the various considerations now suggested, we may endeavor a perfectly fair judgment upon his conduct during the next two years, and the treatment which he received therefor, from the government.

I have intimated that, at the least, a year elapsed after he commenced labor, in a sort, at Salem, before Mr. Skelton died, and he took his place as pastor. History is not wholly silent concerning him, however, during this interval. In November, 1633, we find him joining Mr. Skelton in taking exception to a ministers' meeting, which had been established by the pastors and teachers of the churches of the Bay, for every fortnight, at each others' houses;—"as fearing it might grow, in time, to a presbytery, or superintendency, to the prejudice of the churches' liberties."[102] While at Plymouth, Mr. Williams had written a "treatise"[103]—unreferred to, indeed, by the Plymouth men, except as we get a veiled reference to it as classed under the "strang oppinions" which, as we have seen,[104] Gov. Bradford attributed to him; and the knowledge of it came to the authorities of Massachusetts, on whose request (a very natural one, since the matter clearly had become so noised abroad, as to be a subject of remark and

---

their offence pardoned." [*Ibid*, 70.] In July, 1632, the elders of the churches in the Bay, and at Plymouth (with the brethren) were consulted as to whether a person might be a civil magistrate, and a ruling elder of the church at the same time. [*Ibid*, 81.] In the autumn of 1632, the ministers ended a "difference between the Governor and Deputy." [*Ibid*, 88.] In February, 1632-3, three elders went to Nantasket, with the Governor and four Assistants, to see if it were a good place to build a fort. [*Ibid*, 99.] The Governor and Council called all the elders together 17-27 Sept. 1633, to consult as to where John Cotton should settle. [*Ibid*, 112.] The advice of the elders was taken 27 Dec.-7 Jan. 1633-4, by the Governor and Assistants in regard to Roger Williams's opinion about the patent. [*Ibid*, 122.] Some of the elders were called in to the conference of Bradford, Winslow and Winthrop, 9-19 July, 1634, about the case of Kennebeck. [*Ibid*, 136.] Twenty days thereafter, "divers of the ministers" took part in the discussion which ended in fortifying Castle Island. [*Ibid*, 137.] In November, 1634, John Eliot, having taken occasion to blame the government for making peace with the Pequots without consulting the people, the Court ordered him to be "dealt with" by Messrs. Cotton, Hooker and Welde, to bring him "to see his errour, and to heal it by some public explanation of his meaning; for the people began to take occasion to murmur against us for it." They brought him "to acknowledge his errour" and to promise to "express himself in public next Lord's Day." [*Ibid*, 151.] I have already cited the fact that, in Feb. 1634-5, all the ministers were summoned to advise the Court what to do if a General Governor should be sent over. [*Ibid*, 154.] So "all the ministers" were summoned to act with the Governor and Assistants in hearing and deciding the case of Roger Williams. [*Ibid*, 158, 162, 170.] Dr. Palfrey, writing of 1634, says: "the clergy, now thirteen or fourteen in number, constituted in some sort, a separate estate of special dignity. Though they were excluded from secular office, the relation of their functions to the spirit and aim of the community, which had been founded, as well as their personal weight of ability and character, gave great authority to their advice, etc." [*Hist. N. Eng.* i: 384.] The case of Mr. Cotton, in connection with the sad troubles of Antinomianism in 1636-7, is too familiar to need more than this allusion here.

[102] Winthrop's *Journal*, i: 117; Cotton's *Way of Cong. Churches Cleared, etc.*, 55.

[103] William Coddington says Williams had written "a large Book in Quarto" against the patent. It is not known to what production of Williams's busy pen this averment can refer, unless it be to this. [See Appendix to Fox and Burnyeat's *New-Eng. Firebrand Quenched*, 246.]

[104] See p. 8. The quotation is from Bradford's *Hist. Plym. Plant.* 310.

discussion)[105] the "treatise" was submitted to the examination of the Governor and Assistants at a meeting held 27 Dec.–6 Jan. 1633–4. Gov. Winthrop indicates its quality, as follows:[106]

Wherein, among other things, he disputes their right to the lands they possessed here, and concluded that, claiming by the king's grant, they could have no title, nor otherwise, except they compounded with the natives. . . There were three passages chiefly whereat they [that is, the Court] were much offended: (1.) for that he chargeth King James to have told a solemn public lie, because in his patent he blessed God that he was the first Christian prince that had discovered this land; (2.) for that he chargeth him and others with blasphemy for calling Europe Christendom, or the Christian world; (3.) for that he did personally apply to our present King, Charles, these three places in the Revelations, viz.: [blank].

A letter has lately been discovered among the Winthrop family papers, in the possession of the present noble representative of that family, Hon. Robert C. Winthrop, LL.D., bearing date 3–13 Jan., 1633–4—written, therefore, just one week after the meeting above referred to—from Gov. Winthrop to Mr. Endecott; who was a parishioner and friend of Roger Williams at Salem, as well as one of the Assistants of the Court. This letter gives a fourth specification of the argument of the "treatise," as follows:[107]

---

105 More than one respectable writer has been led into heavy censure of the authorities of Massachusetts for their action in this thing. Gammell says: "the act of the General Court can be regarded as nothing less than a despotic exercise of absolute power. It demanded from the privacy of his own desk an unpublished manuscript which he had written within another jurisdiction, on a great subject of abstract right and natural law, and summoned him to appear and receive censure for the opinions it contained," [*Life*, 32]; and Gov. Arnold says: "the arbitrary action of the Court, in calling for a paper written beyond the jurisdiction of Massachusetts, 'for the private satisfaction of the Governor of Plymouth,' and which had never been published, would have been properly resented by refusing to obey the summons, etc." [*Hist. R. I.* i: 28.] All this is clearly founded upon misapprehension of the facts, and mistake in the meaning of a word. There is no evidence of any "action of the Court"; certainly none appears upon its Records. All we know of the circumstance is from Winthrop's *Journal*. He says they "took into consideration a treatise which Mr. Williams (then of Salem) had sent to them, etc." Farther on, he says Williams pleaded that he should not "have stirred any further in it, if the Governour [Winthrop] had not *required* a copy of him." [i: 122.] So that, at most, there was only this action of the Governor, and I submit that a just rendering of the narrative resolves that action purely into a friendly solicitation, instead of an official demand. Every student of our language knows that the word "require" has an old sense which is exactly synonymous with "desire," or "request": and a reference to the authorized version of the Scriptures, to Shakspeare, and other cotemporary writers, will make it clear that that sense was common in our fathers' time. Take, for example, these texts: *Esther ii:* 15, "she *required* [asked for] nothing but what Hegai the king's chamberlain, the keeper of the women, appointed"; and 2 *Sam. xix:* 38, "and whatsoever thou shalt *require* [the marginal reading says, '*Heb.* choose'] of me, that will I do for thee"; and *Ezra viii:* 22, "I was ashamed to *require* [request] of the king a band of soldiers and horsemen to help us against the enemy in the way." Examine also *Macbeth* [Act iii: Scene 4] where Macbeth says of Lady Macbeth:

"Our hostess keeps her state; but in best time
We will require [request] her welcome."

Still more clear is this, in *King Henry VIIIth* [Act ii: Scene 4], where Cardinal Wolsey says to the King:

—— "most gracious Sir,
In humblest manner I require [supplicate of] your Highness,
That it shall please you to declare, etc."

106 *Journal*, i: 122.

107 See the Letter in *Proceedings of the Massachusetts Historical Society*, 1871–73, p. 343.

(4.) for concluding us all heere to lye under a sinne of unjust usurpation upon others possessions.

This letter also supplies us with the missing passages from the Apocalypse; citing them in its margin as: Rev. xvi: 13–14; xvii: 12–13, and xviii: 9.[108] These were, therefore, as follows:

And I saw three vncleane spirits like frogs come out of the mouth of the dragon, and out of the mouth of the beast, and out of the mouth of the false prophet.

For they are the spirits of deuils working miracles, which goe forth vnto the Kings of the earth, and of the whole world, to gather them to the battell of that great day of God Almighty.

And the ten hornes which thou sawest, are ten Kings, which haue receiued no kingdome as yet; but receiue power as kings one houre with the beast.

These haue one minde, and shall giue their power and strength vnto the beast.

And the Kings of the earth, who haue committed fornication, and liued deliciously with her shall bewaile her and lament for her, when they shall see the smoke of her burning.

Taking these two statements of Winthrop together, it seems evident that this "treatise" was chiefly to the Court objectionable, and in their thought dangerous, because it tended to weaken the confidence of the freemen of the Company in the validity of the Charter in which all their legal rights as a plantation were bound up; because, in its logical conclusion, — which implied that the whole fabric of their organic life was founded on a fraud, and an usurpation — it tended directly and inevitably toward anarchy; and because, in a manner to their view as offensive as it was uncalled for,[109] it insulted the last, and the reigning monarch, by the charges of siding with Antichrist, of falsehood and of blasphemy. All this was aggravated by an apparent insincerity. Mr. Williams had cast in his lot with them, knowing — or having the means of knowing — fully what the character of the patent was before he left England; and although he never became a freeman of the Corporation,[110] he had already

108 This verse is clearly set down here, and where again referred to in the body of the letter, as xviii: 19. But the description of it in the letter, proves that this is a mistake, and that the verse really intended was xviii: 9, as above.

109 "For I would gladlye knowe to what good ende, & for what use of Edification, he should publishe these thinges in this lande (if they were as he supposethe them) — doth he see any pronenesse in this people to joyne with the Beast or the Whore? or dothe he feare least our Kinge beinge upon such a designe, would sende for our Assistance?" [*Letter*, as above, p. 344.]

110 Elton [*Life*, 15], Gammell [*Life*, 19], Knowles [*Memoir*, 49], and Underhill [*Introduction to Bloudy Tenent, etc.*, in *Hanserd Knollys Society's Publications*, p. x,] all declare that Roger Williams took the "Freeman's Oath" 18–28 May, 1631, [Underhill says 12–21 May.] But that was *another* Roger Williams, who had come over in the "Mary and John" in 1630, and was at Dorchester among the earliest. He served on a jury to inquire into the cause of the death of Austen Bratcher 28 Sept.–8 Oct. 1630; applied to be admitted a freeman 19–29 Oct. 1630 — or 109 days before *our* Roger arrived at Nantasket; had charge, with another, of the goods of Christopher Ollyver 7–17 Nov. 1634; was one of the arbitrators about the ship "Thunder" in the summer of 1635, and was one of the selectmen of Dorchester the same year; but soon removed to Windsor, Conn.; within ten years sold his land there to Capt. Benjamin Newberry, and returned to Boston; and joined the An-

become a landholder, owning ten acres besides the lot and the house in which he dwelt at Salem,[111] and thus he seemed by his practice to give the lie to some, at least, of these professions.[112]

The Court advised with those whom they esteemed the most judicious of the elders — as was their custom in cases of doubt — and cited Mr. Williams to appear at their next session "to be censured;" but as Mr. Endecott had not been present, the Governor wrote to him (it would seem the very letter, the rough draught of which has been cited above) to let him know what had been done, and "withal added divers arguments to confute the said errors, wishing him to deal with Mr. Williams to retract the same."[113] Whether in consequence of Mr. Endecott's labor in response to this request, or not, Mr. Williams seems on this occasion to have exhibited a submission to the mental influence of others which was extraordinary in his history. He wrote privately to the Governor, and officially to him and the Court, "very submissively;" intimating that he had no intention of pushing these views, and "withal offering his book, or any part of it to be burnt."[114] On the 24 Jan.–3 Feb. 1633–4,

---

cient and Honorable Artillery Company in 1647. [*History of Dorchester*, 92; Savage's *Gen. Dict.* iv: 567; *Hist. Anct. and Hon. Art.* 155; Stiles's *Hist. Ancient Windsor*, 135; *Mass. Col. Rec.* i: 77, 133, 151.] *He* was sworn in freeman, in accordance with his previous application, on the 18-28 May, 1631, [*Mass. Col. Rec.* i: 636]; but Roger Williams, who was pastor at Salem, and the founder of Providence, was never a freeman of Massachusetts. In this he differed from the others who exercised the Christian ministry in the Colony at the same time with him. Wilson and Cotton of Boston, Warham and Maverick of Dorchester, Welde and Eliot of Roxbury, Hooker and Stone of Newtown (Cambridge), Phillips of Watertown, James of Charlestown, Batcheller of Saugus, and even his associate Samuel Skelton of Salem, all had taken the freeman's oath. [*Ibid*, 366–369.]

[111] There is a deed at Salem, of date October, 1635, of the sale by John Woolcott unto William Lord, both of Salem, of "all and every part of my house and misteed [merestead] in Salem (*formerlie in the occupation of Mr. Roger Williams*) & from him by order from Mrs. Higenson sould vnto mee, as by a quittance vnd Mr. Wms. hand doth appear." This house stood on ground now covered by the south-eastern portion of the "Asiatic Building," 56 ft. south of the present meeting-house of the First Church. It is not certain that Mr. Williams *owned* this house; nor when he left it. But by a letter of his from Providence, which seems to have been written in June. 1638, [4 *Mass. Hist. Coll.* vi: 230] it is made clear that he did subsequently own a "howse at Salem," and that he had made arrangements to pay with it a debt of between £50 and £60 due to Mr. Cradock, and that he had "long since" put it into Mr. Mayhew's hands (as agent for Mr. Cradock) for that purpose. A previous letter [conjecturally assigned to October, 1637] alludes to the same transaction: "I yet know not where that tobacco is; but desire if Mr. Cradock's agent Mr. Jolly [Jolliffe] would accept it, that it may be delivered to him in part of some payments *for which I haue made over my howse to Mr. Mayhew.*" [*Ibid*, 216.] This house in which Mr. Williams seems to have passed the latter part of his residence in Salem, is supposed by the Essex antiquaries to have formed a portion of what was long known as the "Curwen House"; now, or lately, standing on the western corner of North and Essex Sts., in that city. [*Hist. Coll. Essex Institute*, viii: 257.] Curiously, some of the private preliminary examinations of the witch-craft times, are thought to have been held in that house. [*Ibid*, 258.] Mr. Williams also owned a ten acre lot "in the North Field," as appears by the deed of adjoining land from Philip Cromwell to Thomas Cole, of date 13–23 Feb. 1650. [*Ibid*, 257.]

[112] As Gov. Winthrop puts it: "But if our title be not good, neither by Patent, nor possession of these parts as *vacuum domicilium*, nor by good liking of the natives, *I mervayle by what title Mr. Williams himselfe holds?*" [*Letter*, as above, 345.]

[113] Winthrop's *Journal*, i: 122.

[114] This seems to have been thought the suitable fate for pernicious literature. The Court, in the spring of 1635, voted: "Whereas Mr. Israell Stoughton hath written a certaine booke wch. hath occasoned mch trouble &

the Governor and Council met again; when, with the advice of Rev. Messrs. Cotton and Wilson, and finding, on further consideration, that, by reason of the obscurity with which the "treatise" was written, its influence might not be so evil as they had feared, they agreed to deal gently with the offender, and to pass over the offence, "upon his retractation, etc., or taking an oath of allegiance to the king, etc."[115] It is not altogether clear from this statement, what, precisely, Roger Williams finally did at this time, or whether he took the oath demanded. But it *is* clear that the authorities manifested no desire to fault him; but appeared rather anxious to avoid, so far as they consistently might do so, all severe dealing, and to accept his explanations and concessions in the most amicable spirit; and it is clearly involved in what Winthrop afterwards says, as well as in the general tenor of the narrative, that the Salem preacher was understood on this occasion, at least to promise not further to advocate publicly these notions about the patent, and not openly to assail the churches of England as being anti-Christian.[116] While that representation often given, which makes the Governor and Assistants the aggressive party, watching perpetually for Mr. Williams's halting, and now and then just giving him a chance to breathe between their foreordained attacks; is seen to be, here, at least, not only injurious, but absurd.[117] He was the aggressor. If he had been able to restrain himself from attacking the fundamental basis on which all their institutions rested, there is no hint of any wish on their part to trouble him. They did not insist that he should violate the liberty of his own convictions, and surrender his peculiar opinions; but only that he should refrain from "teaching publickly" in a way to undermine the foundations of their social order; and from assaulting openly institutions at home in a way to bring the settlement into disfavor there, and so to imperil its, as yet uncertain, life.

Six weeks now passed, during which we hear nothing of Mr. Williams, or

---

offence to the Court, the sd. Mr. Stoughton did desire of the Court that the sd. booke might forthwith be burnt, as being weake and offensiue." [*Mass. Col. Rec.* i: 135.] The same thing happened to William Pynchon in 1650, and nearly the same to the revered John Eliot, in 1661. [*Ibid*, iii: 215; iv. (2): 5.]

115 *Winthrop's Journal*, i: 123.

116 *Ibid*, 151.

117 Knowles says: "He was now *permitted, for a while*, to continue his ministry at Salem, without interruption from the magistrates." [*Memoir*, 61.] Elton uses almost the same expression: "Williams was now *permitted, for a short period*, to exercise his ministerial labours at Salem in peace." [*Life*, 22.] Underhill's language looks the same way. He prefaces his account of the dealing of the Court with him as to this "treatise" with this sentence, which insinuates a purpose, of the existence of which there is absolutely no evidence: "Matter for complaint *was soon discovered against Mr. Williams*;" as if the Massachusetts Company spent its time in doing little else than in hunting for such "matter;" and he appends to the statement of the dismissal of the subject the invidious declaration: "It will be seen, however, that this accusation was *revived*, and declared to be one of the causes of his banishment." [Introduction to *Bloudy Tenent*, etc. xiii.] And Arnold states it, with an equally unwarranted intimation, in these words: "Thus the subject rested for a few months, *until it was found convenient again to call it up*." [*Hist. R. I.* i: 28.]

his opinions. But on the 7–17 March 1633–4, a question was raised, on Lecture-day at Boston, as to whether it were the duty of all females to veil themselves on going abroad? Cotton thought not: "that where (by the custom of the place) they [veils] were not a sign of the women's subjection, they were not commanded by the apostle." Endecott took the other side, and we learn from Hubbard that he had gained his learning, and his bias, from Mr. Williams, who had been preaching to his congregation their obligation in that respect.[118] The incident is an unimportant one, save as it illustrates the man's astonishing ability to see things in some light of duty different from that usual to the good people by whom he was surrounded.

During the summer following, in which Mr. Skelton died, we hear nothing directly of Mr. Williams, though we fancy it as having been most likely about this time, that he gave utterance to the judgment that: "Of all Christian Churches, the Churches of New England were accounted, and professed by him, to be the most pure: and of all the Churches in New England, Salem (where himselfe was Teacher) to be the most pure." As the autumn drew on, with its ill tidings from England of the danger threatening the patent, and all the interests of the plantation, the Government appointed Wednesday, the 17–27 September, to be "kept as a day of publique humiliacon" throughout the jurisdiction. Mr. Williams improved the occasion by preaching; in which he "discovered eleven publike sins for which he beleeved it pleased God to inflict, and further to threaten publike calamities; most of which eleven (if not all) that Church then seemed to assent unto."[119]

Early in November (5–15) complaint was made to the Court of Assistants that the flag of England had been mutilated at Salem, by the removal of the cross from it. Inquiry was instituted, and, three weeks after, the subject came up again, and it became evident that Endecott had ordered the act to be committed, on the ground that "the red cross was given to the King of England by the pope, as an ensign of victory, and so a superstitious thing, and a relique of Anti-Christ."[120] It was scarcely two months since the Griffin had brought over the alarming news that the Commission had been appointed over the

---

[118] Winthrop's *Journal*, i: 125; Hubbard's *Gen. Hist. N. E.* 204; Felt's *Eccl. Hist. N. E.* i: 177. Hubbard adds the statement that Mr. Cotton about this time spending a Sunday at Salem, preached on that subject in the forenoon, "which discourse let in so much light into their understandings, that they, who before thought it a shame to be seen in the public without a veil, were ashamed ever after to be covered with them." Readers who remember, or will look up, the cases named in the Old Testament, of Tamar, and Ruth, will find assistance in imagining the grim humor of Mr. Cotton's discourse, and its surprising effect upon his female auditors. [*Gen. xxxviii:* 14, 15; *Ruth iii:* 8–15. Compare *Ezek. xvi:* 16, 25.]

[119] Cotton's *Reply to Mr. Williams his Exam., etc.* 2, 142; *Way of Cong. Churches Cleared, etc.* 28 *Magnalia*, Book vii: 8. The Fast is recorded in *Mass. Col. Rec.* i: 128; and Williams's account of his sermon is in *Mr. Cotton's Letter Examined, etc.* 2.

[120] Winthrop's *Journal*, i: 147.

colonies, with power to call in their patents, and that there was danger of the speedy loss of all their civil and commercial rights ; and the colonists were at this very time hard at work in fortifying Castle Island, Charlestown and Dorchester, in view of possible contingencies. They were much alarmed therefore at this sudden and unauthorized action, "as fearing," that just at this juncture, "it would be taken as an act of rebellion, or of like high nature, in defacing the king's colors."[121] It turned out that a considerable popular feeling had been awakened against the cross in the ensign, so that it was some months before the matter was quieted, although Endecott was admonished, and disabled for a year from bearing office.[122] Winthrop is reticent in regard to the reasons of this act of the Salem Assistant, but Hubbard[123] distinctly lays the origin of the business at Mr. Williams's door, saying, that "in his zeal for advancing the purity of reformation, and abolishing all badges of superstition, he inspired" the movement; while Cotton Mather[124] reiterates a charge having in itself, it must be confessed, strong elements of probability.

Three weeks had scarcely passed, when (27 Nov.–7 Dec. 1634) the Court was informed that "Mr. Williams of Salem had broken his promise to us, in teaching publickly against the king's patent, and our great sin in claiming right thereby to this country, etc., and for usual terming the churches of England anti-Christian."[125] Summons was accordingly granted for his appearance at the next Court. The next Court met on the 3–13 March 1634–5.[126] But there is no trace of any action in regard to Mr. Williams in the record of its doings ; none in the Governor's own private Journal, which preserved a note of so many things which slipped through the pen of the secretary. We are left therefore to the necessary inference that some reason arose for postponement in the case. That reason I find in the statement of John Cotton : "I presented (with the consent of my fellow-Elders and Brethren) a serious Request to the Magistrates, that they would be pleased to forbeare all civill prosecution against him, till our selves (with our Churches) had dealt with him in a Church way, to convince him of sinne: alledging, that my selfe and brethren hoped his violent course did rather spring from scruple of conscience (though carried with an

---

[121] *Ibid.*

[122] *Ibid*, i: 158.

[123] *Gen. Hist. N. Eng.* 205.

[124] "One in some authority, under the heat of some Impressions from the Ministry of Mr. Williams, did, by his own Authority, cut the Red-Cross out of the King's Colours, to Testifie a Zeal against the Continuance or Appearance of a Superstition." [*Magnalia*, Book vii: 9.] William Coddington, more than forty years after, refers to this, in his blunt and rough, but seemingly honest way. He says: "Another time you may have him [R. W.] a Teacher, or Member, of the church at Salem in New England: O! Then a great deal of Devotion is placed in Women wearing of Vails in their Assemblies, as if the Power of Godliness was in it; and to have the Cross out of the Colors, etc." [Letter, of 28 June, 1677, in the Appendix of *A New England Firebrand Quenched, etc.* 246.]

[125] Winthrop's *Journal*, i: 151.

[126] *Mass. Col. Rec.* i: 134.

inordinate zeale) then from a seditious Principle."[127] This proposal "was approved and allowed," and several of the churches, with their elders, appear to have gone about the work of friendly labor with the church in Salem, and its acting pastor; it would seem with no result which promised to be adequate to the emergency—none, at any rate, which convinced him of any duty of quietness.

Accordingly we find that when the Court met, on the 30 April–10 May 1635, the Governor and Assistants sent for Mr. Williams, and dealt with him in relation to a new difficulty which had arisen in regard to his teaching. In the extremely miscellaneous condition in which the colony found itself; liable to the influx of strangers from other settlements along the coast from Newfoundland to Virginia, as well as from the Bermudas and the mother-country, and with the knowledge that many influences were at work against them; it had seemed to the authorities expedient to require some pledge as a condition of residence on the soil, which should engage new comers, at least, to such degree of subordination and coöperation as might ensure the plantation against many evils otherwise liable to threaten it. Accordingly the Court of 1–10 April previous, had ordered that every man above the age of twenty years, who was, or proposed to be, resident within the jurisdiction for six months, or more, and who did not become a freeman of the corporation, should take what they named the "Resident's Oath," on pain of being sent out of the territory should he refuse (after having been twice requested to do so by the Government) to enter into the obligations it imposed; which were, to be obedient to the laws, to promote the peace and welfare of the plantation, and to reveal any plots against it, which should come to his knowledge.[128] The next Court, on the 14–24 May

---

[127] *Reply to Mr. Williams his Exam., etc.* 38. Mr. Cotton goes on to state the Governor's answer to this request: "That wee were deceived in him [R.W.], if we thought he would condescend to learne of any of us: And what will you doe (saith he) when you have run your course, and found all your labour lost? I answered for the rest, we hoped better things; if it fell out contrary to our hopes, we could not helpe it, but must sit downe, and quiet our conscience in the Lord's acceptance of our will and endeavour for the deed." See also Cotton Mather [*Magnalia*, Book vii: 8.]

[128] The form of the oath was, as follows: "I doe heare sweare, and call God to witnes, that, being nowe an inhabitant within the lymitts of this jurisdiccon of the Massachusetts, I doe acknowledge myselfe lawfully subiect to the aucthoritie and gouerm^t there established, and doe accordingly submitt my pson, family, and estate to be ptected, ordered, & governed by the lawes & constitucions thereof, and doe faithfully pmise to be from time to time obedient and conformeable therevnto, and to the aucthoritie of the Goun^r & all other the magistrates there, and their successrs, and to all such lawes, orders, sentences & decrees, as nowe are or hereafter shalbe lawfully made, decreed, & published by them or their successrs. And I will alwayes indeav^r (as in duty I am bound) to advance the peace & wellfaire of this body pollitique, and I will (to my best power & meanes) seeke to devert & prevent whatsoeuer may tende to the ruine or damage thereof, or of ye Goun^r, Deputy Goun^r or Assistants, or any of them or their successrs, and will giue speedy notice to them, or some of them, of any sedicon, violence, treacherie, or othr hurte or euill wch. I shall knowe, heare, or vehemently suspect, to be plotted or intended against them, or any of them, or against the said Comonwealth or Goum^t, established. Soe helpe mee God." [*Mass. Col. Rec.* i: 115.]

following, proceeded to modify the existing form of the Freeman's Oath, making some slight changes suggested by the exigencies sought to be guarded against in the other.[129] There was surely nothing unusual to the time in this action; as there appears to be nothing to an ordinary conscience objectionable in the intent of these oaths, or the phraseology in them employed. It is indeed hard to see in what way the authorities could more wisely have provided for obvious duties, and against possible dangers, which thronged the difficult path along which they were called, in God's providence, to walk.

But Mr. Williams thought otherwise, and immediately began to preach against this Resident's Oath.[130] He scrupled all such endeavors to bind those who were not Christians. He took the ground that for a magistrate to tender an oath to an unregenerate person, was thereby to "have communion with a wicked man in the worship of God, and cause him to take the name of God in

---

[129] As modified, it was as follows: "I, A. B. being, by God's providence, an inhabitant & ffreeman within the jurisdiccon of this comonweale, doe freely acknowledge my selfe to be subiect to the govermt. thereof, & therefore doe heere sweare, by the greate & dreadfull name of the euerlyyveing God, that I wilbe true & faithfull to the same, & will accordingly yeilde assistance & support therevnto, with my pson, & estate, as in equity I am bound, & will also truely indeav[r] to mainetaine & preserue the libertyes & previlidges thereof, submitting my selfe to the wholesome lawes & orders made & established by the same; and furthr., that I will not plott nor practise any evill against it, nor consent to any that shall soe doe, but will timely discover & reveale the same to lawfull aucthority nowe here established, for the speedy preventing thereof. Moreouer, I doe solemnely bynde myselfe, in the sight of God, that when I shalbe called to giue my voice touching any such matter of this state, wherein ffreemen are to deale, I will giue my vote & suffrage, as I shall iudge in myne owne conscience may best conduce & tend to the publique weale of the body, without respect of psons., or fav[r] of any man. Soe helpe me God, in the Lord Jesus Christ. [*Ibid*, i: 117.]

[130] Mr. Cotton goes into this matter more fully, I believe, than any other cotemporary writer. He says [*Reply to Mr. Williams his Exam., etc.* 29]: "This Oath, when it came abroad, he [Mr. W.] vehemently withstood it, and disswaded sundry from it, partly because it was, as he said, Christ's Prerogative to have his Office established by Oath; partly because an oath was a part of God's worship, and God's worship was not to be put upon carnall persons, as he conceived many of the People to be. So by his Tenent neither might Church-members, nor other godly men, take the Oath, because it was the establishment not of Christ, but of mortall men in their office; nor might men out of the Church take it, because in his eye they were but carnall."

Backus—in his *History* [i: 66, etc.], and still more especially in his pamphlet of 1778, entitled *Government and Liberty Described; and Ecclesiastical Tyranny Exposed*, [9] charges that the object of this change in the oath was to get rid of the phrase "lawfully made," and substitute for it the phrase "*wholesome*," as describing those statutes to which it pledged its taker; and that this was done because they had "set out to frame and enforce a new religious establishment, very contrary to that of England," and found that the old oath stood in the way of it. The evidence of this last assertion he finds in the fact that, in "the following year, the Court sent out to all their ministers and brethren, for advice and assistance, about one uniform order of discipline in their churches, etc." But Dr. Backus clearly did not stop to consider the European aspect of American matters at that time, nor what the pressure then was from over sea; in a sense compelling them, not merely to venture upon some regulations and procedures which might not bear a close examination in the light of English law, and their Charter; but to take every precaution to secure the enforcement of those regulations. Since Dr. Backus's time our nation has learned that in days of war, and revolution, red tape must take its chance. He who reads carefully Dr. Palfrey's lucid exposition of New England affairs of that period, will see, I think, that Backus was in error; that the change in the oath had no relation whatever to any plans about an unlawful establishment; and that Williams opposed the oath—as he said he did, and as others say he did—for what he conceived to be the intrinsic sin of *any* oath so administered; and not because he wished to protest against, and forestall, the possible founding of a New England national church.

vain."[131] Playing thus directly into the hands of that small but active, and malcontent if not seditious, element of the population which was ready to respond with active coöperation to those "Episcopall, and malignant practises against the Countrey"[132] which were then menacing from without; his course threatened the authorities with serious embarrassment, the more as his reputation for unusual sanctity, especially among the weaker and more influential sex,[133] drew not a few good people towards his conclusion. Mr. Cotton, indeed, goes so far as to represent that his adverse influence was so considerable as to force the Court to retrace its steps, and "desist from that proceeding."[134] But I find no cotemporary corroboration of this representation; while the fact, that Winthrop's Journal, Morton's Memorial, Hubbard's History, and the Court Records, show no trace of any such retrograde action, inclines me to the opinion that Mr. Cotton here erred by over-statement. Most likely what took place really was, that the magistrates for a time used the discretion which the law gave them, in not "conventing" before them those who neglected or declined to take the oath, and sending out of the jurisdiction all who should the second time refuse to do so; which course would practically amount to a suspension of the statute. And that this was the case, is made the more probable by the fact that seventeen years later (in May, 1652), the Court, taking notice of the fact that "divers inhabitants," who were receiving the protection of the Government, had said and done things whereby their fidelity might justly be suspected; ordered the administration of the old oath (evidently never unrepealed, but practically disused by many) to "*all* settled inhabitants amongst vs who hath not already taken the same."[135]

It was for this action of Mr. Williams that the Court, on this occasion, called him to account. He argued the matter with them, and with the other ministers. The opinion of the Court was that he was "very clearly confuted;"[133] and Endecott, who had at first sided with his minister, acknowledged himself convinced. Here, for more than two months, the matter rested; Mr. Williams being left—it would seem—to think the subject over, under the protest of the magistrates, and of his brother ministers, against his views; and he and his church remaining still under the process of dealing with them, and him, commenced at Mr. Cotton's suggestion, to which reference has been made.

---

[131] Winthrop's *Journal*, i: 158.

[132] *Reply to Mr. Williams his Exam.*, *etc.* 28.

[133] "The people being, many of them, much taken with the apprehension of his godliness" [Winthrop's *Journal*, i: 175]; "many, especially of devout women, did embrace his opinions." [*Ibid*, i: 176.]

[134] *Reply to Mr. Williams his Exam.*, *etc.* 29. But he himself in the same *Reply*, elsewhere feels it to be quite sufficient to say [4]: "upon this, *sundry* refused the Oath."

[135] *Mass. Col. Rec.* iii: 263.

[136] Winthrop's *Journal*, i: 158.

Just at this time, and during these two months of May and June, 1635—if I am right in my theory of resolution of the chronological difficulties involved in the subject—the major part of the church in Salem; which had desired Mr. Williams as its teacher when the interposition of the magistrates, and other influences had led him to go, instead, to the Old Colony, and which for some twenty months had been hearing him since his return from Plymouth; in the face of his position of practical — not to say factious — hostility toward the Government; and in the face of the dealings with him, and with them, of the other churches of the jurisdiction still going on; proceeded formally to complete his thus far informal pastoral relation, and ordain him over them according to the simple rites which the early Congregationalism of New England had already adopted. My reasons for venturing to differ with all previous writers, as to the date of this event, and as to one of the most important circumstances connected with it, I have fully stated below.[137]

---

[137] It has been usual to set down the date of this ordination, as Gammell does [*Life*, 37], as in August 1634. But I find no such date given in the earliest authorities. Hubbard [*Gen. Hist. N. E.* 204] says that "in *one year's* time" he had filled Salem with principles of rigid separation, etc., and represents the ordaining to have taken place some time after that; and Morton [*N. E. Mem.* 79] makes a statement almost identical with this; from which Gammell and others, assuming the date of his return to Salem to have been in August, 1633, appear to have fixed upon August, 1634, as the time of ordination. But Backus [*Hist. N. Eng.* i: 57] says "all agree that he was not ordained till after Mr. Skelton's death," which we know took place 2–12 Aug. 1634; and Hubbard [204] says it was "after some time" subsequent to Mr. Skelton's death, that the Church called Mr. Williams to office. Dr. Bentley [Description of Salem, etc. 1 *Mass. Hist. Coll.* vi: 247] indeed represents that "Mr. Skelton's sickness gave him [R. W.] an opportunity to renew his public labours in the pulpit, *for the pastoral relation had not been dissolved.*" But we have already seen [*ante* p. 5] the improbability that Mr. Williams was settled at Salem before going to Plymouth; and, if he had been, the relation — by the strict construction of those days — would have been terminated by his departure. It so happens that the most conclusive evidence exists not only that Mr. Williams was not ordained, as Mr. Gammell claims, in August, 1634, but that his ordination had not taken place at as late a period as in December of that year. There is among the British Colonial State Papers, a letter from Capt. James Cudworth of Scituate to Dr. Stoughton, of Aldermanbury, London, dated "Citewat the — of December, 1634," in which, in giving an account of the ministers then laboring in the vicinity, he says: "at Salem theare Pastore old Mr. Skelton is ded; theare is Mr. Williames *who doe exersies his giftes, but is in no office.*" [*Colonial*, viii: No. 39.] Being thus thrown wholly out of the old ruts of opinion as to this date, we are quite at liberty to look around for whatever hypothesis may offer most of probability. My notion is that where no Court records are available, Winthrop's Journal always furnishes us the most trustworthy data for settling the early chronology of Massachusetts. His habits appear to have been methodical, and he was accustomed to jot down his memoranda of occurrences before time enough had elapsed to blur the exactness of memory; so that it is not easy to believe in any essential error in the order of his records. His interest in topics of religious and patriotic moment was, moreover, such as to make it as difficult for us to think that he would overlook, as that he would misplace the mention of any such. But we find no allusion, whatever, to any such event as Mr. Williams's ordination in the pages of Winthrop, until we get down to the date of 8–18 July, 1635; where we are told that "the other churches were about to write to the church of Salem to admonish him of these errors; notwithstanding, *the church had since called him to the office of a teacher.*" [*Journal*, i: 162.] If I understand this language correctly, it indicates that the calling of Mr. Williams to be a teacher had taken place after the churches had commenced arrangements to labor with his church and with him. If so, that calling must have been after the early spring of 1635 [see p. 33 *ante*], and in all probability after the 30 April–8 May of that year, or Gov. Winthrop would have referred to it in his statement of that date [*Journal*, i: 157]; for had such an event already happened, it seems almost incredible that he

It was not reasonably to be expected that this high-handed course on the part of the church of Salem and its pastor, amounting to something very like open contempt of the public sentiment and feeling of the vast majority of the ablest and best men in the colony, should go free of rebuke; and we are therefore prepared for the information which Governor Winthrop gives us, of the citation of Mr. Williams to the General Court of 8–18 July next succeeding, to answer to complaints made against him. It was natural also that the Court should, on this occasion, go more fully than before into the detail of his offensive teachings. It was laid to his charge, that he advocated opinions dangerous to the common welfare, viz.:[138]

1. That the magistrate ought not to punish the breach of the first table,[139] except when the civil peace should be endangered.

2. That an oath ought not to be tendered to an unregenerate man.

3. That a man ought not to pray with the unregenerate, even though it be with his wife or child.

4. That a man ought not to give thanks after the sacrament, nor after meat.

---

should make no allusion to it, there and then. Mr. Cotton says, moreover [*Reply to Mr. Williams, etc.* 29], that the action of the Court about the Marblehead land — to which we shall soon come in the story — was "soone after" his settlement by "the major part of the Church." But this action about the land took place apparently in July 1635 [Winthrop's *Journal*, 164], so that if my idea that his ordination was in May or June of 1635, be correct, Cotton's "soon after" would be exact.

The other circumstance above referred to, is the question whether there was at this time any interference of the magistrates, to prevent the ordination, if possible. It is to be conceded that Mr. Cotton [*Reply, etc.* 29] says there was: "The Magistrates discerning by the former passages, the heady and turbulent spirit of Mr. Williams, *both they*, and others, advised the Church of Salem not to call him to office, etc." Cotton Mather also declares [*Magnalia*, Book vii: 7]: "the Government again renewed their Advice unto the People to forbear a thing of such ill Consequence;" and Hutchinson [*Hist. Mass.* 1: 41] following Hubbard [*Gen. Hist. N. Eng.* 204] says as much. On the other hand, Winthrop — who surely must have known the fact, if any such action of the Government took place — says nothing about it, when there was every reason that he should have done so, if such were the fact; and we find no sign of any action on the official records. It is my impression therefore that Cotton and Hubbard confused the interference of the elders and the other churches, which clearly did take place, with interference by the Court; and that the only "interference" of which the Court was guilty, was that afterward of adjudging his ordination, under the circumstances of his attitude of hostility to them on the question of the Resident's Oath, and of the dealing of the other churches, to be "a great contempt of authority." [Winthrop's *Journal*, 1: 163.] It is clear from Cotton [*Reply, etc.* 4] that the action of the church was by no means unanimous.

[138] Winthrop's *Journal*, i: 162.

[139] This is the first time, since the spring of 1631, in the whole history thus far, that any hint is given that the doctrine of "soul-liberty" had anything to do with these disturbances. This Backus [*Hist. N. Eng.* 1: 69] interprets as "denying the civil magistrates right to govern in ecclesiastical affairs." Doubtless the charge might include some such denial. But Dr. Palfrey [*Hist. N. Eng.* 1: 407] fairly shows how much more than merely this was involved: "The 'first table' of the Decalogue, consisting of the first four precepts, was understood to forbid four offences, idolatry, perjury, blasphemy and Sabbath-breaking. Of these the last two stand as penal offences on the statute-book of Massachusetts at the present day; the second, there is no government that does not punish; while, in the judgment of the age and the place now treated of, a denial of the right to suppress idolatry, was a denial of the right to provide securities against an irruption of Romanism. It should not excite surprise that the magistrates thought it would be hazardous to good government and the public peace to have their authority in matters of such moment denounced, by a hot-headed young man, from the first pulpit of the Colony."

Earnest debate followed. The elders were called in to give the aid of their judgment. Mr. Williams seems not to have gained a single convert on the occasion; but all, magistrates and elders, with one accord, judged his positions "to be erroneous, and very dangerous"; while all was aggravated by the fact of his ordination in what looked like defiance of the reasonable protest of the ministers and churches, if not of the magistrates. All ended by requesting him, and his church, to take the whole matter into reconsideration until the next General Court, to meet eight weeks thereafter; with the understanding that unless the causes of complaint should by that time be removed, the Court must then be expected to take some final action thereon.[140]

It so happened, that at this same Court some reply was to be made to a petition which the Salem people had previously sent in, for the assignment to them of "the lande betwixte the Clifte and the Forest Ryver, neere Marble Head."[141] Considering the exasperation which was felt — and, I submit, naturally felt, by the tribunal — at the, as it seemed to it, seditious and harmful posture assumed by Mr. Williams; aggravated by the almost scornful disregard, by his church, of the constitutional protests of the other churches, in sealing him, just at this time, to be their pastor, and thereby doing their utmost to endorse, dignify, and spread abroad principles advanced by him which appeared to the Court subversive of the very foundations of all government, and especially dangerous just at that time, because of the aid and comfort given by them, on the one hand, to the factious element within the plantation, and, on the other, to their various enemies in England who needed just such arguments as Mr. Williams and his church were furnishing them, to succeed in crushing the Charter and destroying the plantation; one feels no surprise whatever in learning that this petition was laid on the table for the

---

140 Gov. Winthrop appends here the statement that the elders were very decided in advising the Court, on this occasion, "that he who should obstinately maintain such opinions (whereby a church might run into heresy, apostacy, or tyranny, and yet the civil magistrate could not intermeddle) were to be removed, and that the other churches ought to request the magistrates so to do." [*Journal*, 1: 163.] At first glance this looks very much like a conflict between the doctrine of toleration on the one side, and its opposite on the other. But when it is remembered that by the fundamental law of the plantation, to be a church-member was to acquire eligibility to become a voter in the State; it will be seen that in such an abnormal condition of affairs it must fairly be expected that the government, in granting to the churches such a privilege, would claim some correspondent right to insist that the churches should not ride roughshod over the rights and privileges of the State. Or, to make the matter specific to the case in hand: the Court had said, for substance, that if a man joined the church in Salem he could have the accompanying privilege of becoming a freeman of Massachusetts. Hence it felt that it was no hardship, but a just and fair thing, that it should demand of the church in Salem not to admit to its communion men who would not themselves take, and who used all their influence to prevent others from taking, those oaths by which alone the State could — under the pains and penalties of perjury — bind its citizens, and residents who were not its citizens, to a faithful and fruitful coöperation in its affairs, and to due obedience and subordination to its rule. So it seems to be very clear that the naked question of toleration was, after all, involved here but indirectly, if at all.

141 *Mass. Col. Rec.* 1: 147.

present, in order to see how all these things were to be finally adjusted.[142] Salem people wanted from the Court the favor of the legal confirmation of a right which they claimed in this Marblehead Neck; the government wanted of the Salem people the favor of a quiet and faithful submission to an existing order of things, which others (presumably as perspicacious and devout as Salem people) felt to involve no hardship to any reasonable conscience. Was it strange that the government should say, not in the way of threat or the mood of bribery, but in the remembrance of what was due to their own self-respect, and to the integrity of an imperilled sway: "we will wait before giving answer to your request, until there shall be time to test more fully the quality of your allegiance to the power, which you desire should be interposed on your behalf?"[143]

Roger Williams was never the meekest and coldest of men. Nor had he reached his own maximum of these qualities, at the youthful period when these events occurred. This action of the Court kindled his indignation, and he lost no time in returning the blow which seemed to him to be struck at him, and his people, by this action of the magistrates. In the then inchoate condition of Church Polity in the Colony, the communion of the churches was largely exercised through what afterward came to be distinguished, in the Cambridge Platform, as the "Way of Admonition."[144] Availing himself of this right, Mr. Williams procured the consent of his church to letters of admonition, written and sent by himself, in their name,[145] to other churches of the plantation, admonishing them of the "heinous sin"[146] thus committed by their members, the magistrates.[147] Doubtless the most was made of the matter, and there may have been many different specifications of offence; but the

---

[142] Winthrop's *Journal*, i. 164.

[143] Prof. Knowles [*Memoir*, 70] says: "here is a candid avowal that justice was refused to Salem, on a question of civil right, as a punishment for the conduct of the church and pastor. A volume could not more forcibly illustrate the danger of a connection between the civil and ecclesiastical power." Gov. Arnold [*Hist. R. I.* i: 34] calls this action of the Court "the punishment inflicted upon the people of Salem for the alleged contempt of installing Roger Williams." It is safe to think that neither of these interesting writers would have phrased matters thus, if they had been living in Massachusetts to see with their own eyes the events which they describe; or, if writing in the 19th century, they could have succeeded in following the motto: "put yourself in his place," until it should have led them into the very midst of the 17th.

[144] *Chap.* xv: 2 (3).

[145] Morton's *N. Eng. Mem.* 79; Hubbard's *Gen. Hist. N. Eng.* 206.

[146] Hubbard (206) says "of sundry heinous offences," copying Morton's words exactly. Winthrop [*Journal*, i: 164] says "of this as a heinous sin."

[147] Winthrop seems to speak as if the deputies were included, as well as the Magistrates, but others do not mention them, nor is it certain that they had anything to do with the offence. If they had, all the churches would have been involved. If not, the churches would be the following six, viz: *Boston* (Dep. Gov. Bellingham, Winthrop, Coddington and Hough); *Newtown* [*Cambridge*] (Gov. Haynes, Dudley and Bradstreet); *Charlestown* (Nowell); *Roxbury* (Pynchon); *Lynn* (Humfrey); and *Newbury* (Dummer). John Winthrop, Jr. (*Ipswich*) was absent from the country, and took no part in the legislation of the year. [*Mass. Col. Rec.* i: 145].

gravamen of the charge centered in the accusation of an open and scandalous transgression of the rule of justice in such a treatment of that petition;[148] and there is evidence that bitter, if not insulting, language characterized these epistles;[149] while the exact practical thing which they asked for, was that each of these churches should put its members, who as magistrates had been guilty of a share in this transaction, *under the discipline of admonition therefor!*[150] In plain English, Roger Williams undertook, in the name, and by the authority of his church, to compel these churches to constrain their members who were magistrates, under penalty to vote to give Marblehead Neck to the people of Salem! That is, he sought to use the machinery of the Church, to secure a certain desired result in the State. What is sauce for the goose ought to be sauce for the gander; and by this action Mr. Williams debarred himself—and would debar his modern apologists and advocates, did they comprehend the facts, and exercise a perspicacity like his own in regard to them—from all consistent objection to any mixture of action between Church and State, if any had been subsequently taken, as the result of what he thus had done.

Much of Mr. Williams's previous teaching and conduct had tended toward sedition; had manifestly cheered the enemies of good order in the plantation, and put arguments into the mouths of those who were seeking its ruin; *this* had a look like open rebellion. This young man—not of age yet ten years; not a freeman of the Company; unsettled in judgment; advocating one new scheme to-day and another to-morrow; who did not believe their patent gave them a legal right to the soil which they occupied, or that any man's house thereon could be his own, who still owned a house which he claimed as his own; who had headed such an onset against the Company's right to administer an oath of fealty to those who yet claimed the protection of its laws, and

---

148 Cotton Mather says, [*Magnalia*, Book vii: 8]: "Mr. Williams Enchants the Church to join with him in Writing Letters of Admonition unto all the Churches, whereof any of the Magistrates were Members, *that they might Admonish the Magistrates of Scandalous Injustice for denying this Petition.*" John Cotton says [*Reply to Mr. Williams, etc.*, 29]: "to admonish them of their *open transgression of the Rule of Justice*"; and Winthrop speaks of the letters as "complaining of the magistrates *for injustice, extreme oppression, etc.*" [*Journal*, i: 170].

149 The next General Court declared that in these letters the church of Salem "*exceedingly reproched and villifyed the magistrates, etc.*" [*Mass. Col. Rec.* i: 156.]

150 This is clearly stated by John Cotton, writing within twelve years of the occurrence, [*Reply to Mr. Williams, etc.* 5] thus: "in writing Letters of Admonition to all the Churches, whereof any of the Magistrates were members, *to admonish their Magistrates of their breach of the rule of Justice*, in not granting their Petition." Cotton Mather [as cited above, *note* 148,] repeats the statement; which is indeed necessarily involved in all the testimony; for of what value could be any church dealing which should not result in some action, and in what way could these churches responsively act, unless by such dealing with the offenders as should repair the offence? Mr. Cotton himself returns to the subject in his *Reply*, and more fully explains the facts, as follows: "Mr. Williams witnesseth that in such a case the Church [whose town has petitioned for land, etc.] whose Petition is so delayed, may write Letters of Admonition to all the Churches, whereof such Magistrates are members, *to require them to grant, without delay, such Petitions, or else to Proceed against them in a Church-way*" [p. 55].

all the advantages of residents under it, as had almost compelled that wise and essential provision to drop into disuse; this young man, who had so "enchanted"[151] the church in Salem as to persuade it to take him to be its pastor by formal rites, at the very moment when the other churches of the plantation were dealing with it in the endeavor to prevent such a step, and in cool defiance of their judgment and desire; this young man was now undertaking to compel the magistrates to administer the civil government as he, and those under his influence, desired, under pain of church discipline—involving of course, as the Massachusetts system then was, the risk of excommunication (then carrying with it, as I suppose, the loss of civil rights) should they prove contumacious. John Haynes, Esq., had been *chosen* Governor for that year, and the contemplated administration of the affairs of the plantation for 1635, involved the coöperative action of Lieut. Governor Bellingham, with eight Assistants and from twenty to thirty Deputies; but it was really beginning to look as if the *actual* Governor of Massachusetts for the time being might prove to be Roger Williams, with the assistance of "the major part"[152] of the church of Salem, and no deputies whatsoever!

The issue was squarely joined. But there could be essentially but one result of such a conflict. Either the Governor and Company of Massachusetts must abdicate in favor of this young Salem pastor, or he must abandon his preposterous endeavors, or take himself out of the way. And no man can reasonably claim that it would be presumable in such a case for the greater to yield to the less; for nearly or quite five thousand Englishmen with more than five hundred freemen, with twelve churches, and from fifteen to twenty highly educated ministers, all sturdily engaged in pushing forward the heavy work of a plantation which included three or four thriving towns, with more than twenty hamlets, grouped around the shores of the Bay, and already stretching inland as far as Ipswich and Newbury on the north, and Weymouth and Hingham on the south, to surrender at discretion to the wild earnestness of a single visionary stripling, however finely endowed, with however much of method in his madness, and with however fervid a female following![153]

The General Court did not meet again until September, so that assuming—as it is reasonable to think they did—that Mr. Williams's letters in the name of his church went out quickly after the Court action which caused them, six weeks or more would intervene between their reception by the churches, and any action of the authorities which might take influence from the public feel-

[151] *Magnalia*, Book vii: 8.

[152] John Cotton's *Reply to Mr. Williams, etc.* 29.

[153] These statistics are estimated from the Colony Records, and from Savage's Edition of Winthrop's *Journal*, with the assistance of the tenth chapter of Dr. Palfrey's first volume.

ing in regard to them. It is not certain, indeed, that, in every instance, these letters reached the direct attention and action of the bodies to which they had been addressed. The church in Boston certainly did not at once come to the knowledge of theirs, for its elders sent a communication to the Salem church, of date 22 July–1 Aug. 1635, in which they gave their reasons for not "seeing their way clear" to "publish to the body" the Salem document.[154] Roger Williams and Samuel Sharpe replied in the name of their church, endeavoring to show the insufficiency and inaptness of these reasons, and to persuade the Boston elders to deliver their "humble complaint" to the consideration of the body of their brethren.[155] It is quite possible that some of the churches had not yet reached the end of the friendly labor with the Salem church on which they had entered some time before Mr. Williams's ordination; there is evidence that others utilized the interval before the General Court should reassemble, in the endeavor, by correspondence and personal intercession, to persuade Mr. Williams and his flock to retreat from their offensive and untenable position.[156] Prominent among these were the two important churches of Boston and New-town [Cambridge].[157] Mr. Hooker and Mr. Cotton personally were very active

---

[154] These reasons were three: (1) that the admonition of the Salem Church was a "gift" which should not be offered until that church had reconciled itself to the magistrates [with reference to Matt. v: 23, 24]; (2) that the act of the magistrates was rather a private than a public offence; and (3) that it was not fitting to deal on the Lord's day in a worldly business, nor to bring a civil matter into the church. [See these reasons quoted, that they may be replied to, in a Letter of the elders of Salem Church, to elders of Boston Church, *Publications of the Narragansett Club*, vi: 71–77].

[155] Their reply to the third reason is characteristic. They first disclaim the "civil" aspect of the matter of their complaint altogether, referring to it only as it is a spiritual offence. Then they say: "again, we are not bold to limit you (our beloved) to the Lord's day; we leave it to your wisdom, and the wisdom of the church, *when* to consider of the matter; yet hitherto we have conceived that the kingly office of our Lord Jesus ought to be as well administered on the Lord's day as his Priestly and Prophetic office; and also that He is as much honored in the act of censuring or pardoning of sinners from his throne, *Zach.* vi: 13, in case of transgression against His crown, as against the administration of other his sweet and blessed ordinances." [*Ibid*, 76.]

[156] "But to prevent his sufferings (if it might be) it was mooved by some of the Elders that themselves might have liberty (according to the Rule of Christ) to deale with him, and with the Church also in a Church-way. It might be the Church might heare us, and he the Church; which being consented to, some of our Churches wrote to the Church of Salem, to present before them the offensive Spirit and Way of their Officer (Mr. Williams) both in Judgement and Practise." [Cotton's *Reply to Mr. Williams, etc.* 29.] "The neighboring Churches, both by Petitions and Messengers, took such Happy Pains with the Church of Salem, etc." [*Magnalia*, Book vii 8.]

[157] Cotton's *Reply to Mr. Williams*, 38. Morton [*N. Eng. Mem.* 82] gives a copy of a portion of the "Writing" which was signed by John Cotton, Teacher; and Thomas Oliver and Thomas Leveret, elders [the pastor, John Wilson, being then "absent upon a voyage to England"], which was sent by the Boston church to the church at Salem. It recounts five specific "Errours" in Doctrine; the fifth of which is: "it is not lawful for Magistrates to punish the breaches of the first Table, unless thereby the Civill Peace of the Commonwealth be disturbed," from which it draws the inference that a portion of the Salem church held "that a Church wholly declining into Arianism, Papism, Familism, or other Heresies, being admonished, and convinced thereof by other Churches, and not reforming, may not be reformed by the Civil Magistrate in a way of Civil Justice unless it break the Civil Peace." This makes it probable that Williams had some disciples in his views in regard to liberty of conscience, and that that subject did have a certain share in all these troubles; while it does not demonstrate that—except in the most general way—it had anything to do with the action now soon resulting in his banishment.

in laboring with Mr. Williams; the latter subsequently calling him to witness to the fact, thus: "he knoweth I spent a great part of the Summer in seeking, by word and writing, to satisfie his scruples."[158]

The result of all appears to have been to harden the purpose and judgment of the pastor, and to soften those of the majority of the church. That "Holy Flock," in Cotton Mather's stately phrase, was "presently recovered to a Sense of his Aberrations."[159] In Mather's maternal grandfather Cotton's milder way of putting it: "it pleased the Lord to open the hearts of the Church to assist us in dealing with him."[160] In plainest English, the churches of the Bay, so far from responding favorably to these admonitory letters, and proceeding to discipline their magistrate-members for what had been done in laying on the table, for a time, the Salem petition in regard to the Marblehead land; retorted in kind, and commenced counter-labor with the Salem Church, and its minister, for sending them such letters; for many of his teachings, and for other things; with the result of speedily winning to the view they took the majority of that church, and persuading it to unite with them in dealing with him. When Mr. Williams comprehended this result, and saw that the majority of his own people had forsaken him; were actually now ready to take sides with his opponents; and were even, in point of fact, about to commence church labor with him, in the endeavor to bring him to the abandonment of the advocacy of his peculiar views; he turned upon them with a sudden — almost a fierce — denunciation.

By one of those remarkable coincidences which deeply impress some minds as with a certain weird sympathy between man and nature, the Massachusetts Sabbath of the 16–26 August 1635, dawned upon a troubled world. All day long on Saturday the elemental forces had been raging up and down the New England coast, in a manner whose furious equal was not within the memory, or the traditions, of the most venerable living Algonkin. It had been blowing, through the whole previous week, almost a gale from a Southerly direction, when suddenly, on the morning of the 15–25th, a North-easter set in, with torrents of rain, with a gusty violence which raised the tides by as many as twenty feet of perpendicular height, sending many of the Narragansetts into the trees to avoid drowning, which fate — flood-tide coming before the usual time — many did not escape; which foundered ships at sea, and stranded vessels anchored near the shore; which prostrated many houses, and

---

[158] *Reply to Mr. Williams his Exam., etc.* 47.

[159] *Magnalia*, Book vii: 8.

[160] *Reply to Mr. Williams, etc.* 39. Hubbard says, [*Gen. Hist. N. Eng.* 206] "divers of them that joined with him in these letters, afterwards did acknowledge their error, and gave satisfaction." Morton [*N. Eng. Mem.* 79] says "divers did acknowledge their error and gave satisfaction."

unroofed many more; which beat down flat the whole crop of Indian corn; which twisted off tall, thrifty oaks, and tough hickories, as a farmer twists a slender withe in binding his rail-fence together, and snapped stately pines and goodly firs in the midst, and uprooted hundreds of thousands of forest trees; leaving the scar-marks of its desolation scored deep upon the fair face of the land, during a large portion of the half-century that followed.[161] As the Salem congregation picked their devious way on that Sabbath morning, between the pools, and among the gulleys, and over the broken branches, and around the prostrate trees, and fragments of dwellings and fences which cumbered the rude and narrow ways, to their humble meeting-house,[162] they did not find Mr. Williams in the pulpit. It is quite likely that most of them did not expect to see him there, having heard that he was sick. The elder, Samuel Sharpe, it is to be inferred, conducted the service.[163] And, as one part thereof, he read a letter from the pastor. It had been doubtless written while the storm had been raging on the Saturday, and — whether in language or not — in spirit it was as tempestuous as the day of its birth had been. It was a solemn protestation. He had made up his mind fully. He could hold Christian communion with the churches of the Bay no longer. They were unclean by idolatrous pollutions. They were defiled with hypocrisy and worldliness. They needed cleansing from anti-Christian filthiness and communion with dead works, dead worships, dead persons in God's worship. They ought to loathe themselves for their abominations, and stinks in God's nostrils (as it pleaseth God's Spirit to speak of false worships); for they were false worshipers of the true God, liable to God's sentence and plagues; guilty of spiritual drunkenness and whoredom, of soul-sleep and soul-sickness, in submitting to false churches, false ministry, and false worship. They were ulcered and gangrened

---

161 Winthrop's *Journal*, i: 164; Morton's *N. Eng. Mem.* 94; Hubbard's *Gen. Hist. N. Eng.* 199. This was the storm which Richard Mather mentions in his Journal, which came upon his ship when it was at anchor off the Isles of Shoals; and the same in which, by the breaking up of a pinnace of Mr. Allerton's off Gloucester, the Rev. John Avery was drowned, with twenty others; only Rev. Anthony Thacher and his wife being saved, by being cast up upon what has hence always since gone by the name of Thacher's Island. [See *Magnalia*, Book iii: 77; Mather's *Journal*, and Thacher's *Narrative* in Young's *Chronicles of Massachusetts*, 473–486.] Joshua Scottow, [Narrative of the Planting of the Mass. Col., 4 *Mass. Hist. Coll.* iv: 29] calls it "an Hurricane before, or since, not known in this Country." Winthrop says, "it was not so far as Cape Sable, but to the South more violent."

162 From 1629 to 1634, the church had met for worship in an unfinished building. In 1634 a framed house was erected, 20 feet long and 17 feet wide, with a gallery across the end over the door. It was four years before a bill was paid for glazing it, so that most likely oiled paper at first served instead of glass in the windows. It is a remarkable fact that this building still essentially exists, having been ten years since reclaimed from some base use; removed to the rear of Plummer Hall, and there renovated and restored, to be handed down as a sacred relic to the far future. [*Hist. Coll. Essex Institute*, ii: 145–148; vii: 116–118.]

163 Samuel Sharpe was at this time Ruling Elder of the church, and his name appears as signed, with Mr. Williams's, to the letter which had a little while before been sent to the Boston Church. [*Pub. Narragansett Club*, vi: 77.]

with obstinacy. Their ministry was false, and a hireling ministry. Their doctrines were corrupt. They were asleep in abundant ignorance and negligence, in gross abominations and pollutions; which the choicest servants of God, and most faithful witnesses of many truths, were living in, more or less. And the breath of the Lord Jesus was sounding forth in him (a poor despised ram's horn) the blast, which in His own holy season should cast down the strength and confidence of all these inventions of men, in the worshiping of the true and living God. Solemnly he gave his testimony against those churches; solemnly he separated from them as unworthy to be fellowshiped as true churches of the living God. He should communicate with them no more. And, further, he should communicate with *them*, to whom his letter was addressed, no more; unless they were prepared to follow whither now he led, and renounce Christian communion with all other professing followers of God in the Massachusetts Colony![164]

This was explicit, as well as emphatic; but "the whole church was grieved herewith!"[165]

Subsequent reflection did not, on either side, essentially modify this condition of affairs. The great majority of the church remained firm in their refusal to separate from their sister churches of the Bay; by and by humbling themselves before their brethren who had admonished them, acknowledging the justice of the admonition, and confessing the faults into which Mr. Williams had led them.[166] A few—"divers of the weaker sort," who "had been through-

164 Winthrop [*Journal*, i: 166]; Morton [*N. Eng. Mem.* 80]; and Hubbard [*Gen. Hist. N. Eng.* 206]; who does little more than copy Morton, are the direct authorities for the nature of this communication of Mr. Williams. Neither of them gives more than the substance of it. I have thought that I could not go wrong in endeavoring a little more fully to reproduce it, if I scrupulously made use of Mr. Williams's own language elsewhere employed (and preserved) in regard to the same subject. All the epithets, and the invectives, given above, are scattered through his little tractate entitled *Mr. Cotton's Letter, lately printed, Examined and Answered.* [See pp. 5, 9, 12, 18, 20, 27, 29, 30, 33, 34, 35, 38.] Even Mr. Knowles is constrained to admit as much as this, here: "in this conduct he was doubtless wrong, yet who will venture to say, that if he had been placed in the situation of Mr. Williams, he would have maintained a more subdued spirit." [*Memoir*, 71.]

165 So says Winthrop [*Journal* i: 166]. Morton says [*N. Eng. Mem.* 80], "the more prudent and sober part of the Church, being amazed at his way, could not yield unto him." Hubbard again repeats Morton.

166 Winthrop [*Journal* i: 171]. Cotton says [*Letter to Mr. Williams*, London 1643], that he has little hope that the man will hearken to his voice "*who hath not hearkened to the body of the whole Church of Christ* with you, etc." [p. 1]; implying, of course, the charge that the great majority, at least, of the church, did not sympathize with Mr. Williams; but had labored with him to change his course. To which Mr. Williams, in his reply, [*Mr. Cotton's Letter Examined and Answered*, London 1644] concedes: "in my troubles the *greater part* of that Church *was* swayed and bowed (whether for feare of persecution or otherwise) to say and practise what, to my knowledge, with signes [sighs?] and groans many of them mourned under," [p. 2]. Cotton says, in replication [*Reply to Mr. Williams, his Examination, etc.* 38]: "the issue was when the church of New Towne, with our owne, and others, had endeavoured to convince both Mr. Williams of these offences, and the Church of Salem of their indulgent toleration of him therein; it pleased the Lord to open the hearts of the Church to assist us in dealing with him: but he, instead of hearkening either to them or us, renounced us all as no churches of Christ; and therefore not at all to be hearkened unto."

ly leavened with his Opinions, of which number were divers women that were zealous in their way[167]" — by degrees fell off to him. Mr. Williams himself was as good as his word. He seems never to have entered the meeting-house again. He gathered the skirts of his garments close about him, that they might not be defiled even in Salem; renouncing communion with all the churches, and with his own church, and with all who would not renounce communion with his own church; insomuch that he would neither pray with his own wife at the family altar, nor give thanks in her presence to God for food upon the family table, so long as she persisted in attendance upon the church assembly![168] He opened a "pure" service on Sundays, and lecture-days, in his own house;[169] in the way of separation from, testimony against, and opposition to, the services of the church of which he was still the ordained pastor.

Two Sabbaths — most likely of this separate service — intervened between that stormy one which followed the storm, and the reassembling of the Court; — long time enough to develop the spirit and intentions of this impetuous young enthusiast, and to suggest the probabilities of the results of the course which he had elected to take. It is easy to believe that the tidings of what was thus happening in Salem, was, during that fortnight, pretty thoroughly noised abroad, and that any excitement formerly existing, was in no way soothed, or quelled, by the news. When the Court met at Newtown, on Wednesday 2–12 September, there was, however, no unseemly haste manifested in approaching the subject. Nothing whatever was done about it on the first day of the session. On Thursday the fact was recognized that the Salem church, by its letters to the other churches of endeavor to admonish them into direct ecclesiastical interference with the civil government for its course in reference to the Marblehead land, had indicated an insubordinate, not to say a rebellious, spirit, which called for inquiry if not for rebuke; and the three Deputies of the town, Capt. William Traske, and Messrs. John Woodberry and Jacob Barney, were sent home to the freemen whom they represented; who were, of course, so far

---

[167] Morton's *N. Eng. Mem.* 80.

[168] Winthrop's *Journal*, i: 175; Morton's *N. Eng. Mem.* 80; Hubbard's *Gen. Hist. N. Eng.* 207. Cotton says, [*Reply to Mr. Williams, etc.* 30]: "Soone after sundry began to resort to his Family, where he preached to them on the Lord's day." Cotton Mather says: "His more considerate Church not yielding to these lewd Proposals, he never would come to their Assemblies any more; no, nor hold any Communion in any Exercise of Religion with any Person, so much as his own Wife, that went unto their Assemblies; but at the same time he kept a Meeting in his own House, whereto resorted such as he had infected with his Extravagances" [*Magnalia*, Book vii: 8]. Cotton adds [*Reply, etc.* 9]: "which occasioned him for a season to withdraw communion in spiritual duties even from her [his wife] also, till at length he drew her to partake with him in the errour of his way."

[169] It seems to have been Mr. Williams's practice, during his ministry in Salem, to "exercise" during the week remarkably for those days. In speaking of his various labors, he says that they were "on the Lord's dayes, and *thrice a week* at Salem." [*Mr. Cotton's Letter Examined, etc.* 13.]

as they went, (all freemen being church-members, though all church-members were not freemen) identical with the offending parties; to procure some satisfactory explanation of those letters; or, if none were to be had, to report to the Court the names of such Salem citizens as endorsed that offensive procedure.[170]

It has been usual to stigmatize this action as a tyrannical endeavor on the part of the Court to punish the Salem church, and compel the Salem people to take sides against Mr. Williams, on pain of losing their common civil rights.[171] But it is my impression that what was really done has been overstated. It will be remembered that Mr. Williams, his church consenting and coäcting, had distinctly accused the General Court of "heinous sin" in laying on the table the Marblehead petition; and had deliberately demanded of the several churches of which its members were members, that they enter upon a course of discipline with those deputies, for that great moral wrong; and that this demand had been couched in language which seemed to the Court most unexampled and offensive. It could hardly be expected that on its first reassembling that body should take no notice of this remarkable, and — if we put ourselves into their place, we shall perhaps be able to think — perilous procedure. The very least which, with self-respect, it could do, would be to demand the justification, or withdrawal, of those letters. It did that very thing, emphasizing its demand by bidding the three Salem Deputies to go home and carry it, in place of raising any other committee, or trusting to letter, when as yet there was no post.[172] It is particularly noticeable, on the face of the transaction, that the Court order enjoining this, is radically different in terms from those usual when Deputies were unseated. Mr. John Humfrey, in 1629, had been "discharged of his Deputy-shipp."[173] Of Mr. William Aspinwall, in 1637, it was said: "the Court did discharge him from being a member thereof;"[174] and, at the same time, Mr. John Coggeshall was "in like sort dismissed from being a member of the Courte."[175] In 1638 Ralfe Mousall, "being questioned about speaches, etc.,

[170] *Mass. Col. Rec.* i: 156.

[171] Elton [*Life*, 28] calls it "an atrocious violation of their rights," and talks about "the inquisitorial spirit of that tribunal." Knowles [*Memoir*, 71] styles it "punishing with rigor" the Salem people. Gammell [*Life*, 46] terms it "disfranchisement." And Arnold [*Hist. R. I.* i: 35] names these "arbitrary measures," and says the Court "*disfranchised* the Salem deputies"; which it surely did not do, as they remained as fully freemen of the company after the vote, as before.

[172] The first symptom of public provision for the carriage of letters which I have found, is the order of 5–15th Nov. 1639, making Richard Fairbanks's house in Boston the place where letters were to be left for forwarding over sea, or were to be delivered by incoming ships, he to have a penny a letter for taking care "that they bee delivered, or sent, according to their directions." [*Mass. Col. Rec.* i: 281.] It was not until June 1677, that any symptoms of a Post Office appear [*Ibid*, v: 148]; and not until Nov. 1687, that a post seems to have been established between Boston and Connecticut. [*Conn. Col. Rec.* iii: 393, 398.]

[173] *Mass. Col. Rec.* i: 70.

[174] *Ibid*, i: 205.

[175] *Ibid.* In September 1636, when the new town of "Waimoth" had sent three Deputies to the Court, when so small a town was entitled to only one, "at the request of the said Deputies, two of them were *dismised* by Court, viz: Mr. Bursley & John Vpham." [*Ibid*, i: 179.]

was dismissed from being a member of the Courte."[176] Such, if I mistake not, was the invariable formula of record;[177] while disfranchisement, (that is, the taking away from a freeman of his right of membership in the Massachusetts Company) was much more than this; and, as in the case of Aspinwall and Coggeshall above named,[178] was effected by a separate vote. But the Court did not "discharge" Traske, Woodberry, and Barney, "from being members thereof;" it did not "dismiss" them; it simply ordered that they "shalbe sent backe to the ffreemen of their towne that sent them, to fetch satisfaccon for their lettres, etc., or els the arguments of those that will defend the same, etc." So far from there being any hint in this language that the Deputies were not expected to return, or that they would not be entitled to their seats again when they should return; they are expressly directed to "fetch" either an acknowledgment for, or a vindication of, the letters which were the ground of offence. I cannot help thinking that this formal and conspicuous sending home upon a mission which involved return, was all that was in the mind of the Body when passing the order, or that could legitimately stand upon the terms employed.

But a scene of excitement followed. Endecott was present. It is not clear in what capacity he could be there, because in the previous May, he had been expressly "disinabled for beareing any office in the Commonwealth, for the space of a yeare nexte ensueing,"[179] for cutting the cross out of the king's flag. He was a man whose impetuous temper more than once involved him in serious trouble; and he seems on this occasion to have lost his self-control and stormed suddenly and violently against the course which matters had taken, until the Court, incensed beyond endurance, retorted, by directing "by generall ereccon of hands," that he be committed for contempt. It does not appear, however, that he actually went to jail; as, at a later hour, "upon his submission and full acknowledgement of his offence, he was dismissed."[180] But further on in the record of the same day's session we find a supplementary order of the Court, to the effect that "if the major part of the ffreemen of Salem shall disclame the lettres sent lately from the Church of Salem to severall churches, it shall then be lawfull for them to send Deputyes to the Generall Court;"[181] which looks like a move-

---

176 *Ibid*, i: 236.

177 Notice the same term employed some years after, when the Deputy of Hingham was allowed at his own request, and for his own convenience, to give up his seat. [*Ibid*, ii: 258.]

178 *Ibid*, i: 207.

179 *Ibid*, i: 146. Gammell [*Life*, 46] calls Endecott "the principal *Deputy*." He had been an *Assistant* before his degradation from office. Elton [*Memoir*, 28] repeats the same blunder.

180 *Ibid*, i: 157. I am aware that Winthrop [*Journal* i: 166] says "for which he was committed; but, the same day, he came and acknowledged his fault and was discharged;" but that may merely mean that he was "committed" so far as the order of the Court went. He who "stands committed" is as fairly spoken of in that manner after sentence has been pronounced, before leaving the Court room, as he could be after the cell-door has been locked upon him.

181 *Ibid*, i: 158.

ment, prompted by the heat of the fire which Endecott had kindled, to get into a postscript an important modification of the tone of an epistle, or to stiffen a will by a codicil. It may be questioned whether, if Endecott could on this occasion have exercised the grace of silence, any clause implying the termination of the official life of the Salem Deputies, would have found place upon the record of that day's doings.

The most noticeable feature, however, of this session of the Court, is that although more than eight weeks before the date of its assembling Mr. Williams had been charged to "consider of" the "erroneous and very dangerous" opinions which he had avowed, until it should meet; and had been cited then to appear before it to "give satisfaction, or else to expect the sentence;" and although this consideration instead of reducing him to penitent inoffensiveness had goaded him on to new outbreaks of the most exasperating character; still no mention whatever of his name appears in connection with it. Possibly he was still sick, or again sick. But had that been the case, in all likelihood, Mr. Winthrop would have noted the fact in his Journal. So that, when we find the Court adjourning, after a two days' session, to "the Thursday after the next Particular Court";[182] which would carry them, over an interval of exactly five weeks, to the 8–18 October; and—even in all the heat of the three Deputies' ejection, and of Endecott's "committal"—saying nothing about the head and front of all, but leaving him to try his conscientious experiments of anarchy in Church and State for another month unmeddled with; I conceive that we discover, in place of a pack of legal hounds thirsting for the blood of a victim after whom they have been for months pressing in full cry, the calm, deliberate, and even noticeably lingering, processes of an anxious, conscientious, yet reluctant, tribunal.

I am not aware of much light from any quarter upon this five weeks' interval, by which we may see with any minute accuracy what Mr. Williams, or his church, were doing. We can infer that new excitement would inevitably follow the Court action in reference to Mr. Endecott and the Deputies. It is easy to guess that those members of the church who had already committed themselves against Mr. Williams, would be tempted to great exertions in the endeavor to bring others to think with them; while his separate service, aided by his marked popular ability, would more and more influence all whose prepossessions were in the direction he had taken. So that, beyond question, the excitement must daily have increased, rather than diminished. Hubbard says:

---

[182] The next Particular Court met on Tuesday 6–16th October, at New Town, that is, Cambridge. [*Mass. Col. Rec.* i: 162.] The Thursday following would be, of course, the 8–18th.

"things grew more and more towards a general division, and disturbance."[183] As the day of the adjourned meeting of the Court approached, it is clear that this subject largely occupied men's minds, and was especially upon the conscience of those by whose final action it must be determined.[184]

Let us here endeavor some clear idea as to what, precisely, was this "Greate and Generall Court," whose session was to end all this. The Charter — and I again beg the reader to remember that it was, as yet, the charter of a *company*, and not of a commonwealth; and that the said charter expressly styled the body the "Greate and Generall Court *of the saide Company*"[185] — made provision that there should be "one Governor, one Deputy Governor, and eighteene Assistants," "to be from tyme to tyme constituted, elected, and chosen out of the freemen of the saide Company," etc.[186] It further provided that four times in each year a General Court should be held, when "the Governor, or, in his absence, the Deputie Governor, of the saide Company for the tyme being, and such of the Assistants and freemen of the saide Company as shalbe present, or the greater nomber of them soe assembled, whereof the Governor or Deputie Governor, and six of the Assistants, at the least to be seaven, shall have full power and authoritie to choose, nominate, and appointe" new freemen, to elect officers, and "to make lawes and ordinances for the good and welfare of the saide Company, and for the government and ordering of the said landes and plantacon, and the people inhabiting, and to inhabite the same, as to them from tyme to tyme shalbe thought meete,"[187] the same not being repugnant to the laws of England. When these provisions of the Charter came to be applied on the ground to the practical exigencies of the life of the young plantation, some modifications were found expedient. The number of Assistants yearly chosen was reduced to eight — two more than the number necessary, with the presiding officer, to make a quorum. These met often as a "Particular" Court, or Court of Assistants, or Magistrates, to adjudicate upon matters of organiza-

---

[183] *Gen. Hist. N. Eng.* 207.

[184] Mr. Cotton says that one of the magistrates of Boston, who was to attend the Court, asked him what he thought of the whole matter as it then stood. He replied: "I pitie the man, and have already interceded for him, whilest there was any hope of doing good. But now, he having refused to heare both his own Church, and us, and having rejected us all as no Churches of Christ, before any conviction [that is, on his own individual assumption, without any orderly trial of such a charge, issuing in conviction], we [that is, the elders, in whose name — see note 127 — Mr. Cotton had a year before interposed] have now no more to say in his behalfe, nor hope to prevaile for him. Wee have told the Governour and Magistrates before, that if our labour was in vaine, wee could not helpe it, but must sit downe. And you know they are generally so much incensed against his course, that it is not your voyce, nor the voyces of two, or three more, that can suspend the Sentence. Some further speech I had with him of mine own marvell at the weaknesse and slendernesse of the grounds of his [Mr. W.'s] opinions, motions and courses, and yet carried on with such vehemency, and impetuousnesse, and prefidence [previous confidence] of Spirit." [*Reply to Mr. Williams's Examination, etc.* 39.]

[185] *Mass. Col. Rec.* i: 11.

[186] *Ibid*, i: 10.

[187] *Ibid*, i: 11.

tion, criminal and civil jurisprudence, probate and police.[188] Then, as the number of freemen became largely increased, in the spring of 1634 it was arranged that the freemen of each town should have the right to choose two or three of their number to be their Deputies, who should take from those sending them full power to perform in their stead all their proper functions; except in the election of Magistrates and other officers.[189] So that the General Court which met at New Town on the 8–18 Oct., 1635, was made up of the Governor, Deputy Governor, eight Assistants and — there being now ten towns to send Deputies — from twenty-five to twenty-eight Deputies. The names of those having the right to be present are easily identified.[190] John Haynes of New Town, who had been an opulent land-holder in Essex, was Governor. Richard Bellingham of Boston; bred a lawyer, and who had been Recorder of Boston in Lincolnshire, was Deputy Governor. John Winthrop, Atherton Hough (who had been Mayor of Boston on the Witham), and William Coddington (Treasurer) of Boston; Simon Bradstreet of New Town; Thomas Dudley of Roxbury; Increase Nowell of Charlestown; John Humfrey of Lynn, and Richard Dummer of Newbury, were the eight Assistants. Leaving out the three Salem men, whose *status* was now something more than doubtful, there remained twenty-five Deputies, from nine towns, to wit: John Talcott, John Steele and Daniel Dennison of New Town; Richard Brown, Ensign William Jennison, and Edward Howe of Watertown; William Hutchinson, William Colburn, and William Brenton of Boston; Dr. George Alcock, John Moody, and William Park of Roxbury; John Mousall, Thomas Beecher and Ezekiel Richardson of Charlestown; Nathaniel Duncan, Captain John Mason, and William Gaylord of Dorchester; Joseph Metcalf, Humphrey Bradstreet and William Bartholomew of Ipswich; Captain Nathaniel Turner, Edward Tomlyns and Thomas Stanley of Lynn; and John Spencer of Newbury.

It would probably be safe to assume, from the felt importance of some of the business to come before the Court, and the extent of the public interest in the same, that all, or nearly all, of these gentlemen were present.

Anxious for the benefit of the utmost available light upon a question perplexing in proportion to the magnitude of the various issues seen to be involved, the Court had again invited "all the ministers in the Bay"[191] to attend, for consultation with them on this occasion. There were, at that time, within the limits of the Massachusetts plantation, ten churches in full working

---

188 Palfrey's *Hist. N. Eng.* i: 325.

189 *Mass. Col. Rec.* i: 118.

190 *Mass. Col. Rec.* i: 156.

191 Winthrop's *Journal*, i: 170.

condition,[192] having among them fifteen pastors and teachers. In the order in which they were formed, those churches were, and were at this time officered, as follows: *Salem*, Roger Williams; *Dorchester*, John Warham and John Maverick; *Boston*, John Wilson and John Cotton; *Watertown*, George Phillips; *Roxbury*, Thomas Welde and John Eliot; *Lynn*, Stephen Bachiler; *Charlestown*, Thomas James; *New Town*, [Cambridge], Thomas Hooker and Samuel Stone; *Ipswich*, Nathaniel Ward; and *Newbury*, Thomas Parker, and James Noyes. It is possible that the two last named, who were, as yet, fresh from their consecration under the "majestic oak" of *Quascacunquen*,[193] and who then were, and, as is well known, remained, in some slight want of ecclesiastical harmony with their brethren in the Bay, might not have been present; probably there had hardly yet been time to count them fairly in to the older company. Since Winthrop notes the absence of no other one — as, in a somewhat similar previous case, he had done[194] — I incline to think that the remaining twelve were there.[195] Nine of these we know to have been graduates of Cambridge University.[196] Nine of them we know to have held rectorships — some of them positions of exceptional importance — in the father-land.[197] Thomas Hooker, in addition to his experience in the ministry in Essex, and on the Continent, had taught a school at Little Baddow, where John Eliot had acted as his assistant.[198] Three of them must have worn that crown of glory which the way of righteousness puts upon the hoary head.[199] Five, at least, of their juniors were in the fullest maturity of manly strength.[200] While the remaining four, if young enough to come into special sympathy with the fervid zeal of the man whose peculiarities had called them together, were also old enough to have outgrown, perhaps, some of his crudities.[201] Altogether it was a distinguished

---

[192] As has been before remarked [p. 41] there were *twelve* churches actually existing; one having been formed at Weymouth in the previous July, and one at Hingham in the previous September. But these were hardly yet fully organized, the latter, certainly, not as yet having any pastor.

[193] Coffin's *Hist. Newbury*, 9, 17.

[194] *Journal*, i: 154.

[195] There would be twelve without Mr. Williams.

[196] These were Wilson, Cotton, Hooker, Stone, Welde, Eliot, Phillips, James and Ward. Of Bachiler, Warham and Maverick, we lack details. Parker and Noyes had both studied at Oxford.

[197] Cotton had been beneficed at Boston, Lincolnshire; Warham, at Exeter, Devon; Wilson, at Sudbury, Suffolk; Phillips, at Boxted, Essex; Weld, at Terling, Essex; Hooker, at Chelmsford, Essex, and afterwards at Delft and Rotterdam; Ward, at St. James's, Dukes place, London, and afterwards at Stondon Massey, Essex; Maverick, at some place about forty miles from Exeter, and James somewhere in Lincolnshire.

[198] *Magnalia*, Book iii: 59.

[199] Bachiler must have been now about 74 (I know his character was much spoken against, and there were unfortunate facts in his history; yet the obvious confidence of good men in him inspires in my mind the hope that his way, on the whole, was one of righteousness); Ward was not far from 65, and Maverick near 60.

[200] Cotton was about 50, Hooker perhaps a year younger, Wilson 47, and Phillips and James each not far from 42.

[201] Eliot, who was but 32, seems to have been the youngest. Stone was 35, while Weld and Warham, whose birth-dates have not, to my knowledge, been identified, would, from various circumstances, appear to have been at this time between 30 and 40.

company; and it may well be doubted whether the Massachusetts of to-day,—even under the classic shades of that great university which makes the spot where this Court was held now almost as well known to the learned world as is that ancient shrine of knowledge whose scholastic robes so many of them were entitled to wear—could call together, out of its hundreds of pulpits, twelve pastors and teachers who should be their equals in intellect and worth, and in all those imperial qualities which fit men to be the founders of States.

It has been the habit of a certain class of writers to regard, and speak of, the trial of Mr. Williams at this time thus before the General Court in the presence of these ministers, as affording an odious instance—in its worst form—of the coworking of Church and State. Even the accomplished historian of Rhode Island, to whom I have already more than once referred, sees in it: "a practical commentary on the danger of uniting the civil and ecclesiastical administrations. It suggests the reflection that, of all characters, the most dangerous and the most despicable, is the political priest."[202] But I submit—with all respect—that there was here, strictly, neither Church nor State. There was, on the one hand, the board of directors and managers of a great trading and land company, administering the affairs of their corporation, and in so doing growing insensibly to be a commonwealth, assembled to consider whether a person—whom, for many of his qualities and much of his influence, they respected and esteemed;[203] who was not a member of the company, but, though holding land by their grant, was living among them on sufferance; who had formed the opinion that their charter was invalid, and that they had no right to their territory; that they had no authority to govern, no warrant to administer the judicial oath whether for civil cohesion, to secure the ends of justice, or as a safeguard against insubordination; that their churches were standing on an unauthorized basis; and so that their procedure in every department, and on all subjects, was null before the law, and reprehensible before the gospel; and who scrupled not, in the face of all their endeavor, to advocate and push these opinions in a way which, in the perilous juncture of affairs at home, threatened the very existence of the plantation—could be safely allowed longer to remain among them? And there was, on the other hand, invited by a body impressed with the gravity of the occasion, and because they were at once their best educated and wisest men, and the peers of the offending elder—gathered in no ecclesiastical

---

[202] Arnold's *Hist. R. I.* i: 38.

[203] Nothing is more noticeable in all this history than the kindness of feeling which, in the midst of and in spite of all the trouble, was manifested toward Mr. Williams. Knowles says: "it is due to the principal actors in these scenes, to record the fact, of which ample evidence exists, that personal animosity had little, if any, share in producing the sentence of banishment. Towards Mr. Williams, as a Christian and a minister, there was a general sentiment of respect." [*Memoir*, 78.]

fashion, and for no ecclesiastical end, but as experts in the moral and religious bearing of the matters in dispute—the body of the remaining pastors and teachers of the plantation, to give their advice as *amici curiæ*. And this was all.

The rising sun of Thursday, the 8–18 October, 1635, doubtless found the majority of these thirty-five laymen and twelve ministers, with whoever had special occasion to be present with them at the Court, heading for New Town along the field and forest paths which converged thither.[204] Edward Converse must have driven a thriving business with his "fferry betwixte Charlton & Boston, for which he had ij[d] for evy single pson, & i[d] a peece if there be 2 or more;"[205] inasmuch as the travel from Boston to New Town then took that way. Roger Williams made from twelve to fourteen miles of it from Salem to the Court, of which he afterwards complained as a cause of his ill health.[206] We do not know at what hour the session commenced, but it was no doubt at one sufficiently late to make it possible for those living within from five to ten miles to reach the spot without serious inconvenience; and sufficiently early to leave a good share of the day still open for business. The place of assembling was, doubtless, that rude structure which served the Sabbath and other occasions of the New Town church as its meeting-house; inasmuch as no other building of adequate size presumably then existed there, and no scruple as to any special sanctity about the place would hinder.[207]

A large amount of minor legislation was first attended to. One John Holland was authorized to "keepe a fferry betwixte the Capt. Poynte att Dorchestr [now Commercial Point] & Mr. Newberryes Creeke" at Squantum [now Billings's Creek] for which service he was to have four pence for one, and three pence each if there were two or more.[208] Order was taken for aiding Robert Wing, who was from sixty to seventy years of age, and poor, in building a house.[209] Mr. Dummer, Assistant from Newbury, was empowered to adminis-

---

204 Not only did no public conveyance of any sort—with the exception of boats across a few ferries—then offer itself to the traveller; but nearly all locomotion must have been done on foot, as horses were yet very few in New England. [Baylies's *Memoir of Plym. Col.* i: 206.] Two years before, Gov. Winthrop had walked to Ipswich to see his son John jr.: "The Governour went on foot to Agawam, and because the people there wanted a minister, spent the Sabbath with them, and exercised by way of prophecy, and returned home the 10–20th." [Winthrop's *Journal* (under date of Thursday, 3–13th April 1634) i: 130.]

205 *Mass. Col. Rec.* i: 88.

206 "By travells also by day and night to goe and return from their Court, etc., it pleased God to bring me neare unto death." [Williams's *Mr. Cotton's Letter Examined and Answered*, 12.] "The Court being held within twelve or fourteene miles distance from Salem, travell to, and fro, was no likely cause of such distemper." [Cotton's *Reply to Mr. Williams, his Examination, etc.* 56.]

207 We have Lechford's testimony that, years after, the Court met in the First Church in Boston [*Plaine Dealing*, 24]; and it is within the memory of multitudes now living that town-meetings used to be habitually held in the New England Sanctuaries.

208 *Mass. Col. Rec.* i: 159; *History of Dorchester*, 592.

209 *Mass. Col. Rec.* i: 159. From *Ibid*, ii: 216, it appears that in Nov. 1647, this Wing was "above 80

ter the oath of office to a constable in that remote settlement.[210] Robert Long was licensed "to keepe a howse of intertainment att Charles Towne, for horse & man."[211] The bounds of Roxbury "on both sydes the towne" were ordered to be surveyed and reported to the next Court; and Ensigne Jennison and Mr. Aspinwall were appointed to do it. A law which had prohibited merchants from taking more than 33⅓ per cent. profit for their wares; one which had limited the price of wages; one which had regulated the time of going on board ships; and one which had provided for the support of military officers out of the public treasury, were repealed; and in place of the latter it was enacted that each town maintain its own officers. It was decreed that Charlestown and Watertown be two distinct "companyes." Action was taken for the improvement of the highways between Lynn and Ipswich, and between Ipswich and Newbury. It was ordered that Plymouth "be ayded with men and municons to supplant the French att Penopscott," and Capt. Sellanova was to be sent for at the public charge for conference in regard to this.[212] Constables who were behindhand on their rates to the Treasury, were directed to pay up at once, on pain of attachment.[213] John Winthrop, jr., "being formerly chosen an Assistant, did nowe take an oath to his said place belonginge."[214] Ordnance and ammunition were voted to be sent to the plantations

---

years of age & 4 smal children, & nothing to live upon." But Savage [*Gen. Dict.* iv: 595] says he was 60 in 1634; and he certainly was put down at 60 on the shipping list of the *Francis*, in which he came from Ipswich, Eng., in April 1634. [Hotten's *Original Lists of Persons of Quality, Emigrants, etc.* 279.] One may find additional facts about him in Drake's *Hist. Boston*, i: 791, 793, 796.

[210] *Mass. Col. Rec.* i: 159. The strict Charter provision in regard to this matter required the administration of the oath of office to "all officers" to be *before the Governor of the Company*. In this, as in some other matters, the great inconvenience attending a growth of the company not anticipated, and provided for, in the Charter, led to legislation which comported with its spirit better than its letter. [Charter, *Mass. Col. Rec.* i: 13; Lecture of Judge Joel Parker on the Charter, etc. *Lowell Lectures by Members of Mass. Hist. Soc.* 1869, 367].

[211] He had been an inn-keeper at Dunstable, Bedfordshire; had just arrived with his wife Elizabeth and ten children, and purchased the "Great House;" which had been built in 1629 by Thomas Graves for the Governor to live in, and for the accommodation of the courts; and which had subsequently been used as a meeting-house. In 1632 it had been purchased of the company for £10. Robert Long now gave £30. [Frothingham's *Hist. of Charlestown*, 29, 65, 96; *Savage*, iii: 108.]

[212] A trading house belonging to Plymouth had been captured by the French, who, on being overhauled by a vessel sent from Plymouth, prepared for defence and refused to surrender, whereupon the Plymouth men applied to Massachusetts for help. [Baylies's *Hist. Mem. Plym. Col.* i: 218; Bradford's *Hist. Plym. Plant.* 332; Palfrey's *Hist. N. Eng.* i: 540.]

[213] It seems to have been a part of the constables' duty to collect all taxes which they received warrants from the Treasury to gather. Considerable explicit legislation was called for from time to time to secure prompt action of this sort; leading to the suspicion that our fathers had a reluctance to pay their taxes, quite as decided as that which is sometimes manifested by their sons. [*Mass. Col. Rec.* i: 160, 179, 302.]

[214] John Winthrop, jr., had commenced the settlement of Ipswich in 1633, and buried his first wife there in the summer of 1634. He sailed for England in company with John Wilson, there married again, and had just two or three days previous arrived back from England, in company with Wilson, Thomas Shepard, Hugh Peter, Henry Vane, and others, with a commission "to begin a plantation at Connecticut, and to be governour there." As the usual number of Assistants was com-

at Connecticut "to ffortifie themselues withall." On second thought, to prevent ill consequences from the repeal of the laws about prices and wages just ordered, it was enacted that any offence of the description which these laws had been intended to repress, might be considered by the Court, and punished at its discretion. A further statute, authorizing the appointment and swearing in of constables, was also passed.

Early in the day, moreover — for the first time for a period of a little more than three years — a man had been ordered out of the jurisdiction. His name, which was John Smyth, — a miller of Dorchester — was even then most unfavorable for individualization;[215] and the general terms of his sentence, which was "for dyvers dangerous opinions, wch he holdeth & hath dyvulged,"[216] together with the fact that we do not find the name of *this* John upon the Records of the Court at any earlier or later date; make it impossible to hazard a conjecture as to the nature of his opinions, or the peculiarities of danger which attended his case. Nor does the fact that he afterwards accompanied Williams to Moshassuck, and became with him one of the founders of Providence, indicate that he sympathized with Mr. Williams in the quality of his opinions; for Mr. Williams's account of the matter implies that he allowed Smyth to go along with him, rather from pity of his desolate condition, than from any affinity between their views.[217]

The case of Roger Williams was reached at last. It will be remembered, that, having been accused of holding and teaching: (1) that the magistrate ought not to punish the breach of the first table, otherwise than in such cases as did disturb the civil peace; (2) that the oath ought not to be tendered to the unregenerate; (3) that one ought not to pray with the unregenerate, though wife, or child; (4) that one ought not to give thanks after the sacrament, nor after meat; and having also been guilty, with his church, of "a great contempt of authority" in having become their pastor, as he did; all had been referred to this Court for further consideration. Of course, then, these former charges now again came up, aggravated by what had since taken place, and especially

---

plete without him, and as he was simply *in transitu* to Connecticut, and his business required haste, his taking the oath on this occasion would seem to have been rather a matter of courtesy than of business. [Felt's *Ipswich*, 10, 72; Hollister's *Hist. Connecticut*, i: 26.]

[215] Savage names more than 70 John Smiths in his *Genealogical Dictionary of the First Settlers of New England* [iv: 118–124], and thinks, beyond doubt, there must have been several more.

[216] *Mass. Col. Rec.* i: 159.

[217] "My soul's desire was to do the natives good, and to that end to have their language (which I afterwards printed), and therefore desired not to be troubled with English company; yet out of pity I gave leave to William Harris, then poor and destitute, to come along in my company. I consented to John Smith, miller at Dorchester (banished also), to go with me, and at John Smith's desire, to a poor young fellow, Francis Wickes, as also to a lad of Richard Waterman's. These are all I remember." [Williams's Answer to W. Harris, before the Court of Commissioners, 17–27th Nov. 1677, as cited by Gov. Arnold. *Hist. R. I.* i: 97.]

by the letters of admonition, which he had addressed, in the name of his own church, to the other churches "complaining of the magistrates for injustice, extreme oppression," etc., and the letter to his own church to insist upon their withdrawal of communion from all the churches in the Bay, "as full of anti-Christian pollution," etc.[218]

When demanded whether he were prepared to give satisfaction to the Court in these matters, Mr. Williams "justified both these letters, and maintained all his opinions."[219]

They asked him whether he would take the whole subject into still further consideration; proposing that he employ another month in reflection, and then come and argue the matter before them. This he distinctly declined; choosing "to dispute presently."

They then appointed Thomas Hooker to go over these points in argument with him, on the spot, in the endeavor to make him see his errors. One single glimpse of this debate is afforded us, by Mr. Cotton, writing not very long after. He says that Mr. Williams complained, now in open Court: "that he was wronged by a slanderous report up and downe the Countrey, as if he did hold it to be unlawfull for a Father to call upon his childe to eat his meate. Our reverend Brother Mr. Hooker, (the Pastor of the Church where the Court was then kept) being mooved to speake a word to it, Why, saithe he, you will say as much againe (if you stand to your own Principles) or be forced to say nothing. When Mr. Williams was confident he should never say it, Mr. Hooker replyed, If it be unlawfull to call an unregenerate person to take an Oath, or to Pray, as being actions of God's worship, then it is unlawfull for your unregenerate childe to pray for a blessing upon his own meate. If it be unlawfull for him to pray for a blessing upon his meate, it is unlawfull for him to eate it (for it is sanctified by prayer, and without prayer unsanctified, *I Tim. iv:* 4, 5.) If it be unlawfull for him to eate it, it is unlawfull for you to call upon him to eate it, for it is unlawfull for you to call upon him to sinne.—Here Mr. Williams thought better to hold his peace, then to give an Answer."[220]

It is not perhaps surprising, under all the circumstances, that, after spending the rest of the day in discussion, all ended where it had begun, in that neither the Court nor Mr. Hooker found it possible to "reduce him from any of his

[218] Winthrop's *Journal*, i: 171.

[219] Winthrop [*Journal*, i: 171], is our main reliance for the account of this trial, supplemented, in some points, by others. Mr. Knowles has the good sense and magnanimity to style him [*Memoir*, 64, 75] "the mild and candid Winthrop," and frankly acknowledges that "this truly great man wrote without the angry temper which most of the early writers on the subject exhibited."

[220] Cotton's *Reply to Mr. Williams his Examination, etc.* 30. Cotton Mather repeats this from his grandfather's book [*Magnalia*, Book vii: 8], adding the characteristic comment: "such the Giddiness, the Confusion, the *Antocatacritie* of that Sectarian Spirit!"

errors." His positions, to his mind, had a "Rockie strength." He was ready for them, "not only to be bound and banished, but to die also in New England, as for most holy Truths of God in Christ Jesus."[221]

Whereupon adjournment seems to have taken place, for a night's rest and reflection.

The next day — which was *Friday* 9–19 October, 1635 —[222] the Court reas-

[221] I quote here his own language concerning the matter, on a subsequent occasion, which, most likely, samples what he said at the time. [*Mr. Cotton's Letter Examined and Answered, etc.* 5.]

[222] I believe I have the pleasure to be the first writer on the subject to state this date of the banishment of Roger Williams with entire accuracy. A singular variety of times has been assigned to it. Winthrop [*Journal*, i: 170] puts it under the general date of "October." Hubbard [*Gen. Hist. N. Eng.* 202] seems to put it at some time in 1634. Holmes [*Annals*, i: 225] certainly does this. Neale [*Hist. N. Eng.* i: 142] makes the same strange blunder. Morse and Parish [*Compendious Hist. N. Eng.* 86] give no date whatever. Backus [*Hist. N. Eng.* i: 69] simply quotes Winthrop's general date of "October, 1635." Knowles [*Memoir*, 72] does the same. Gammell [*Life*, 52] says the sentence was passed on the 3d November, 1635. Elton [*Life*, 29] follows Gammell, as does Underwood [*Introduction to Bloudy Tenent, etc.* xxi]. Felt [*Eccl. Hist. N. Eng.* i: 231] puts it generally under October, 1635. Palfrey [*Hist. N. Eng.* i: 412] prints "3 Sept." in his margin against the sentence. Ex. Gov. Arnold [*Hist. R. I.* i: 37] and Mr. R. A. Guild, [Biog. Introduc. Works, etc. *Pub. Narragansett Club*, i: 27] fix it on the 3d November, 1635. Prof. J. L. Diman, in editing the second of the series of volumes issued by that Club, shows, [*Ibid*, ii: 239] that the first session of the General Court which passed the sentence was held at New Town on the 2d Sept. 1635, then adjourned to the next day, and then adjourned to "the Thursday after the next Particular Court." He shews that the Particular Court referred to, met at New Town on Tuesday 6 Oct. 1635, which would fix the date of reassembling of the Generall Court for Thursday, 8 Oct. 1635 (although the marginal date of 3 Sept. is carelessly carried through the whole record.) He therefore fixes 8 October as the date of sentence. But Winthrop, after referring to the trial and the debate and its failure, says: "so, *the next morning*, the Court sentenced him, etc." which naturally carries the important date one day further along, to Friday 9–19, where I assign it. Prof. Diman by no means overlooked this statement of Winthrop, but suggests that — writing some time after — his memory may have been at fault, or that the Governor may mean that the vote, which had been determined upon the night before, was officially announced the next morning. To this I reply that, from the appearance of the entries, Winthrop would seem to have made the record between 1 November and 3 November — or about three weeks (only) after the event; so that his memory can hardly be presumed to be then at fault in regard to so distinct a matter as whether the sentence was passed on Thursday night or Friday morning; while the fact that so large an amount of business — some of it of a character to provoke discussion — preceded the trial of Mr. Williams, while that must have occupied, it would seem, a long time; with the further fact that a few other important votes, two of which might have started debate, are on the record following Mr. Williams's sentence; render it eminently probable that more time must have been consumed by the entire sitting of the Court than would have been afforded by what of Thursday remained after the earliest hour of meeting convenient for its assembling. I esteem it, therefore, much more probable that the Court adjourned over until Friday on the conclusion of Mr. Williams's hearing, and that the record of adjournment was omitted (especially as one error of this sort is even now palpable on the page), than that Winthrop forgot, or that the entire of the business could have been crowded into one abbreviated day. I am confirmed in this view by noticing that, in the Court Record of the case of Mr. John Wheelwright, in November, 1637, no change of date is noted in the margin between the trial and sentence, while in the particular account which is given of the trial in *A Short Story of the Rise, Reign, and Ruine of the Antinomians, etc.*, it is distinctly stated that an adjournment over night took place: "although the cause was now ready for sentence, yet night being come, the Court arose and enjoyned him to appeare the next morning. The next morning he appeared, etc." [p. 26]. Precisely the same thing is, moreover, to be noticed in the trial of Mistress Anne Hutchinson. The Court Record [*Mass. Col. Rec.* i: 207] there has the appearance of being unbroken, as if all which is set down before the adjournment to the 15–25 Nov. 1637, had taken place upon the 2–12 November. But the same *Short Story* [p. 36] gives these particulars: "It was neare night, so the Court brake up, and she was enjoyned to appeare againe the next morning. When she appeared the next day, etc." This looks as if it had been the Secretary's custom to count it one

sembled, and, there being no concession on the part of Mr. Williams, and no change in their own convictions of duty — in which they were reënforced by "all the ministers, save one,"[223] — they passed the following sentence:

Whereas Mr. Roger Williams, one of the elders of the church of Salem, hath broached & dyvulged dyvers newe & dangerous opinions, against the aucthoritie of magistrates, as also writt lres of defamacon, both of the magistrates & churches here, & that before any conviccon, & yet mainetaineth the same without retraccon, it is therefore ordered, that the said Mr. Williams shall depte out of this jurisdiccon within sixe weekes nowe nexte ensuing, wch if hee neglect to pforme, it shalbe lawfull for the Gour & two of the magistrates to send him to some place out of this jurisdiccon, not to returne any more without licence from the Court.[224]

Some formality attended the announcement to Mr. Williams of the sentence thus passed upon him. The Governor[225] appears to have summed up the case, and we have Mr. Williams's own report of what he said.[226]

He stood up and spake:

Mr. Williams (said he) holds forth these 4 particulars:

First, That we have not our Land by Pattent from the King, but that the Natives are the true owners of it, and that we ought to repent of such a receiving it by Pattent.

Secondly, That it is not lawfull to call a wicked person to Sweare, to Pray, as being actions of God's worship.

---

session of the Court, so long as it was continuous from day to day, and to allow the date of the assembling to run in the margin, until it was interrupted by adjournment over some intervening day, or days, when the fact was noted, and the marginal date adjusted to correspond.

[223] I am a little at a loss to decide whether this solitary dissentient were Mr. Cotton. In his letter to Mr. Williams he says: "Let not any prejudice against my person, (I beseech you,) forestall either your affection or judgement, as if I had hastened forward the sentence of your civill banishment; for what was done by the Magistrates, in that kinde, was neither done by my counsell nor consent, although I dare not deny the sentence passed to be righteous in the eyes of God, etc." [*Letter of Mr. John Cotton's, etc., to Mr. Williams, etc.* 1.] To this Mr. Williams replied: ,,that Mr. Cotton consented not, what need he [consent], not being one of the civill Court? But that hee councelled it (and so consented), beside what other proofe I might produce, and what himself here under expresseth, I shall produce a double and unanswerable testimony." This he does, by alleging (1) that Mr. Cotton taught the doctrine of not permitting, but persecuting, all other consciences and ways of worship but his own, and (2) that divers worthy Gentlemen had told him [Williams] they should not have consented to the sentence but for Mr. Cotton's private advice and counsel. He then proceeds: "I desire to bee as charitable as charity would have me, and therefore would hope that either his memory faild him, or that else he meant that in the very time of sentence passing he neither counselled nor consented (as hee hath since said, that he withdrew himselfe, and went out from the rest), . . and yet if so, I cannot reconcile his owne expression." [Mr. Williams's *Mr. Cotton's Letter Examined, etc.* 6.] To this Mr. Cotton rejoined: "I havè professed that I had no hand in procuring or soliciting the Sentence of his Banishment." [Cotton's *Reply to Mr. Williams his Examination, etc.* 8.]

[224] *Mass. Col Rec.* i: 160.

[225] Mr. Williams calls him in one place, [*Mr. Cotton's Letter Examined, etc.* 4] "one of the most eminent Magistrates (whose name and speech may by others be remembered"); and in another, [*The Bloudy Tenent Yet More Bloudy, etc.* 40] "the chief Judge in Court." These expressions confirm the natural judgment that it would be the place of the Governor, as presiding officer, to say what was to be said on such an occasion. But in his letter to Major Mason, written thirty-five years after, Williams says: "that heavenly man, Mr. Hains, Governour of Connecticut, though he pronounced the sentence of my long banishment against me at Cambridge, then Newtown, etc." [1 *Mass. Hist. Coll.* i: 280.]

[226] *Mr. Cotton's Letter Examined, etc.* 4.

Thirdly, That it is not lawfull to heare any of the Ministers of the Parish Assemblies in England.

Fourthly, That the Civill Magistrates power extends only to the Bodies and Goods, and outward State of men, etc.

To this the Governor added[227] the citation of a passage out of Paul to the Romans, as follows:[228] "Now I beseech you, brethren, marke them which cause diuisions and offences, contrary to the doctrine which ye haue learned; and auoyd them."

By way of appendix to the case of Mr. Williams, thus disposed of, the Court proceeded to "enjoyn" Mr. Samuel Sharpe to be in attendance at the next Particular Court, to report progress in regard to the condition of the Salem church, and especially whether they would persist in the attitude which they had assumed, or acknowledge offence in regard to the same.[229]

The six weeks allowed Mr. Williams in which to settle up his affairs before leaving the plantation, expired on Friday, 20–30 November. Previous to that time, however, a new claim for the clemency of delay came into the case, which did not fail of recognition. Soon after the decree of banishment, Mr. Williams fell suddenly, and severely ill. Mr. Cotton had the impression that his sickness was caused by "over-heat" in disputation;[230] but Mr. Williams attributed it to excessive labors in his profession and in manual toil in the fields, aggravated "by travells also by day and night to goe and return from their Court."[231] It was "a sodaine distemper,"[232] and although he had two "skillfull in Physick," it brought him "neare unto death."[233] There is evidence that he was smitten with it in connection with certain warm debates which occurred in the church in Salem, immediately following this action of the Court;[234] debates unquestionably made intense by a letter, or letters,[235] sent to that church about this time, intended to

[227] *The Bloudy Tenent Yet More Bloudy, etc.* 40. See also p. 131, where Williams returns to the subject, and uses this citation, which he claims to refer purely to church offences, as an argument to prove that the Massachusetts men had "made up a kind of national church, and (as the phrase is) a Christian State, and government of Church and Commonweale, that is of Christ and the world together."

[228] *Romans*, xvi: 17.

[229] *Mass. Col. Rec.* i: 161.

[230] *Letter to Mr. Williams*, 2.

[231] *Mr. Cotton's Letter Examined, etc.* 13.

[232] *Reply to Mr. Williams his Examination, etc.* 56.

[233] *Mr. Cotton's Letter Examined, etc.* 13.

[234] Mr. Cotton says in his *Reply, etc.*: "The Court being held within twelve or fourteene miles distance from Salem, travell to, and fro, was no likely cause of such distemper. And whatsoever his Labours were in Towne or Field, on the Lordes Dayes, or weeke dayes, (I detract not from them) but this is all I would say, That that sodaine distemper fell not upon him, neither in the field at his labour, nor on the weeke dayes, or Lord's dayes in his Preaching: but in his vehement publick arguing against the writings and testimonies of the Churches and Brethren sent to him, and to the church of Salem, against his corrupt wayes." [56.]

[235] Cotton in his *Letter* [2] speaks generally of Mr. Williams's disputing being against "the Lord Jesus" in "the mouthes and testimonies of the Churches and Brethren." In the same document he refers to reasons for his banishment, etc., "as may appeare by that answer which was sent to the Brethren of the Church of Salem, and to your selfe" [2]; which must necessarily intend some communication to him and to them, made subsequent to the sentence, yet prior to his departure from the town.

win them back from the way into which Mr. Williams had led them; an endeavor which, with a majority of them, proved successful. Probably because of this sickness, the authorities gave him leave to stay until Spring, on the (under the circumstances far from unreasonable) condition that he should not "go about to draw others to his opinions."[236]

Winthrop—between whom and Williams a life-long friendship existed, notwithstanding all their differences—privately advised him to go into the fertile, comely, and as yet unsettled, Narragansett country;[237] and Cotton says some of his friends went before him thither to make preparation for his coming.[238] As the days began to lengthen for another year, the tonic of the strengthening cold, perhaps, so invigorated the invalid that he quite commenced again his old work as a teacher of the people; so that, disregarding wholly any promise necessarily implied—if never to them publicly expressed—in his acceptance of the lenity of the government in lengthening the period of his tolerated stay; he "did use to entertain company in his house, and to preach to them, even of such points as he had been censured for."[239]

It was not to be expected that this could long be suffered, and so Winthrop tells us, under the general date of January 1635–6, that the Governor and Assistants (that is, the Particular Court) met at Boston "to consider about Mr. Williams." It was reported to them that above twenty persons had been gained to his opinion,[240] and that the leaven was spreading in Salem even to the extent of endangering the neglect of the public ordinances there.[241] It was finally decided to send him to England by a ship then lying at Nantasket, and ready to depart. James Penn, Marshal of the Court,[242] served the warrant upon him to come to Boston for that purpose. Answer was shortly returned by

---

236 Winthrop's *Journal*, i: 175.

237 "That ever honored Governour, Mr. Winthrop, privately wrote to me to steer my course to the Nahigonset-Bay, and Indians, for many high and heavenly and publike ends, incouraging me from the freenes of the place from any English claims or pattents." [Letter of R. Williams to Maj. Mason (1670), 1 *Mass. Hist. Coll.* i: 276.] See also testimony to the same effect in another letter cited by Knowles. [*Memoir*, 74.]

238 "In the meane time, some of his friends went to the place appointed by himselfe before hand, to make provision of housing, and other necessaries for him against his coming, etc." [*Reply to Mr. Williams's Exam. etc.* 8.]

239 Winthrop's *Journal*, i: 175.

240 *Ibid.*

241 "This I have been given to understand, that the increase of concourse of people to him on the Lord's dayes in private, to the neglect or deserting of publick Ordinances, and to the spreading of the Leaven of his corrupt imaginations, provoked the Magistrates, rather then to breed a winter's spiritual plague in the Countrey, to put upon him a winter's journey out of the Countrey. *Gangrænam amoveas, ne pars sincera trahatur.* [Cotton's *Reply to Mr. Williams's Exam. etc.* 57.]

242 "There is a Marshal, who is as a Sheriffe, or Bailiffe, and his deputy is the Gaoler, and Executioner." [Lechford's *Plaine Dealing, etc.* 39.] This was James Penn, who had been chosen beadle at the first session of the Court in Charlestown 23 Aug.–2 Sept. 1630, and marshal 25 Sept.–5 Oct. 1634. Cotton, in writing his name in the margin of the MSS. of his *Reply, etc.*, probably wrote it Penne, which the London compositors and proof-reader transmuted into James *Bonne;* there being no person of that surname, or any resembling it, then in the country. [*Mass. Col. Rec.* i: 74, 128; Cotton's *Reply, etc.* 57. See also *Plaine Dealing, etc.* 28, with its note 97.]

a Salem committee which charged itself with that labor, that he was still too ill to comply with the order without hazard of his life. The Marshal, however, who was a godly man and greatly respected,[243] testified that he saw Mr. Williams and talked with him, and that "he discerned no signe of sicknesse upon him, much lesse of nearnesse unto death." So John Underhill, then one of the two chief officers of the plantation, and who was that year chosen Captain for Boston,[244] was sent with a pinnace to Salem, ordered to take Mr. Williams and put him on board the ship. But when they arrived at his house they were informed that he had been gone three days — nobody could (or would) tell them whither. The event proved that — not altogether alone — he was making his way through the difficult, yet by no means pathless, winter wilderness to the wigwams of some of his Indian friends; whence with opening spring he repaired to Seekonk to commence the clearing which, not long after, circumstances led him to abandon for the more beautiful and hospitable shores of the Moshassuck.[245]

---

[243] "The officer of justice is a man fearing God, and of a tender Conscience, and who dare not allow that liberty to his tongue which the Examiner [Mr. Williams] often useth in his Discourse." [Cotton's *Reply, etc.* 57, 59.] Mr. Penn was, through a long life (dying in 1671), greatly trusted in Boston; was selectman many years, and town treasurer, Deputy, and Elder of the First Church. He was one of the Elders of that Church whose course as to the settlement of John Davenport, in 1668, the seventeen ministers protested against. [Drake's *Hist. Boston,* i: 189, 233, 237, 291, 307, 318, 320, 385, 390; Hutchinson's *Hist. Mass.* i: 246, 248; Savage's *Gen. Dict.* iii: 389.]

[244] Winthrop's *Journal,* i: 176; *Mass. Col. Rec.* i: 75, 77, 191.

[245] Most likely, with his four companions, [See note 217 ante] he went as quickly as he could to *Sowams* (Warren, R. I.), the home of his friend — and the friend of the Plymouth men — *Massasoit.* He says: "I was sorely tost for one fourteen weekes, in a bitter winter season, not knowing what bread or bed did meane." [Letter to Maj. Mason, 1 *Mass. Hist. Coll.* i: 276.] I do not think he meant by this, as seems to have been commonly supposed, that it took him fourteen weeks to make his way from Salem to his place of refuge, and that he was camping out in the snow all that time; but that he meant to say that for fourteen weeks he lived in the wilderness among the savages. If he left Salem, as is commonly supposed, about the middle of January, fourteen weeks would bring him to about the last week in April, by which time he and his little company would naturally have been so far along at Seakonk as to have some civilized, though rude, shelter there. It did not probably take him and his comrades more than four or five days, at the outside, to reach *Sowams,* where they would be sure of the best which the Indians had. But he who reads Edward Winslow's account of his visit to *Sowams* fifteen years before — how he went supperless to bed, and was "worse weary of his lodging than of his iourney" [*Mourt's Relation,* 45] — may well understand that Williams need here use no unwonted exaggeration of speech in declaring his small acquaintance, during all that time, with bread and bed. Mr. Guild [*Pub. Narragansett Club,* i: 32] concludes that he went *by sea* to Seekonk; so interpreting Williams's expressions that he was "sorely tossed," that he "*steered his course* to the Nahigonset-bay from Salem, etc." [*Letter above*], and especially his complaint [*Cotton's Letter Examined, etc.* 12] of "hardships *of sea* and land, in a banished condition." But Prof. Diman has pointed out [*Pub. Narragansett Club,* ii: 87] that the common metaphor of "steering his course" is to be interpreted by his accompanying words: "though in winter snow, etc.;" which would not naturally apply to a voyage by water; while the connection of the phrase "hardships of sea and land, etc.," linking it with "debts, necessities, poverties and miseries," clearly points, not to the incidents of this particular journey, but to his general experiences in the years since he lived at Salem. This theory that Williams went by sea, was propounded years ago by Gen. G. M. Fessenden of Warren, R. I., in an ingenious paper still existing in MSS., in the archives of the R. I. Historical Society [Arnold's *Hist. R. I.* ii: 163]. But to one who considers all that is involved, the notion is intrinsically absurd. A rowing voyage in an open boat in the dead of winter,

It may be added here, in brief, that besides those who immediately identified themselves, and their future, with Mr. Williams, there were three men and eight women left at Salem who cherished and avowed his peculiar views;[246] that the Church, as such, followed him into the wilderness with what it regarded as its appropriate labor;[247] admonished him for wrong-doing when he demitted his ministry;[248] and, finally, after he had repudiated his infant baptism, been rebaptized,[249] and, three or four months after,[250] had renounced his second baptism and become the "Come-outer" from all current sacred rites, and existing religious organizations that he always after remained,[251] they consummated their

---

exposed to those "deangerous shoulds and roring breakers" off the elbow of Cape Cod, which on the 10–20th of November drove the Mayflower back [Bradford's *Hist. Plym. Plant.* 77], would be an act of needless foolhardiness — to say nothing of his risk of running into the jaws of the very pinnace commissioned to arrest him, and within eye-shot of the ship from which he was trying to escape — of which we cannot believe Mr. Williams guilty. Besides, Williams expressly says, [*Mr. Cotton's Letter Examined, etc.* 1] that he was "exposed to winter miseries *in a howling Wilderness*," and again, in the preface of that work, "To the Impartiall Reader," he speaks of himself as "exposed to the mercy of an howling Wildernesse in Frost and Snow;" and still again, [*Ibid,* 33] he calls it "the miserie of a Winter's Banishment amongst the Barbarians." These are expressions entirely germane to the common theory of a land journey, but almost irreconcilable with the fancy that he went by water.

246 This came out in the April following, when the church at Salem asked counsel of the other churches what course should be taken with this minority, and whether it might not be better "to grant them dismission to be a church by themselves;" and it was decided that the number was too small, besides that it was questionable policy "to raise churches on such grounds." [Winthrop's *Journal,* i: 186.] Neal [*Hist. N. Eng.* (1720) i: 143] represents that: "sentence of banishment being read against Mr. Williams, the whole Town of Salem was in an uproar; for such was the Popularity of the man, and such the Compassion of the People, occasioned by his Followers raising a Cry of Persecution against him, that he would have carried off the greatest part of the Inhabitants of the Town, if the Ministers of Boston had not interposed, etc." I have met with the statement, however, in no earlier writer, which is a little remarkable if it be true; as Neal wrote some fourscore years after the occurrences took place, and in another country.

247 There is a passage in Cotton's *Controversie Concerning Liberty of Conscience in Matters of Religion* (1649) [14], which seems to refer to this labor as taking place, by letter, in a somewhat elaborate form; in which he forbears adding extended reasons as to a certain point: "because you may find that done to your hand, in a Treatise sent to some of the brethren late of Salem, who doubted as you do."

248 "If it had been a negligent and proud part in Archippus (as Mr. Williams confesseth) to refuse to hearken to the lawfull voyce of the Church of Colosse, admonishing him of his slacknesse in his Ministery; I know not but it might be such a like part in Mr. Williams to refuse to hearken to the voyce of the Church of Salem, admonishing him to take heed of deserting his Ministery. Whether is a greater sinne in a Minister, not to fulfill his Ministery, or to desert his Ministery?" [Cotton's *Reply, etc.* 20.]

249 Winthrop's *Journal,* i: 293.

250 "I have been his [Roger Williams's] Neighbour these 38 years; I have only been Absent in the time of the Wars with the Indians till this present. I walked with him in the Baptist's Way about 3 or 4 Months but in that short time of his Standing I discerned that he must have the Ordering of all their Affairs, or else there would be no Quiet Agreement amongst them. In which time he brake off from his Society, and declared at large the Ground and Reasons of it — that their Baptism could not be right, because it was not Administered by an Apostle, etc." [*Letter of Richard Scot.* Appendix of *A New England Firebrand Quenched, etc.* 247.] See also a letter from Williams to Winthrop, written in 1649, which gives some account of his views on Baptism, etc., at that time. [4 *Mass. Hist. Coll.* vi: 273.]

251 [Hubbard's *Gen. Hist. N. Eng.* 208.] See also further testimonies, *e. g.* "At Providence, which is twenty miles from the said island [*Aquidnick*], lives Master Williams, and his company of divers opinions; most are Anabaptists; they hold there is no true visible Church in the Bay, nor in the world, nor any true Ministerie." [Lechford's *Plaine Dealing, etc.* 42.] Baillie says, [*Letters and Journals, etc.* (*Letter* 73) ii: 43]: "Sundry of the Independents are stepped out of the church, and follow my

friendly fidelity, according to the best light they had, by passing upon him the great censure, and excommunicating him from their fellowship.[252]

Now, in view of all the facts here hinted, the simple and only question before us must be, not what opinions Roger Williams at this time held which were incongenial with those then dominant in Massachusetts — whether, in point of fact, far in advance of, or far behind, those of others; but for which of those opinions he was thus ordered beyond the jurisdiction of the plantation? Was he sent away specifically for teaching toleration? That question I propose now to consider in the light of such evidence — cotemporary and other — as I have been able to discover, which bears upon it. Some, which would have been of extraordinary value, at least for interpreting the aspect which the subject had, at the time, in the view of the good men of the colony, seems to have utterly perished out of the knowledge of men;[253] enough however remains to indicate, and warrant, a clear judgment in the case.

1. It is necessarily to be presumed, first of all, that the sentence of the Court, ordering the departure of Mr. Williams from the jurisdiction, would state with

---

good acquaintance, Mr. Roger Williams, who says there is no church, no sacraments, no pastors, no church-officers or ordinances in the world, nor has been since a few years after the Apostles." In Mr. W.'s famous debate with the Quakers, in 1672, which he himself reported, John Stubs asked him why he made certain charges against the Quakers, when he was himself so guilty — "not living in church ordinances?" To which he says he replied: "I professed that *if my Soul could finde rest* in joyning unto any of the Churches professing Jesus Christ now extant, I would readily and gladly do it, yea, unto themselves whom now I opposed." [*Geo. Fox Digged out of His Burrowes, etc.* 66.]

252 Hugh Peter was then pastor of the church. After the excommunication he wrote in the church's name to the other churches announcing the fact. His letter to the Dorchester Church has been preserved. It runs thus — under date of 1-11 July, 1639: "Reuerend and deerly beloued in the Lord: Wee thought it our bounden duty to acquaynt you with the names of such persons as haue had the great censure past vpon them in this our church, with the reasons thereof; beseeching you in the Lord not only to reade their names in publike to yours, but also to giue vs the like notice of any dealt with in like manner by you, that so wee may walke towards them accordingly; for some of vs here haue had communion ignorantly with such as haue bin cast out of other churches, 2 Thes. iii: 14. Wee can doe no lesse then haue such noted as disobey the truth." Then follow the names of Roger Williams and wife, and eight others, who have wholly refused to hear the Church, denied it, and all the churches of the Bay, to be true churches, etc. *Hutchinson Papers.* Felt's *Ecc. Hist.* i: 379.]

253 I have in mind especially "a full Treatise" on the subject, twice referred to by Mr. Cotton as having been written by John Eliot. He says, [*Reply to Mr. Williams his Exam. etc.* 7]: "What causes moved the Magistrates so to proceed against him [R. W.] at that time, is fully declared by another faithfull and diligent hand, in another Treatise of that matter." And again, [*Ibid*, 26] he says: "I referre the Reader for Answer to a full Treatise of that Argument, penned by a reverend faithfull Brother (the Teacher of the Church at *Rocksbury*), etc." I have never met with this treatise, nor — after considerable research — ever seen it catalogued as existing in any library. It seems, at first glance, improbable that Cotton should refer English, and other miscellaneous readers of his own book, to such a treatise for information, if it existed only in manuscript; but we have ample evidence that many such tractates did then have a considerable public circulation, which were never printed: *e. g.*, Edwards, in 1644, in his *Antapologia* [201], after enumerating five or six books as supporting a certain view, adds, "and in manuscripts not a few, particularly in a manuscript intituled *A Treatise about a Church, etc.*" Very likely this manuscript had been sent to England to be printed, and Cotton supposed it had been; inasmuch as sometimes years then passed, before it would be known here whether a manuscript forwarded to London for the press had been issued, or not. Cotton says it was so long before his own *Letter* was printed, that he had almost forgotten it. [*Reply, etc.* 1.]

some exactness the reasons in view of which such action was taken. If the reader will turn back to that sentence,[254] and examine it carefully, he will see that three complaints are therein made : (1) of public attacks upon the authority of the magistrates; (2) of defamatory letters concerning them, and the churches, and (3) of contumacious persistence in this course. There is no proof here that the subject of "soul-liberty" came into the question in any manner. Mr. Williams had denied that the magistrates had authority to proceed upon the assumption that their land-patent was good in equity, or to administer the judicial oath to unregenerate citizens; as really as — and more earnestly than — he ever had gainsaid their right to "punish the breach of the first table." And, although it appears from Winthrop that, in the previous July, Mr. Williams had denied to the Court the magistrates' power in matters of religion, it is not in evidence that that point was specifically made in the final trial.

2. Various testimony[255] may be cited from Mr. Williams himself, in proof that it was upon something else than his views on the subject of toleration, that he understood the action of the Court to rest.

(1.) He admitted that Governor Haynes was exact in his summing up of the case;[256] while that only incidentally alluded to the subject of toleration, but laid no stress upon it.[257]

(2.) In one of his communications to Mr. Cotton he narrowed down the causes of his "banishment" to a single one, and that he declared to be "my humble and faithfull, and constant admonishing of them of such unclean walking between a particular Church (which they only professe to be Christs) and a Nationall."[258] Prof. Diman, in annotating this passage, forcibly calls atten-

---

[254] See p. 59.

[255] With so much positive testimony as I am about to present, it seems hardly worth while to detain the reader with negative evidence. I only therefore here raise the question whether, if Mr. Williams's "banishment" was due to any such view of his on the liberty of conscience, as it has been of late years fashionable to assert, it be not a remarkable circumstance that neither Thomas Morton (who published his *New English Canaan* in 1637), nor Thomas Lechford (who published his *Plain Dealing* in 1642), both of whom hated the Colonists, and could have used such a fact with signal force — and would have had no scruples in doing so — did not mention it; although the latter refers to Williams and his opinions? I submit, also, that it seems unaccountable that Capt. Edward Johnson — who was in Charlestown just before, and just after, the occurrence — in writing his *Wonder-Working Providence of Sion's Saviour, etc.*, within twelve or fifteen years, and in referring distinctly to Mr. Williams therein [131], said nothing about a fact — if it were a fact — so well suited to be mentioned by him.

[256] See p. 59.

[257] "I acknowledge the particulars were rightly summed up, etc." [*Mr. Cotton's Letter Examined, etc.* 5.]

[258] By this he means his unceasing endeavors to convict the colonists of sin, because they would not refuse permission to their church members, in revisiting England, to worship in the congregations of the Church of England — the ground of his separation from his own Salem Church. The statement is found in *Mr. Cotton's Letter Examined, etc.* 33; and on the same page he repeats the avowal that he "at last suffred *for such admonitions to them*, the miserie of a Winter's Banishment amongst the Barbarians." Entirely in the same line is his declaration, in his letter to John Cotton, jr., (March 1671), to this effect: "I first withdrew communion from yourselves for [your] halting between Christ and Anti-Christ, the parish churches, and Christian congregations." [*Proceedings Mass. Hist. Soc.* 1858, 315.]

tion to the remarkable fact that Mr. Williams here makes no allusion whatever to his opinions respecting the power of the civil magistrate, "although such allusion would naturally find a place in a discussion respecting 'the evill of a National Church.'"[259]

(3.) In *The Bloody Tenent Yet More Bloody* (1652) Mr. Williams goes somewhat at large into the matter. He says:[260]

I know those thoughts have deeply possessed not a few, considering also the sinne of the Pattents, wherein Christian Kings (so calld) are invested with Right by virtue of their Christianitie, to take and give away the Lands and Countries of other men; As also considering the unchristian Oaths swallowed downe, at their coming forth from old England, especially in superstitious Laud, his time and domineering.

And I know these thoughts so deeply afflicted the Soule and Conscience of the Discusser[261] in the time of his Walking in the way of New Englands Worship, that at last he came to a perswasion, that such sinnes could not be Expiated, without returning againe into England: or a publike acknowledgement and Confession of the Evill of so and so departing: To this purpose before his Troubles and Banishment, he drew up a Letter[262] (not without the Approbation of some of the Chiefe of New England, then tender also upon this point before God) directed unto the King himselfe, humbly acknowledging the Evill of that part of the Pattent which respects the Donation of Land, etc.

This Letter, and other Endeavours (tending to wash off publike sinnes, to give warning to others, and above all, to pacifie and to give Glory unto God) it may be that Councells from Flesh and Bloud supprest, and Worldly policie at last prevailed: *for this very cause (amongst others afterwards re-examined) to banish the Discusser from such their Coasts and Territories.*

The most that could be claimed here is that there may be a veiled reference to the subject of toleration, in the phrase "other Endeavours," etc.; but it lies on the surface of the statement that Mr. Williams did not here intend to make that prominent — least of all to represent that everything hinged upon it.

(4.) Quite analagous to this is another account of the matter, which came from his pen in a letter to Gov. Endecott, written in 1651, in which he puts it thus:[263]

'Tis true, I have to say elsewhere about the Causes of my Banishment: as to the calling of Naturall Men to the exercise of those holy Ordinances of Prayers, Oathes, &c. As to the frequenting of Parish Churches, under the pretence of hearing some Ministers: As to the matter of the Patent, and King James his Christianitie and Title to these parts, and bestowing it on his Subjects by vertue of his being a Christian King, &c.

At present, let it not be offensive in your eyes, that I single out another, a fourth point, a

---

[259] *Publications of the Narragansett Club*, ii: 165.

[260] Page 276.

[261] By which word Mr. Williams here means himself.

[262] It has been usual to assume that this "letter" was the "Treatise" [see p. 26 *ante*] which made disturbance at Plymouth, and afterward at Boston. But the internal evidence of such identity, I cannot help thinking to be rather slight.

[263] *The Bloody Tenent Yet More Bloody, etc.* (Appendix) 305.

cause of my Banishment also; wherein I greatly feare one or two sad evills, which have befallen your Soule and Conscience.

The point is that of the Civill Magistrates dealing in matters of Conscience and Religion; as also of persecuting and hunting any for any matter meerly Spirituall and Religious.

It is clear now, from these four citations, that he who should take Mr. Williams's own version of the case as unbiassed, complete and accurate, would necessarily conclude that the subject of liberty of conscience was considered by him to have been among the causes which led to his exclusion from the Massachusetts territory. It is equally clear that he would never get so much as the hint that it was, specifically and solely, *the* cause thereof. Nothing can be plainer from his own statements, than that Mr. Williams lived and died in humiliating ignorance of the fact which his biographers and eulogists have since discovered, that "the *head and front of his offending*" consisted in his "maintaining the great doctrine which has immortalized his name: *that the civil power has no jurisdiction over the conscience!*"[264]

Mr. Williams, moreover, was so near a party in interest that it would not be strange if even this very moderate claim which he himself has made, should suffer some deduction, when submitted to the cross-light of the testimony of those who saw the matter from a wholly different point of view. Let us see what that cross-light may be.

3. John Cotton is a voluminous, while he certainly meant to be a candid, witness. And I call attention to his statements, first, because he distinctly traversed some of these very pleadings of Mr. Williams, and that, at length.

(1.) In his *Reply to Mr. Williams his Examination, etc.*,[265] he says:

Whom that eminent Magistrate was,[266] that so summed up the grounds of Mr. Williams his Banishment in those foure Particulars above mentioned, Mr. Williams doth wisely conceale his name, lest if he were named, he should be occasioned to beare witnesse against such fraudulent expression of the Particulars: whereof some were no causes of his Banishment at all, and such as were causes, were not delivered in such generall Tearmes. For *in universalibus latet Dolus.* It is evident the two latter causes which he giveth of his Banishment, were no causes at all, as he expresseth them. There are many knowne to hold both these Opinions, *That it is not lawfull to heare any of the Ministers of the Parish Assemblies in England*, and *That the* Civill *Magistrates power extendeth onely to the bodies, and goods, and outward estates of men:* and yet they are tolerated not onely to live in the Common-wealth, but also in the fellowship of the Churches.

The two former, though they be not so much noysed, yet there be many, if not most, that

---

[264] Prof. Gammell's *Life*, 55; Knowles's *Memoir*, 80; Elton's *Life*, 30.

[265] Page 26.

[266] The reference is to Williams's report of Governor Haynes's summarizing of the points in his case when pronouncing sentence, [see p. 59 *ante*]. Williams had not mentioned his name; simply saying, "one of the most eminent magistrates" (whose name and speech may by others be remembered) stood up and spake, etc." *Mr. Cotton's Letter Examined, etc.* 4.]

hold, *That we have not our Land, merely by right of Patent from the King, but that the Natives are true ouners of all that they possesse, or improve.* Neither doe I know any amongst us, that either then were, or now are, of another minde.

And as for the other Point; *That it is not lawfull to call a wicked Person to sweare, or pray:* Though that be not commonly held, yet it is knowne to be held of some, who yet are tolerated to enjoy both Civill, and Church-liberties amongst us.

To come therefore to Particulars: Two things there were, which (to my best observation and remembrance) caused the Sentence of his Banishment: and two other fell in, that hastened it.

(*a*) His violent and tumultuous carriage against the Patent. By the Patent it is, that we received allowance from the King to depart his Kingdome, and to carry our goods with us, without offence to his Officers, and without paying custome to himselfe. By the Patent, certain select men (as Magistrates, and Freemen) have power to make Lawes, and the Magistrates to execute Justice, and Judgement amongst the People, according to such Lawes. By the Patent we have Power to erect such a Government of the Church, as is most agreeable to the Word, to the estate of the People, and to the gaining of Natives (in Gods time) first to Civility, and then to Christianity.

To this Authority established by this Patent, English-men doe readily submit themselves: and foraine Plantations (the French, the Dutch, and Swedish) doe willingly transact their Negotiations with us, as with a Colony established by the Royall Authority of the State of England.

This Patent, Mr. Williams publickly, and vehemently preached against, as containing matter of falsehood, and injustice: Falsehood in making the King the first Christian Prince who had discovered these parts: and injustice, in giving the Countrey to his English subjects, which belonged to the Native Indians. This therefore he pressed upon the Magistrates and People, to be humbled for from time to time in dayes of solemn Humiliation, and to returne the Patent back againe to the King. It was answered to him, first, That it was neither the Kings intendment, nor the English Planters, to take possession of the Countrey by murther of the Natives, or by robbery: but either to take possession of the voyd places of the Countrey by the Law of Nature (for *Vacuum Domicilium cedit occupanti:*) or if we tooke any Lands from the Natives, it was by way of purchase, and free consent. A little before our coming, God had by pestilence, and other contagious diseases, swept away many thousands of the Natives, who had inhabited the Bay of Massachusetts, for which the Patent was granted. Such few of them as survived were glad of the coming of the English, who might preserve them from the oppression of the *Nahargansets.* For it is the manner of the Natives, the stronger Nations to oppresse the weaker.

This answer did not satisfie Mr. Williams, who pleaded: the Natives, though they did not, nor could subdue the Countrey (but left it *vacuum Domicilium*) yet they hunted all the Countrey over, and for the expedition of their hunting voyages, they burnt up all the underwoods in the Countrey, once or twice a yeare, and therefore as Noblemen in England possessed great Parkes, and the King, great Forrests in England onely for their game, and no man might lawfully invade their Propriety: So might the Natives challenge the like Propriety of the Countrey here.

It was replied unto him: (i) that the King, and Noblemen in England, as they possessed greater Territories then other men, so they did greater service to Church and Common-wealth; (ii) That they employed their Parkes, and Forrests, not for hunting onely, but for Timber, and for the nourishment of tame beasts, as well as wild, and also for habitation to sundry Tenants;

(iii) That our Townes here did not disturb the huntings of the Natives, but did rather keepe their Game fitter for their taking; for they take their Deere by Traps, and not by Hounds; (iv) That if they complained of any straites wee put upon them, wee gave satisfaction in some payments, or other, to their content; (v) We did not conceive that it is a just Title to so vast a Continent, to make no other improvement of millions of Acres in it, but onely to burne it up for pastime.

But these Answers not satisfying him, this was still pressed by him as a Nationall sinne, to hold to the Patent; yea, and a Nationall duty to renounce the Patent: *which to have done, had subverted the fundamentall State, and Government of the Countrey.*

(*b*) The second offence which procured his Banishment, was occasioned as I touched before. The Magistrates, and other members of the Generall Court, upon Intelligence of some Episcopall, and malignant practises against the Countrey, they made an order of Court to take tryall of the fidelitie of the People (not by imposing upon them, but) by offering to them an Oath of Fidelitie: that in case any should refuse to take it, they might not betrust them with place of publick charge, and Command. This Oath when it came abroad, he vehemently withstood it, and disswaded sundry from it, partly because it was, as he said, Christ's Prerogative to have his Office established by Oath: partly because an Oath was a part of Gods worship, and Gods worship was not to be put upon carnall persons, as he conceived many of the People to be. So by his Tenent neither might Church-members, nor other godly men, take the Oath, because it was the establishment not of Christ, but of mortall men in their office; nor might men out of the Church take it, because in his eye they were but carnall. So the Court was forced to desist from that proceeding: which practise of his was held to be the more dangerous, because it tended to unsettle all the Kingdomes, and Common-wealths in Europe.

These were (as I tooke it) the causes of his Banishment: two other things fell in upon these that hastened the Sentence. [These Mr. Cotton goes on to specify—at a length which need not be here minutely followed—as being (i) the provocation given by his "heady and violent Spirit" in the Letters of Admonition to the Churches to which the Magistrates belonged, urging the discipline of those Magistrates for their course about the Marblehead land;[267] and (ii) his subsequent renunciation of, and separation from his own Church, and from all the Churches in the Bay, with his preaching in his own house.[268] He then concludes]: Thus have I opened the grounds, and occasions, of his Civill Banishment; which whether they be sandy, or rocky, let the servants of Christ judge.[269]

(2) Again, in criticising a statement upon the 38th page of Mr. Williams's *Mr. Cottons Letter Examined, etc.*, Mr. Cotton says:[270]

Here be many extenuations, and mincings of his own carriage, and as many false aggravations of Guilt upon his sentence of Banishment, and the Authors of it. As:

i. In that he was cut off, he and his, branch and roote, from any Civill being in these Territories, because their Consciences durst not bow downe to any worship, but what they beleeve the Lord had appointed: Whereas the truth is, his Banishment proceeded not against him, or

---

[267] See *ante* p. 38.

[268] See *ante* p. 46.

[269] Earlier in the same *Reply*, he had glanced at the subject in the same spirit as in the more elaborate view given above. He there says, (a) he opposed "the King's Patent with much vehemency"; (b) he "vehemently withstood" the Oath; (c) he "aggravated the former jealousies" by becoming "incensed" about the Marblehead land, etc. [4].

[270] *Ibid*, 113.

his, for his own refusall of any worship, *but for seditious opposition against the Patent*, and *against the Oath of fidelitie offered to the people.*

ii. That he was subject to the Civill estate, and Lawes thereof, when yet he vehemently opposed the Civill foundation of the Civill estate, which was the Patent: And earnestly also opposed the Law of the generall Court, by which the tender of that Oath was enjoyned: and also wrote Letters of Admonition to all the Churches, whereof the Magistrates were members, for deferring to give present Answer to a Petition of Salem, who had refused to hearken to a lawfull motion of theirs.

(3) Further we find Mr. Cotton testifying thus:[271]

The casting of him [Mr. Williams] out of the Commonwealth, sprung not from his difference in matters of Church Discipline. It was well knoune that whilest he lived at Salem, he neither admitted, nor permitted, any Church Members, but such as rejected all Communion with the Parish Assemblies, so much as in hearing of the Word amongst them. And this libertie he did use, and might have used to this day, without any disturbance to his Civill, or Church-Peace (save onely in a way of brotherly disquisition); but it was his Doctrines and Practises which tended to the Civill disturbance of the Common-wealth, together with his heady and busie pursuite of the same, even to the rejection of all Churches here. *These they were* that made him unfit for enjoying Communion either in the one state, or in the other.

(4) Still further, Mr. Cotton says again, in another place,[272] that the reasons for which the Court proceeded against Mr. Williams, were:

offensive and disturbant Doctrines, and Practises against the Patent, and against the oath of fidelitie; and against the Magistrates delay of the Petition of Salem, *which he himselfe knoweth.*

(5) And, once again, he reverts to the subject in a Letter sent to England, and printed there in 1641, as follows:[273]

It has been reported unto you (as it seemeth) that we receive none into our Church-fellowship untill they first disclaime their Churches in England as no Churches, but as limbs of the devill; now, I answer, God forbid, God forbid: It is true, one Sheba of Bickry[274] blew a Trumpet of such a seditious Separation; I meane one Mr. Williams late Teacher of Salem, but himselfe and others that followed stiffely in that way, who were all excommunicated out of the Church and banished out of the Common-wealth; for men in that way, and of such a spirit, are wont not onely to renounce the Churches of England, but ours also, because we held communion with them in England in the things which are of God; see therefore how unjustly wee are slandered for renouncing communion with you, as is mentioned, and *for it they themselves are punished in our Commonwealth,* censured in our Churches, *for such Antichristian ex-orbitures:* by this you may see the Objection cleerely answered.

I pause here only to call attention to the fact that whether, as in the last

---

271 *Ibid*, 64.

272 *Ibid*, 47.

273 *A Coppy of a Letter of Mr. Cotton of Boston, in New England, sent in Answer of certaine Objections made against their Discipline and Orders there*, etc. 1.

274 See the 20th chapter of 2d Samuel, *passim.*

extract, referring to the intensely separative spirit possessed and exercised by Mr. Williams, which had so much to do in bringing the public feeling up to that pitch which demanded action against him; or describing the reasons of law and equity on which the Court acted in decreeing banishment; Mr. Cotton's testimony is clear and absolute to the point that Mr. Williams's opinions in regard to toleration — while they were known and were unpopular — had nothing whatever to do with the conclusion reached. I cannot forbear to add that if Mr. Cotton be correct in his understanding and representation of the facts, Mr. Williams was by no means the first, or the last, man honestly to mistake the intent and quality of judicial action bearing heavily, and, to his thinking, unjustly upon himself.

4. Gov. Winthrop is our next witness, and we have Roger Williams's own cotemporary and abundant endorsement of him, as a prudent, candid and loving one.[275] I find six different references from his pen to the subject.

(1) His statement in his Journal, under date of 8–18 July 1635, of the things at that time laid to Mr. Williams's charge, is this:[276]

> That, being under question before the magistracy and churches for divers dangerous opinions, viz. (i) that the magistrate ought not to punish the breach of the first table, otherwise than in such cases as did disturb the civil peace; (ii) that he ought not to tender an oath to an unregenerate man; (iii) that a man ought not to pray with such, though wife, child, etc.; (iv) that a man ought not to give thanks after the sacrament nor after meat, etc.; and that the other churches were about to write to the Church of Salem to admonish him of these errors; notwithstanding the church had since called him to the office of a teacher.

Nothing, it will be observed, is here said about the matter of the Patent, or about the subject of hearing the ministers of the Parish assemblies, because the minute covers not the entire subject of points of difficulty, but only so much as came under discussion at that particular session of the Court.

(2) His statement, in the same Journal, of the proceedings at the final trial, is this:[277]

> He was charged with the said two letters, viz.: that to the churches complaining of the magistrates for injustice, extreme oppression, etc.; and the other to his own church, to persuade them to renounce communion with all the churches in the bay, as full of antichristian pollution, etc. He justified both these letters, and maintained all his opinions, etc.

---

[275] Within a year after his banishment we find Williams writing to him thus: "Much honored Sir: the frequent experience of your loving care, ready & open toward me (in what your conscience hath permitted), as allso of that excellent spirit of wisedome & prudence wherewith the Father of Lights hath endued you, embolden me to request a word of private advise, etc." [4 *Mass. Hist. Coll.* vi: 186.] A short time after we find him [*Ibid*, 233] saying: "I therefore now thanckfully acknowledge your wisedome & gentlenes in receaving so lovingly my late rude & foolish lines: you beare with fooles gladly, because you are wise. I still waite vpon your loue and faythfullnes, etc." Many like expressions might be quoted.

[276] i: 162.

[277] i: 171.

There is surely no evidence here that any emphasis was placed in the last and decisive session of the Court, on the tenet as to toleration; if (under this "all his opinions") it came up at all.

(3) At the time of Mr. Williams's flight from Salem, Gov. Winthrop writes, as follows:[278]

He had so far prevailed at Salem, as many there (especially of devout women) did embrace his opinions, *and separated from the churches for this cause, that some of their members, going into England, did hear the ministers there, and when they came home the churches here held communion with them.*

This puts the stress of the matter, practically, solely upon the subject of Separation; as if that were the sum and substance of "his opinions."

(4) Near the middle of the following April, occurs another mention, to this effect:[279]

The Church of Salem was still infected with Mr. Williams his opinions, *so as most of them held it unlawful to hear in the ordinary assemblies in England,* because their foundation was antichristian, and we should, by hearing, hold communion with them; and *some went so far as they were ready to separate from the Church* upon it.

(5) In the letter to Endecott, to which reference was made in its place,[280] Gov. Winthrop says:

The things which will chiefly be layd to his charge are these: (i) that he chargeth Kinge James with a solemn public lye; (ii) that he chargeth both Kinges,[281] & others, with blasphemye for callinge Europe Christendom, or the Christian world, &c.; (iii) for personal application of three places in Rev. to our present Kinge Charles; (iv) for concludinge us all heere to lye under a sinne of unjust usurpation upon others possessions, etc.

It is true that this had relation to the initial stage of the controversy, and yet it is remarkable, if the whole contest were fought with reference to "soul-liberty," that no mention of it finds place here.

(6) After the action which was had two years subsequent to Mr. Williams's case in reference to Mr. Wheelwright, Gov. Winthrop felt called upon to prepare a formal argument in defence of the order of Court. In this he refers to the earlier trial, thus:[282]

If we conceive and finde by sadd experience that his [a Christian man's] opinions are such, as by his own profession cannot stand with externall peace, may we not provide for our peace, by keeping off such as would strengthen him, and infect others with such dangerous tenets?

---

[278] *Ibid*, i: 176.

[279] *Ibid*, i: 186.

[280] See *ante*, p. 27.

[281] By these "Kinges" he means, of course, James I. and Charles I.

[282] *Life and Letters of John Winthrop*, ii: 186.

and if we finde his opinions such as will cause divisions, and make people looke at their magistrates, ministers and brethren as enemies to Christ and Antichrists, etc.; were it not sinne and unfaithfullness in us, to receive more of those opinions, which we allready finde the evill fruite of: Nay, why doe not those who now complayne joine with us in keeping out of such, as well as formerly they did *in expelling Mr. Williams for the like, though lesse dangerous?*

I find in all these statements no evidence that Gov. Winthrop differed from Mr. Cotton in his understanding of the reasons which governed the Colony in its treatment of Mr. Williams, and no suggestion that any doctrine of "soul-liberty" came to the front in the way of affirmation on the one side, or denial on the other.

5. I pass to Samuel Gorton, who landed in Massachusetts within a few months after Williams left it; who was himself a first-class disturber of communities on religious questions; who had experience enough of trouble in regard to his own rights of conscience to make him appreciative of whatever had been done before him in the same line by another, and who seems himself to have been a firm believer in toleration.[283] In his invective against New England men and things published in London, in 1646, entitled *Simplicities Defence Against Seven-Headed Policy, etc.*, he says that, on landing at Boston, he understood[284]

that they had formerly banished one Master Roger Williams, a man of good report both for life and doctrine (even amongst themselves,) *for dissenting from them in some points about their Church Government;* and that in the extremity of winter, forcing him to betake himselfe into the vast wilderness, to sit down amongst the Indians in place, by their own confessions, out of all their Jurisdictions, etc.

As Gorton was not dependent upon the Massachusetts men for his sole account of the matter, but almost immediately made Williams's acquaintance, pitched his own clearing near the place where he was, and, before all ended, gave the Welsh exile quite too much of the pleasure of his company;[285] it seems a little strange that, printing ten years after, he should attribute Williams's banishment entirely to this same matter of Separation — which seems to be the

---

283 Witness the following, written by himself, from lines preliminary to his *Simplicities Defence, etc.*:

Suspend your judgement, all your skill is gone,
And let the Judge of all, his Circuit passe apace,
Who comes not to destroy — such is His grace!
And let that man his own destruction be,
Who breaks that faith with God, cannot be peec'd by thee:
Cease then your prosecutions, seek yee to doe good:
Save life in any, in Church wayes spill not blood:
In Christ, if you consider, the Covenant of God,
Youle find that all compulsion is nought but that Nim-rod.

He kindly explains that by the last word he intends "a meer hunting of men, to worry your own kinde, etc."

284 *Simplicities Defence, etc.* i. This has been republished by Mr. Force, [*Tracts, etc.* iv.] and by the R. I. Hist. Soc. [*Coll.* vol. ii.]

285 Williams, in 1646, accused him of "bewitching and bemadding poor Providence" with "uncleane and foull censures," and of "uncivil and inhuman practices," and complained that almost all Providence "suck in his poison." [*Pub. Nar. Club.* vi: 141.]

natural interpretation of "dissent" as to "points of church government"—if the real cause thereof had been "soul-liberty."

6. Naturally next comes Gov. Winslow, whom Williams styles "my antient friend," and "a great and pious soule."[286] In his *Hypocrisie Unmasked, etc.*, printed in London in 1646, he notices, and replies to, the assertion of Gorton cited above, as if it did not do justice to his knowledge of the case that Williams should be represented as having been sent out of the jurisdiction for Separation, or for anything short of sedition. His version of the matter is:[287]

In answer take notice: I know that Mr. Williams (though a man lovely in his carriage, and whom I trust the Lord will yet recall) held forth, in those times, the unlawfulnesse of our Letters Patents from the King, &c.; would not allow the Colours of our Nation; denyed the lawfulnesse of a publique oath, as being needlesse to the Saints, and a prophanation of God's name to tender it to the wicked, etc. And truly *I never heard but he was dealt with for these, and such like points:* however I am sorry for the love I beare to him and his, I am forced to mention it, but God cals mee at this time to take off these aspersions.

The drift and force of this cannot be mistaken; and, with Winslow's impartiality as a Plymouth man, and his opportunites to know the facts, as a friend of both parties, it adds conclusive weight to what has gone before.

7. My next witness is Thomas Edwards; a Cambridge divine, a voluminous and earnest participant in the religious debates of his time, and an intense and envenomed hater of all who labored for that toleration of which he had an almost insane horror.[288] In his *Antapologia* (1644), intended as an answer to the "Apologeticall Narration" of Goodwin, Nye, Sympson, Burroughs and Bridge, he insists that if they give up some "strong church government" in England, they will find it needful to do as they had done in New England, where:[289]

Not having Classes, Synods, that have authoritative power to call to account and censure such persons [offenders], were necessitated to make use of the Magistrates, and to give the more to them, a power of questioning for doctrines, and judging of errors, and punishing with im-

---

[286] *Letter* [1 *Mass. Hist. Coll.* i: 276, 277.] The fact of Winslow's specially friendly feeling toward Williams, finds illustration in the circumstance mentioned by Williams in this same letter, that he: "kindly visited me at Providence, and put a piece of gold into the hands of my wife for our supply."

[287] *Hypocrisie Unmasked, etc.* 65.

[288] His *Gangræna* (1646) is a remarkable manifestation of his diligence in collecting facts which he supposed to be important, and of his earnestness of feeling, especially against "soul-liberty." "A Toleration," says he, in it, [121] "is the grand designe of the Devil, his Master-peece and chiefe Engine he works by at this time to uphold his tottering Kingdome; it is the most compendious, ready, sure way to destroy all Religion, lay all waste, and bring in all evill; it is a most transcendent, catholique and fundamentall evill: . . as original sin is the most fundamentall sin, all sin; having the seed and spawn of all in it: So a Toleration hath all errors in it, and all evils; it is against the whole streame and current of Scripture both in the Old and New Testament, both in matters of Faith and manners, both generall and particular commands, etc. . . and therefore the Devil follows it night and day, working mightily in many by writing Books for it, and other wayes; all the Devils in Hell and their Instruments being at work to promote a Toleration."

[289] *Antapologia, etc.* 165.

prisonment, banishment; and they found out a prety fine distinction to deceive themselves with, and to salve the contrariety of this practice to some other principles, that the Magistrate questioned and punished for these opinions and errors (which now for want of Ecclesiasticall discipline and censure they knew not what to doe with) not as heresies and such opinions, but as breaches of the civill peace, and disturbances to the Common-wealth — which distinction if the Parliament would have learned from you, and proceeded upon, they might long agoe have put doune all your Churches and Congregations, and justly have dealt with you *as the Magistrates in New England did with Mr. Williams* and the Antinomians, Familists and Anabaptists there, and yet *have said they punished you not for your consciences, nor because of such opinions, but because your opinions, ways, and practises were an occasion of much hurt to the Common-wealth, a breach of civill peace, etc.*

This declaration is valuable simply as showing that it was understood among well-informed persons of that time in the mother country, that the reason published abroad for the banishment of Mr. Williams, was the danger alleged to threaten the civil State of New England from his opinions. And that Mr. Edwards conceived this to be "a prety fine distinction," does not diminish the importance of that fact; while we may be very sure that the slightest suspicion on his part that the banishment was suffered in the cause of toleration, would have kindled him, at once, into a heat of hate.

8. Robert Baillie, of Glasgow, confirms the statement just made as to the current English opinion of this case, in his *Dissvasive from the Errours of the Time*, (1645). He refers in his various writings more than once to Mr. Williams, and seems to have been familiar not only with his history, but with him.[290] He says:[291]

Let men only look over to the fruits of their principles in New England. Not many yeares agoe there, upon a very small, and so farre as I know very groundlesse suspition, to have somewhat of their Government altered by the King contrary to their Patent, they did quickly purchase and distribute Armes among all their people, and exact of every one an Oath for the defence of their Patent against all impugners whosoever: *Mr. Williams opposition to this Oath, as he alledgeth, was the cheife cause of his banishment.*

9. Nathaniel Morton, Secretary and historian of Plymouth Colony, and who had some special facilities for accurate knowledge of the facts, makes the following condensed statement of the affair:[292]

the prudent Magistrates . . seeing things grow more and more towards a general division and disturbance, after all other means used in vain, they passed a sentence of Banishment against him out of the Massachusets Colony, *as against a disturber of the peace, both of the Church and Common-wealth.*

10. William Hubbard, although he did not complete his *General History of*

---

[290] See this affirmed in the extract from his *Letters, etc.* in note 251 *ante.*

[291] *Dissvasive, etc.* 126.

[292] *New England's Memoriall* (1669) 80.

New England until some five and forty years after the banishment of Williams had taken place, did not lack the best advantages for information; having been a member of the first class graduating, soon after, at Cambridge, and having personal intercourse with most of the prominent actors in that transaction, with many original manuscripts of that day in his hands.[203] He devotes considerable space[204] to Mr. Williams and his career, which is largely filled with extracts from Winthrop, Morton, Cotton, and Williams himself. He says:

> Forasmuch as sundry have judged hardly of New England for their proceedings against him, by a sentence of banishment, it is thought needful, in this place, to give a more particular account thereof to the world. [He then goes on, very nearly in Mr. Cotton's words,[205] to declare that Mr. Williams's action about the Patent, and that concerning the Oath of Fidelity, were the two real causes of the Court action; exaggerated and hastened by his letters to the churches, his renunciation of his own church and of all the others, and his setting up a separate service; and concludes thus]: Thus men of great parts and strong affections, for want of stability in their judgments to discern the truth in matters of controversy, like a vessel that carries too high a sail, are apt to overset in the stream, and ruin those that are embarked with them.

Mr. Hubbard adds another testimony which is worthy of consideration, as showing in what light the authorities of Massachusetts regarded the banishment, when looking back upon it from a distance of nearly ten years. Having occasion, in 1644, to take Boston in his way from England, Mr. Williams brought a letter signed by His Grace the Duke of Northumberland, and others, asking for him permission for passage through Massachusetts. Mr. Hubbard says:

> Upon the receipt of the said letter the Governor and Magistrates of the Massachusetts found, upon examination of their hearts, they saw no reason to condemn themselves for any former proceedings against Mr. Williams; but for any offices of Christian love, and duties of humanity, they were very willing to maintain a mutual correspondency with him. *But as to his dangerous principles of Separation*, unless he can be brought to lay them down, they see no reason why to concede to him, or any so persuaded, free liberty of ingress and egress, lest any of their people should be drawn away with his erroneous opinions.

Why this emphasis still upon Separation, if he had been banished for his advocacy of universal toleration — whose spirit is as nearly the opposite of Separation as may well be conceived?

11. Joshua Scottow, less known than many others, deserves, nevertheless, our utmost confidence as a witness. Coming hither in the year after the banishment; an eminently devout man; one of the founders of the Old South Church;

---

[203] See *Proceedings Mass. Hist. Soc.* 1858, 321; Sibley's *Biographical Sketches of Graduates of Harvard Univ. etc.* 1: 57.

[204] *Gen. Hist. N. Eng.* 202–213. The second extract is on p. 349.

[205] See p. 67 *ante*.

and Chief Judge of some of the Courts of the then Province of Maine; he was the author of two tracts, one of which was *A Narrative of the Planting of the Massachusetts Colony, etc.* In this he says:[206]

This Heterodoxy was preached publickly; that there was no Communion to be held with the Church of England; and that if any of our Church-members had transiently heard a Minister which Conformed to the Church of England without declaring Repentance for it, he was to be Excommunicated; and that no Communion was to be held with any Unregenerate Person; that they ought not to Pray or Crave a Blessing at Meals before Wife or any Relation Unconverted, of which Conversion their Opinion was the Test; and not only so, but that the Oath of Allegiance to his Majesty was not to be taken, nor was it lawful to take any other kind of Oath, because no Power [was] to be Settled by Oath but Christ's Kingly Power only; and that our Pattent ought to be sent back to our King, nor ought we to have to do therewith. Thus was New England Attackt by Satan; and this from an Eminent Preacher, noted for Piety in his Life and Conversation, as his strictest Observers characterised him. This Child of Light [Roger Williams] walked in Darkness about Forty Years, not only by Rejecting the Church of England and its Baptism, but his second Baptism also.

Here again it is to be marked that the subject of "soul-liberty" is not even named, in connection with Mr. Williams's history in Massachusetts, by one the bent of whose mind was such as apparently to have awakened his special attention to that question.

12. Cotton Mather, who, though he himself belonged to the next generation, yet lived, in a sense, in that of Mr. Williams in his distinguished ancestors on both sides; in his *Magnalia Christi Americana* (1702) speaks as if from decisive knowledge in regard to this trial.[207] Referring to several of Mr. Williams's singular opinions he says: "these things were, indeed, very Disturbant and Offensive, but there were Two other things in his Quixotism, that made it no longer Convenient for the Civil Authority to remain unconcerned about him." Proceeding to explain that these were his position with regard to the Patent, and the Oath, he continues:

these Crimes, at last, procured a Sentence of Banishment upon him. [To this he adds a reference to Williams's action when the churches dealt with him, and concludes]: the Effect was, that he renounced them all as no Churches of our Lord Jesus Christ. Whereupon the Court ordered his Removal out of the Jurisdiction.

13. Governor Thomas Hutchinson is the last witness I shall call.[208] Though

---

[206] 4 *Mass. Hist. Coll.* iv: 295.

[207] Book vii: 7–11.

[208] He is the last who can be regarded as, in any sense, approximately a cotemporary. The judgment of later historians has its value mainly in the way of comment upon, and deductions from, the earlier authorities. I cite a few words to indicate the judgment of the most prominent of them — in the order in which they wrote.

Neal (1720): "banished the Mass. Colony as a Disturber of the Peace of the Church and Commonwealth." [*Hist. N. Eng.* i: 142.]

Callender (1739): [enumerating the matters about the

he was but a youth when Cotton Mather was an elderly man, he could rightly claim that his ancestors "for four successive generations had been principal actors in public affairs;"[200] he was connected with the Mathers by marriage; he amassed a great collection of manuscripts bearing upon early New England

---

Patent, the Oath, Separation, etc.] "for these things, he was at length banished the Colony, as a disturber of the peace of the Church and Commonwealth. [*Historical Discourse. Coll. R. I. Hist. Soc.* iv: 72.]

Douglass (1753): "because of his Antinomian, Familistical, Brownist, and other fanatical Doctrines, though in other respects a good man, he was excommunicated and banished from Mass. Colony by their Assembly or Legislature, as a Disturber of the Peace of the Church and Commonwealth." [*Summary, etc.* i: 77.]

Backus (1777): "By the first and last of this account it is evident that the grand difficulty they had with Mr. Williams was, his denying the civil magistrates right to govern in ecclesiastical affairs." [*Hist. N. Eng.* i: 69.]

Morse and Parish (1804): "On account of these sentiments [the Oath, the Patent, the civil magistrates, etc.], and for refusing to join with the Massachusetts churches, he was at length banished the Colony, as a disturber of the peace of the Church and Commonwealth." [*Hist. N. Eng.* (ed. 1808) 86.]

Graham (1827): "Had Williams encountered the severities to which the publication of his peculiar opinions would have exposed him in England, he would probably have lost his senses; the wiser and kinder treatment he experienced from the Massachusetts authorities was productive of happier effects." [*History of U. S.* (ed. 1856) i: 163.]

Baylies (1830): "The magistrates, fearful of distractions amongst the people, after attempting, with much earnestness, to reclaim him, proceeded at length to banish him from the colony 'as a disturber of the peace both in the Church and Commonwealth.'" [*Hist. Mem. of Plym. Col.* i: 269.]

Bancroft (1834): [after more than seven pages of graceful rhetoric, in which he adroitly manages to evade most of the main points at issue]: "let there be for the name of Roger Williams at least some humble place among those who have advanced moral science, and made themselves the benefactors of mankind." [*Hist. Col. of U. S.* (ed. 1840) i: 377].

Bradford (1835): "They were inexcusable in their treatment of Roger Williams, who was an honest, though an eccentric character . . merely for his honest independence of opinion driven out of the colony in the midst of a severe winter." [*Hist. Mass.* 33.]

Hildreth (1849): "This threat of schism filled up the measure of his offences." [*Hist. U. S.* i: 228.]

Felt (1855): "It is not easy to perceive how our General Court could have abstained, consistently with their solemn engagement to seek for the preservation and highest good of the State, from dealing with Williams as they had." [*Eccles. Hist. N. Eng.* i: 232.]

Barry (1855): "it was because his opinions differed from the opinions of those among whom he lived, and were considered by them as dangerous and seditious, tending to the utter destruction of their community, that he was a sacrifice to honest convictions of truth and duty." [*Hist. Mass.* i: 241].

Oliver (1856): "Roger Williams was cast out into the wilderness, because he taught that it was unlawful even 'to hear the godly ministers' of the Church of England." [*Puritan Commonwealth*, 192.]

Elliott (1857): [after considerable fine writing]: "it is difficult to see how they could resist Williams's position," but "it must be remembered that it is not uncommon for religious controversy to debauch the intellect and to paralyze the affections, and that Williams was himself injured by it." [*N. Eng. Hist.* i: 205.]

Palfrey (1858): "The sound and generous principle of a perfect freedom of the conscience in religious concerns, can scarcely be shown to have been involved in this dispute. . . The questions which he raised, and by raising which he provoked opposition, were questions relating to political rights, and to the administration of government. . . There is no reason whatever to doubt, that, correctly or otherwise, they [the Court] considered themselves to be proceeding in the way which the safety and well-being of the Colony, as a civil community, required. . . In fact, the young minister of Salem had made an issue with his rulers and his neighbors upon fundamental points of their power and their property, including their power of self-protection against the tyranny from which they had lately escaped. . . But it was not to be thought of by the sagacious patriots of Mass., that, in the great work which they had in hand, they should suffer themselves to be defeated by such random movements." [*Hist. N. Eng.* i: 413, 414, 415, 417.]

[200] *Hist. Mass.* (ed. 1795) i: *Preface*, v; 41.

history, and became the first comprehensive narrator thereof; so that what he says claims always careful and respectful consideration. Naturally, in the perspective inhering in the time when he wrote (publishing in 1764), he dwarfs the trial of Mr. Williams, and its results, to little more than a single page. What is remarkable about his generalization, is, that, reducing the whole case to a single issue, he makes that issue — not one of toleration, but — one unnamed before, in that connection. He says:

But what gave just occasion to the civil power to interpose, was his influencing Mr. Endecot, one of the magistrates and a member of his church, to cut the cross out of the King's colours, as being a relique of antichristian superstition. . . Endeavours were used to reclaim him, but to no purpose; and at length he was banished the jurisdiction.

Studying carefully now all this evidence, I find it conducting the mind with irresistible force straight toward one conclusion. It is true that Mr. Williams did hold, in an inchoate form, and had already to some extent advocated, that doctrine of liberty of conscience, with which his name afterward became prominently identified. It is true that the language of the official sentence is susceptible of a construction which might include this among his "newe and dangerous opinions." It is true that Mr. Williams did himself claim that it was so included. But it appears to be also true that he himself never claimed more than this; and that, in his own view, his banishment was only incidentally — in no sense especially — for that cause. While the careful and repeated statements of Mr. Cotton, with their reiterated endorsement by Gov. Winthrop, go to show that Mr. Williams was mistaken in supposing that the subject of the rights of conscience had anything whatever to do with the action of the Court upon his case; action, in reality, solely taken in view of his-seditious, defiant, and pernicious posture toward the State. This, it appears from the testimony of Mr. Gorton, and of Gov. Winslow, supported by that of Secretary Morton, of Mr. Hubbard, of Judge Scottow, of Cotton Mather and of Gov. Hutchinson, was the general understanding had of the matter by the New England public of that day; while Edwards and Baillie speak to the same point from over sea. And, as I am aware of nothing purporting to be proof to the contrary, other than the (necessarily biased, and presumably ill-informed and partial) opinion of Mr. Williams himself, before cited; I cannot help thinking that the weight of evidence is conclusive to the point that this exclusion from the Colony took place for reasons purely political, and having no relation to his notions upon toleration, or upon any subject other than those, which, in their bearing upon the common rights of property, upon the sanctions of the Oath, and upon due subordination to the powers that be in the State, made him a subverter of the very foundations of their government, and — with all his worthiness of character, and general soundness of doctrine — a nuisance which it seemed to them they had no alternative but to abate, in some way safe to them, and kindest to him!

Let it here be distinctly remembered that Roger Williams was, in 1635, a Congregational minister in good and regular standing; and so remained without any taint of doctrinal heresy for months, almost for years, after his banishment; so that he was not driven away because he was a Baptist. Nor was his offence, as so many seem to think, that he was too tolerant in spirit for his times; for the most grievous thing about him, and that which clearly most exasperated his enemies, was that he was so intensely rigid in his principles of Separation, that almost two years after John Robinson's treatise *Of the Lawfulnes of Hearing of the Ministers in the Church of England*, "found in his studie after his decease, and now published for the common good," had seen the light, he refused even to commune with his own church, because it would not break off from communing with the other churches in the Bay — for that they would not decree that if their members, when now and then visiting home in Old England, should go inside the parish churches, and listen to the preaching of the Establishment, they must undergo Ecclesiastical censure on their return for so doing!

The intelligent reader will not fail to perceive that the question which I have been laboring to settle, is one solely of fact, and not of casuistry; whether the General Court of the Governor and Company of the Massachusetts Bay did, or did not, banish Roger Williams for a certain alleged reason; rather than whether they acted wisely in what they did, or whether he deserved banishment for any reason? These are separate ranges of investigation. That which may furnish satisfactory reply to the former, may shed no gleam of light upon the latter. And having disposed of the one, it is not my purpose to enter upon any conclusive discussion of the other. I can hardly close, however, without putting on record a few further suggestions which have come to me in the study of the literature of the case, and which are perhaps worthy of being noted as contributions to any exhaustive consideration of the equity of the subject.

1. All candid inquiry must fairly weigh the true character of the plantation. I have shown that it was not an ordinary colony. It was a select settlement upon a vast, lonely, and almost empty continent, open on every side to the choice of other settlers of different affinities. It was first of all intended to afford its undertakers an opportunity to live together in the free and unmolested enjoyment, and following, of certain spiritual ideas which were very dear to them. There can be no question that they were entrusted with the legal prerogative to purge themselves of alien elements; while their right in courtesy

and justice to do so, stood essentially on the same ground on which a pleasure party of special friends may properly eject an incongenial intruder. And, that one of radically hostile opinions, under these circumstances, and with the world all before him where to choose, should persist in forcing himself upon them ; and, being resident among them, should spend his strength in decrying their fundamental principles, not merely, but in doing his utmost to cut the very bands by which their social order was held together ; was a thing as much more intolerable to them than would be a similar procedure to the Vineland settlement, or either of those close "communities" which now exist among us; as the necessary perils of an experiment in process of trial two centuries and a half ago under nearly every conceivable disadvantage, upon the edge of a savage wilderness, must overweigh the petty risks of a modern pleasure venture in the science of sociology. And how long even Vineland would tolerate the presence of one who should disturb its peace in any manner kindred to that in which Roger Williams disturbed that of the Massachusetts Colony ; and how much the well-informed community would pity such a disturber upon his consequent ejectment; I leave others to judge.

2. Not less essential is some careful consideration of the essence of the man. It is difficult to look over the grand hights of the achievements, and the loftiness of the mature quality, of some who have filled large space in the public eye, to note minutely the follies of their early days. And there was so much of sweetness, wisdom, and true nobility in the adult development of Mr. Williams, as to make it hard for us to remember that he always had great faults, and that those faults were of a kind to make his immaturity uncomfortable to others. In itself, no student could desire to go back now to

draw his frailties from their dread abode ;

but if the justification of others become his inculpation, the truth must be spoken. It would be a curious study of character to follow exhaustively the traces he has left of himself upon the history of his time — in what he did and said, and wrote ; and in what others wrote to, and of him, and said about him.[300] Those were days of free and rugged speech, when even the best of men sometimes allowed themselves to suspect and stigmatize the motives of others, and to employ bitter words in so doing ; and just allowance must be made for this. But after all due deduction, it will unquestionably be concluded that Mr. Williams did somehow exceptionally provoke the censures of the good.

[300] I find upon my memoranda a considerable number of such "testimonies" of various cotemporaries in regard to him, and will transcribe here enough to indicate their quality:

Mr. Cotton says "judicious members" of the Salem church found him to be "selfe-pleasing, selfe-full, etc." [*Reply*, 4]; he says "the judicious sort of Christians" complained of the "selfe-conceited, and unquiet, and

When he lived in Massachusetts, he was evidently a hot-headed youth,[301] of determined perseverance, vast energy, considerable information, intense con-

unlambelike frame of his Spirit" [*Ibid*, 5]; and he affirms that many were "grieved at the unmoveable stiffeness and headinesse of his Spirit" [*Ibid*]; at his "offensive Spirit and Way, both in Judgement and Practise" [*Ibid*, 30], and "the rocky flintinesse of his selfe-confidence" and the "heady unrulinesse of his Spirit, and the incorrigiblenesse thereof by any Church-way" [*Ibid*]. He speaks also of "his usuall exorbitant Hyperboles" [*Ibid*, 64]; says his charges are "vehement and peremptory, and in a manner sorbonicall," and that he "obtruded upon the Churches of Christ his unwritten imaginations and censorious Decrees, as the very Oracles of God" [*Ibid*, 86]; and stigmatizes the "liberty and boldnesse of his tongue in calumniations" [*Ibid*, 142]. So he says: "Mr. Williams is too too credulous of surmises and reports brought to him, and too too confident in divulging of them" [*Way of Cong. Chhs. Cleared, etc.* 55]; and I regret to add that once he says of Mr. Williams: "it is no new thing with him, to say I did that, which I did not." [*Bloudy Tenent Washed, etc.* 150.] *William Coddington* says Mr. Cotton called Mr. Williams: "a Haberdasher of small Questions against the Power." [*N. E. Firebrand Quenched*, 246.]

Mr. Winthrop thought him guilty of "presumption" as well as "errour" [*Journal*, i: 122], yet Mr. Williams said he wrote to him: "Sir, we have often tried your patience, but could never conquer it" [*Letter to John Cotton, jr. Proceedings Mass. Hist. Soc.* 1858. 314.] *Gov. Bradford* thought him "godly and zealous, having many precious parts, but very unsettled in judgmente" [*Hist. Plym. Plant.* 310]; and said he ought to "be pitied and prayed for," that the Lord would "shew him his errors, and reduse him into the way of truth, and give him a setled judgment and constancie in the same." [*Ibid*, 311]. *Elder Brewster* was afraid of him, and glad to have him leave Plymouth, "fearing that his continuance amongst them might cause divisions," and forecasting that "he would run the same course of rigid Separation and Anabaptistry which Mr. John Smyth, the Sebaptist, at Amsterdam, had done." [Morton's *N. Eng. Mem.* 78.] *Sir William Martin* wrote most affectionately of him to Gov. Winthrop, but said: "he is passionate and precipitate, which may transport him into error, but I hope his integrity and good intentions will bring him at last into the waye of truth, and confirme him therein." [*Hutchinson Papers*, 106.] *Cotton Mather* said he had "a Windmill in his head" [*Magnalia*, vii: 7]; said he was "a Preacher that had less Light than Fire in him" [*Ibid*]; styles his opinions "turbulent and singular" [*Ibid*], and calls him a "Hot-headed Man" and "an Incendiary." [*Ibid*, 8.] *Hubbard* thinks "he had a zeal, and great pity it was that it could not be added, according to knowledge" [*Gen. Hist. N. Eng.* 202]; says "the more judicious sort of Christians, in Old and New England, looked upon him as a man of a very self-conceited, unquiet, turbulent and uncharitable spirit" [*Ibid*, 203]; calls his zeal "overheated" [*Ibid*, 205], and had heard that "they were wont to say in Essex, where he lived, that he was divinely mad." [*Ibid*, 206.] But whosoever wishes to see abuse come down in showers, may be advised to examine the way in which the mild and peaceful Quakers free their mind concerning Roger, in the *New England Firebrand Quenched* of Geo. Fox and John Burnyeat (1679). The very title-page promises "a Catalogue of his Railery, Lies, Scorn and Blasphemies, and his temporizing Spirit made manifest," and the 488 quarto pages that follow quite redeem that promise. Two or three extracts of his "Neighbour-these-38-years's" letter, will show its general quality: "he must have the Ordering of all their Affairs, or else there would be no Quiet Agreement amongst them" [247]; "that which took most with him, and was his Life, was, to get Honor amongst Men, especially amongst the Great Ones" [*Ibid*]; "he was too forward in spreading False Reports abroad" [*Ibid*, 248]; "though he professed Liberty of Conscience, and was so zealous for it at the first coming home of the Charter, that nothing in Government must be Acted, till that was granted; yet he could be the Forwardest in their Government to prosecute against those that could not Join with him in it: as witness his Presenting of it to the Court at Newport." [R. Scot, *Ibid*, 247.] *William Coddington* contributed to the same book the following: "I have known him [R. W.] about 50. Years—a meer Weather-Cock, Constant only in Unconstancy. . . One while he is a Separatist at New Plymouth, . . another time you may have him a Teacher, or Member of the Church at Salem, . . against the King's Patent and Authority, . . and another time he is Hired for Money, and gets a Patent from the Long Parliament; . . one time for Water-Baptism, Men and Women must be plunged into the Water; and then throw it all down again, etc." [*Ibid*, 246.]—With all this may be compared the summarizing of a writer of the present century, of his character: "a stubborn Brownist, keen, unpliant, illiberal, unforbearing and passionate; seasoning evil with good, and error with truth." [Grahame, *Hist. U. S.* i: 166.]

301 It appears as if Winthrop—who knew him especially well—supposed him to be but about twenty-five years old, when he was banished; at any rate such is the inference which I draw from an expression in the earliest letter from Williams to Winthrop which has been preserved: "among other pleas for a young councellour (which I feare will be too light in the ballance of the

victions, a decided taste for novelty, a hearty love of controversy, a habit of hasty speech with absolute carelessness of consequences, and a religious horror of all expediency; whose logical instincts and whose mobile sensibilities acted and reacted upon each other with intensifying power; whose convictions of moral obligation were as likely to be the result of sudden flashes of feeling as of calm and well balanced consideration; and whose eyes were so intently fixed upon a great ideal line of duty stretching onward through the far future, and upward toward the judgment seat, as to withdraw his consciousness largely from the path that was under his feet, and so to permit him to stumble into entangling inconsistencies which might have been avoided if his attention had been more recalled to the practical obligations of the hour. He forgot, too, that God's ships seldom have a wind fair enough to speed with a flowing sheet straight into port; and that the most pious seamanship must often manifest itself in sailing close-hauled as near toward the desired point as may be, and in getting, in the face of adverse gales ever and anon well about from the starboard to the lar-board tack, and the reverse; while the highest, devoutest skill of all may sometimes show itself in laying to, in the face of a storm which, for the time being, forbids all progress. John Quincy Adams happily characterized him as "conscientiously contentious."[302] Equally felicitous is Prof. Masson's phrase describing him as "the arch-Individualist."[303]

With all, were an abiding patience under trial, and meekness toward reproof; a calm courage, a noble disinterestedness and public spirit, and a predominant good temper in every strait, and toward every opponent, which were the crown and glory of his remarkable character; and which — abating, to be sure, a little of the "modum" — well entitled him to the eulogy which Lucan gave to Cato:[304]

——hi mores, hæc duri immota Catonis
Secta fuit, servare modum, finémque tenere,
Naturámque sequi, patriæque impendere vitam,
Nec sibi, sed toti genitum se credere mundo.

It is not, necessarily, a hyperbole to say that the better, the more devout — and Mr. Williams was devout, "the people being, many of them, much taken with the apprehension of his godliness"[305] — such a man might be; the more dangerous, under certain circumstances, his influence might become.

Holy One), you argue from 25 in a Church Elder;" taken in connection with the fact that he goes on to reply (1) that he [R. W.] is not a Church Elder, and (2) that he is "in the dayes of my vanitie neerer vpwards of 30 then 25." [4 *Mass. Hist. Coll.* vi: 184.]

302 3 *Mass. Hist. Coll.* ix: 206.

303 *Life of John Milton, and History of his Time*, ii: 600.

304 Lucan, *Pharsalia*, ii: 380.

305 Winthrop's *Journal*, i: 175.

3. It may be well, moreover, for the student who desires to go to the bottom of the subject of the banishment of Mr. Williams, to expend a little thought upon the question whether the importance of the transaction itself has not been overestimated and overstated. Clearly the action of the Court, at the time, notwithstanding the local excitement at Salem, made small general sensation.[306] It was merely the renewed exercise, for cause, of a power repeatedly before asserted.[307] In the February following, the event was lumped with some petty troubles in the church at Lynn, and with the existing scarcity of corn, as occasioning the proclamation of a fast in the Colony.[308] Thomas Lechford, who published his *Newes from New England* in 1642, although he speaks of Williams, says nothing of it. Capt. Edward Johnson, in the *Wonder-Working Providence of Sions Saviour in New England*, in 1654, makes only slight and obscure reference to this, although he devotes considerable space to the disturbances occasioned by Samuel Gorton and Mistress Hutchinson. Quaint Cotton Mather — with an obvious suggestion — entitles his chapter which is mainly devoted to Mr. Williams and Samuel Gorton, "Little Foxes."[309] Dr. Backus was the first of our historians to develop the modern idea of the vast significance of the trial, and he was writing "A History of New England with particular reference to the Denomination of Christians called Baptists." While those biographers of our day who have acted on the hints which he gave, and drawn attention to that rude court-room at New Town on the 9–19 Oct. 1635, as if it were one of the focal points of modern history, — Knowles, Gammell, Elton and Underwood — have all been Baptists. On the whole, perhaps Dr. Palfrey is nearer right, when he styles the disturbance produced by it, "limited, superficial, and transient," and goes on to add:[310]

> Had it not been for later transactions, which revealed him in more favorable lights, and for the connection of his exile with the origin of a State, that exile, instead of taking the place in history in which it presents itself to us, might have been recorded simply as the expulsion of one among several eccentric and turbulent persons. His controversy speedily narrowed down to a merely personal dispute; not a half-score of friends followed when he went away, nor were they of a character to show that he inspired confidence in the best and soberest men; scarcely a larger number of persons who remained behind adhered to his peculiarities; and the returning waters presently closed over the track his dashing bark had made.

It is the son of Sirach who says:[311] "there is an exquisite subtilty, and the same is unjust; and there is one that turneth aside to make judgment appear."

---

[306] I have called attention [see note 246 *ante*] to the untrustworthy character of the only statement which I have observed, making against the view taken above.

[307] See p. 14 *ante*.

[308] Winthrop's *Journal*, i: 181.

[309] *Magnalia*, Book vii: chap. 2.

[310] *Hist. N. Eng.* i: 501.

[311] *Ecclesiasticus*, xix: 25.

4. It is indispensable, further, that one note the temper of those times. For half a century there had been a religious commotion in England which had effectually stirred up the masses of the people, and in the general confusion, dangerous elements had now and then manifested themselves. Most adult New Englanders could then remember the Gunpowder plot, and shared that intense and stinging hatred of Popery, as politically synonymous with treason, as well as odious in its superstitions, which has not even yet died out of the hearts of the London populace; whom one sees still fiercely handling their effigies of Guy Fawkes on the 15th November.[312] One hundred years before, a terrible fanaticism had raged over Germany and the Netherlands, which had left in the general conservative mind a vague, yet vivid, horror of all claims to special light from heaven, all particularly loud-voiced accusations of public sin, and especially all plans looking towards civil reconstruction, and all denunciations of the regular magistracy, and the usual sanctions of justice; as being — all ills in one — Anabaptism![313] The settlers of Massachusetts, as a class, were moderate reformers; as anxious, on the one hand, not to wreck their enterprise and imperil its reputation among the sober-minded at home, by excesses in the name of liberty;[314] as, on the other, to avoid being forced back into the old conformity, or — still further back — into the clutch of the Man of Sin.[315] We have seen, moreover, that Mr. Williams's advent, and busy activity in Massachusetts affairs, had taken the plantation in an evil time in respect to the fact that the arrogant Court of England was just then looking toward it with some intent

---

312 It may be questioned whether the feeling against Romanists, which our fathers had, was not due more to political than to religious considerations. It had come to be common in England to regard a Romanist as, almost necessarily, a traitor against the Crown, and a conspirator — the more dangerous, in fact, the more quiet might be his seeming — against it. *Selden* said: "Amsterdam admits of all religions but Papists. . . The Papists where e're they live, have another King at Rome, etc. [*Table-Talk* (1689), Arber's reprint, 87.]

313 "We are accused of rigidness to such as differ from us in matters of religion. To this we say that, from the first settling this plantation, these heterodoxes of Familism, Anabaptism, and of late Quakerism, have been looked upon by the godly here as great errors, and the promoters of them disturbers of peace and order. *Those awful and tremendous motions of that sort of people in Germany, and elsewhere,* hath sufficiently alarmed all pious and prudent men to provide a defensative against them." [*Letter of Gov. Leverett, et al.* (10–20 May 1673) *to Mr. Boyle.* Birch's *Life of Hon. Rob. Boyle*, 456.]

314 "Democracy I do not conceyve that ever God did ordeyne as a fitt government eyther for Church, or Commonweath. If the people be governors, who shall be governed? As for monarchy, and aristocracy, [*his* idea of Congregationalism made it, essentially, the latter], they are both of them clearely approoved, and directed in Scripture; yet so as referreth the soveraigntie to Himselfe, and setteth up Theocracy in both, as the best forme of government in the Commonwealth, as well as in the Church." [*John Cotton, to Lord Say and Seal.* Appendix. Hutchinson's *Hist. Mass.* i: 437.]

315 It was then scarcely ten years since all fears that Prince Charles — now reigning king — would make a Spanish marriage, had been put at rest; and, in the condition of affairs then existing, no wise man could deny that such a turn of the tide as should throw England back (so far as her political and official-religious relations might go) into the condition of a Roman Catholic country, was among the possibilities; and I think the careful reader of New England history will be now and then reminded that many of the leading minds of the colony were wise enough to keep that, and its probable relations to public affairs here, in memory.

against its charter; that disaffected persons, who had been sent home for the colony's good, were doing their utmost to play into the hands of the King by accusing the settlers of intending rebellion, of proposing entire and absolute separation from the mother country, of habitually railing against the State, Church and Bishops, and of revolutionary and anarchical behavior, in general. Only by remembering that at every step the chief actors in Mr. Williams's case would feel themselves compelled to inquire what the effect of all was likely to be in London, can one hope to arrive at any entirely fair judgment upon the quality of their action.[316]

Preëminently is it essential that the dread, and almost horror, with which a general toleration of religious beliefs was then conscientiously regarded by most good men, be recalled;[317] because it is conceded on all hands that Mr. Williams was already to some extent a believer in, and an advocate of this doctrine;[318] although, as we have seen, the subject entered only in the most unimportant manner, if at all, into the conflict of opinion which led to his removal.

---

[316] The remark of the interesting anonymous writer to Gov. Winthrop, soon after this banishment, has great significance in this connection: "your disclayming of Mr. Williams's opinions, & your dealing with him soe as we heare you did, tooke off much preiudice from you with vs, & hath stopt the mouths of some." [4 *Mass. Hist. Coll.* vi: 445.]

[317] What was then thought in England of toleration, has been already indicated in the extract from Edwards's *Gangræna*, before cited [see note 288 *ante*]. That the colonists here had much the same opinion, is well known, and that they were prepared to act upon that judgment in civil things seems probable from Winthrop's statement that the obstinate maintenance of such opinions, "whereby a church might run into heresy, apostacy, or tyranny, and yet the civil magistrate could not intermeddle," would be ground for public action. [*Journal*, i: 163.] Dr. George E. Ellis has stated what I conceive to be the fact on this subject with admirable accuracy. "To assume," he says, "as some carelessly do, that when Roger Williams and others asserted the right and safety of liberty of conscience, they announced a novelty that was alarming, *because* it was a novelty, to the authorities of Massachusetts, is a great error. Our Fathers were fully informed as to what it was, what it meant; and they were familiar with such results as it wrought in their day. They knew it well, and what must come of it; and they did not like it; rather, they feared and hated it. They did not mean to live where it was indulged; and, in the full exercise of their intelligence and prudence, they resolved not to tolerate it among them. They identified freedom of conscience only with the objectionable and mischievous results which came of it. They might have met all around them in England, in city and country, all sorts of wild, crude, extravagant and fanatical spirits. They had reason to fear that many whimsical and factious persons would come over hither, expecting to find an unsettled state of things, in which they would have the freest range for their eccentricities. They were prepared to stand on the defensive." [Lecture on *Treatment of Intruders and Dissentients by the Founders of Mass., etc.*, in *Lowell Lectures by Members of Mass. Hist. Soc.* 84.]

[318] I find no proof that Mr. Williams, at the time of his residence in Massachusetts, had advanced to the holding of the full doctrine of liberty of conscience, which he afterwards avowed, and—subsequently modified. The germ of it appears in his idea with regard to the "first table;" but it is not clear that he himself had then accepted it in all its length, and breadth, and consequences. The leisure which he had in the wilderness, after leaving Salem, seems to have borne fruit, especially in that direction; and to have led him on to a position unoccupied before. But the claim that Mr. Williams was, in any sense, the originator, or first promulgator, of the modern doctrine of liberty of conscience, though often made, is wholly without foundation. Robert Brown—the founder of the Brownists—distinctly advocated it as early as 1582—or from fifteen to twenty years before Williams was born. [See his *Booke which sheweth the Life and Manners of all True Christians, etc.* 26; *Treatise on Reformation Without Tarrying for Any, etc.* 12.] Mr. Felt [*Ecc. Hist. N. Eng.* i: 294] calls attention to the action of the Diet of Augsburg, in 1555, to the effect that "no attempt shall be made toward terminating religious differences, except by persuasion and

5. It would be well, also, that some consideration be given to the necessity, and the alternative, then existing, into which Mr. Williams himself had forced the Company. Matters had been pushed by him to such a pass that, so far as his influence extended, all were really standing on the very edge of chaos. Had he been permitted to remain, and been able to carry out his views, it is not easy to see how some grand catastrophe could have been averted. The patent would have been surrendered to the King with repentance and humiliation that any use had ever been made of it;[319] which would have dropped the bottom at once from under all commercial foundations, destroyed all land-titles, and disorganized business among them in every department; while in the existing condition of the royal mind, they could have hoped for no redressive grant, or legislation. The administration of the Freemen's and Resident's Oath[320] would have been abrogated; and the way thereby opened to a disintegration of civil affairs rivaling in disastrous completeness that which would have been wrought upon their commerce by the other. In a religious point of view, their Congregational liberality would have been transmuted into an unlovely, unreasonable and bitter Separatism; which would have made the colony odious, as well as ridiculous, in the eyes of all intelligent and high-minded men, even of that day; in that it would insist on disfellowshiping every New England church which should decline to excommunicate one of its own members, who, revisiting Old England, should drop in to hear a sermon, even from the godliest rector, in an Established church, without avowing his repent-

---

conference," and the fact that this was the principle of Menno, who died in 1561. It is clear, moreover, that Sir Thomas More developed the principle as early as 1516. In the second Book of his *Utopia* (I quote from Ralphe Robinson's translation of 1556, in Mr. Arber's admirable reprint) he speaks as follows: "Firste of all he [Kyng Utopus] made a decree, that it should be lawfull for euerie man to fauoure and folow what religion he would, and that he mighte do the best he could to bring other to his opinion, so that he did it peaceablie, gentelie, quietly, and soberlie, without hastie and contentious rebuking and inuehing against other. If he could not, by faire and gentle speche, induce them vnto his opinion, yet he should vse no kinde of violence, and refraine from displeasaunte and seditious woordes. To him that would vehemently and feruentlye in this cause striue and contende, was decreed banishment or bondage. This lawe did Kynge Utopus make, not only for the maintenaunce of peace, which he saw through continuall contention and mortal hatred vtterly extinguished: but also because he thought this decrie should make for the furtheraunce of religion." [145.] Most likely, however, Williams got the idea from Henry Jacob's *Humble Supplication for Toleration, etc.*, in 1609, or Leonard Busher's *Plea for Liberty of Conscience*, in 1614. See for a rapid glance at the rise and growth of this idea, Masson's *Milton*, iii: 98–129.

319 Perhaps sufficient evidence of this statement has been already offered in the body of the discussion which has gone before. I add, however, the following, which gives its testimony in a condensed form. "This, therefore, [the falsehood and injustice of the Patent] he pressed upon the Magistrates and People, to be humbled for, from time to time, in dayes of solemne Humiliation, and to returne the Patent back againe to the King." [*Reply to Mr. Williams his Exam. etc.* 27.]

320 "By his Tenent neither might Church-members, nor other godly men, take the Oath, because it was the establishment, not of Christ, but of mortall men in their office; nor might men out of the Church take it, because, in his eye, they were but carnall. . . Which was held to be the more dangerous, because it tended to unsettle all the Kingdomes and Common-wealthes in Europe." [*Ibid*, 29.]

ance of the act, as of a sin, on his return.[321] While that most hateful and dangerous form of the interaction of Church and State which Mr. Williams — in spite of all his philosophies — had entered upon, in endeavoring, through the medium of the discipline of the churches to which they belonged, to compel the members of the General Court to modify their action in regard to the Marblehead land;[322] endangered an excitement, and an overturning, in those churches, quite as much to be dreaded as any calamities likely to ensue in other departments of the public welfare.

The irresistible fact which confronts the honest and thorough inquirer into the minute history of that time, a fact which cannot be ignored, nor explained away, is that the teaching and influence of Roger Williams — to use the careful language of John Quincy Adams — were "altogether revolutionary."[323] Our fathers felt themselves reluctantly compelled to choose between his expulsion, and the immediate risk of social, civil and religious disorganization. To say otherwise is to confess an amount of ignorance, or a degree of prejudice, sufficient to disqualify one from forming any useful opinion upon the subject.[324]

6. In this connection it is impossible to overlook the marked kindness with which Mr. Williams was treated by the Massachusetts men. They were very patient with him under circumstances eminently calculated to exhaust patience. When complaint had been first made against his teaching, his letter of apology was generously received.[325] And when, some ten months after, the Court were informed that he had broken his promises, and renewed the obnoxious and dangerous teachings, nearly half a year was still allowed to lapse before he was brought to their bar to answer. Even then two months more passed by before any formal trial. That trial ended in the express adjournment of the whole subject, through three further months, to the next General Court; in the hope

[321] "Which he, discerning, renounced communion with the Church of Salem, pretending they held communion with the Churches in the Bay, and the Churches in the Bay held communion with the Parish-Churches in England, because they suffered their members to heare the word amongst them in England, as they came over into their native Countrey, etc." [*Ibid*, 30.]

[322] See p. 40 *ante*.

[323] "His hostility to the foundations of the Massachusetts Colony was neither confined to speculation, nor merely defensive. It was altogether revolutionary. He denied utterly the validity of the Colonial Charter. He refused to take the oath of allegiance, and, in retaliation of the remonstrances of the Massachusetts magistrates against his election, and of their withholding a grant of a lot of land, for which his church [I think it was the town] had petitioned, he prevailed on that church to write letters of admonition and of *accusation* against the magistrates, to the churches of which they were members. This, in the temper of the times, could be considered in no other light than instigation to rebellion. At the next General Court, Salem was disfranchised till an apology should be made. This brought to a crisis the continued existence of the Massachusetts colonial government itself. The people of Salem submitted, apologized, and returned to their allegiance. The insurrection was subdued, tranquility restored,— all was quiet, '*præter atrocem animum Catonis*.'" [*The New England Confederacy of* 1643, in 3 *Mass. Hist. Coll.* ix: 208.]

[324] I desire to say this with all due reverence for one of the newspapers before cited. [See note 1 *ante*.]

[325] See Winthrop's *Journal*, i: 122, 151, 157, 162, 171, 175.

that he would be brought to "give satisfaction." At the final hearing he was tendered still another month's additional delay; was labored with, at length, by one of his peers in the ministry in the vain endeavor to persuade him to abandon his positions; and was then granted six additional weeks — which weeks were subsequently lengthened into months[326] — before the requisition of final departure. It was only from a necessity induced by his own point blank violation of all the conditions on which postponement had been accorded, that his leave to remain was cut short in January. Nor was he even then "driven from the society of civilized man, and debarred the consolations of Christian sympathy . . to find among heathen savages the boon of charity which was refused at home,"[327] — a "solitary pilgrim,"[328] in "the sternest month of a New England winter,"[329] under "great hardship."[330] It was the purpose of the magistrates to send him by ship comfortably home to England;[331] not as a criminal for trial, but as a British subject; who having proved incompatible here, might take other chances of usefulness and happiness there.[332] Evading this by sudden flight, it was still at his option to have sought the near shelter of the Plymouth Colony, where aforetime he had found welcome, and which was never addicted to banishing people; or to have turned his steps northward toward white men, nascent institutions, and comfortable, albeit as yet rude, firesides on the banks of the Cocheco, or under the shadows of Agamenticus.[333]

---

[326] Winthrop says that he received leave to stay "till the spring." [i: 175.] If the first of April be counted as the beginning of spring, from the 9–19 October to 1–10 April, would be but little more than a week less than six months.

[327] Arnold's *Hist. R. I.* i: 39.

[328] Elton's *Life*, 31.

[329] Gammell's *Life*, 57.

[330] Knowles's *Memoir*, 74. Judge Job Durfee, in his pleasant (if not great) poem, entitled *Whatcheer*, elaborated a view much like that of the author's, just quoted above. The fidelity with which his poetry follows in the track of history, may be conjectured from the following extract, which depicts Williams's endeavor to explain to *Waban* the cause of his exile:

"My brethren, then, had persecution fled,
And much I hoped, with them a home to find;
But to our common God whene'er we prayed,
My worship seemed ill-suited to their mind;
It differed greatly from their own, they said;
Their anger kindled, and, with speech unkind,
They drove me from my family and shed,
To rove an exile in this tempest dread."
[Canto I: lxviii. *Complete Works, etc.* 20.]

[331] Winthrop's *Journal*, i: 175. There is no particle of warrant for Dr. Bentley's declaration that the magistrates intended to kidnap Williams and transport him, but friends informed him, so that he could escape; nor for the equally unfounded and unjust statement that his liberty to remain until spring, "was only a snare laid for him." [1 *Mass. Hist. Coll.* vi: 249.]

[332] I am not sure that I am right in interpreting John Quincy Adams's assertion [3 *Mass. Hist. Coll.* ix: 209]: "they would have sent him to England *for a trial far otherwise severe, etc.*," as indicating his belief that the idea of the government was to remit Williams — as they had done some others — to an English tribunal for judgment. If he meant that, I believe he was mistaken, for I am aware of no evidence of such intent, on their part. Prof. Masson puts it thus: "It was proposed to kidnap him in a friendly way, and ship him back to England. This was a process to which the colonists had resorted as the simplest and really the kindliest, in one or two previous cases of refractory obstinates." [*Life of John Milton, etc.* ii: 562.]

[333] "In the meane time, some of his friends went to the place appointed by himselfe before hand, to make provision of housing, and other necessaries for him, against his coming; otherwise he might have chosen to have gone either Southward to his acquaintance at Plymouth, or Eastward to Pascatoque, or Aganimticus." [*Reply to Mr. Williams his Exam. etc.* 8.]

Mr. Gammell intimates an injustice in the proceedings against Mr. Williams, on the ground that "there appears to have been no examination of witnesses, and no hearing of counsel;"[334] and this is echoed by Prof. Elton.[335] It is astonishing that intimations so unfounded should come from gentlemen of such intelligence. One would think they could neither have read the cotemporary account of the trial, nor studied the history of the time. No witnesses are needed where the defendant pleads guilty to all charges, and seeks to justify the acts complained of; while the employment of counsel, in the modern sense, to aid in any trial, was then, and for years after, a thing unknown in the colony.[336]

I insist, then, that forbearance and gentleness of spirit toward Mr. Williams, did characterize the proceedings of the Governor and Company of the Massachusetts Bay. It was his bitterly separative spirit which began and kept alive the difficulty,—not theirs.[337] He withdrew communion from them—not they from him.[338] In all strictness and honesty he persecuted them—not they him;[339] just as the modern "Come-outer," who persistently intrudes his bad manners, and pestering presence upon some private company, making himself, upon pretence of conscience, a nuisance there; is—if sane—the persecutor, rather than the man who forcibly assists, as well as courteously requires, his desired departure.[340]

---

334 *Life*, 49.

335 *Life*, 27.

336 "There was no Atourney to be had in those dayes that I knowe of." [*MS. Letter of Sam. Gorton* (of date 1669) in my possession.] The "Body of Liberties" had the following (the 26th): "every man that findeth himselfe unfit to plead his owne cause in any Court, shall have Libertie to imploy any man against whom the Court doth not except, to helpe him, *Provided he give him noe fee, or reward, for his paines.*" [3 *Mass. Hist. Coll.* viii: 220.] Lechford was himself a solicitor of Clement's Inn, but while in Boston he was forbidden to plead "any man's cause vnlesse his owne," [*Mass. Col. Rec.* i: 270]; and he gave the following advice to the colonists touching that subject: "take heede, my brethren, despise not learning, *nor the worthy Lawyers of either gown*, lest you repent too late." [*Plaine Dealing*, 28.] Winthrop moreover says, in 1641, "no advocate being allowed," [*Journal*, ii: 36]. See, further, Hon. Emory Washburn's *Sketches of the Judicial History of Mass.* pp. 50-55.

337 "It was well knowne that whilest he lived at Salem, he neither admitted, nor permitted, any Church-members, but such as rejected all Communion with the Parish Assemblies, so much as in hearing of the Word amongst them." [*Reply to Mr. Williams his Exam. etc.* 64.]

338 "Sir, the truth is (I will not say I excommunicated you, but) I first withdrew communion from yourselves for halting between Christ and Antichrist,—the parish churches and Christian congregations, etc." [*Letter of R. W. to Rev. John Cotton, jr.*, in *Proceedings Mass. Hist. Soc.* 1858, 315.]

339 "Nor is it to be forgotten, that, as to the narrowness which repels dissentients from sympathy and communion, it was Williams that maintained the exclusive side in this controversy, and the Magistrates and Ministers that maintained the liberal side." [Dr. Palfrey, *Hist. N. Eng.* i: 420.]

"Can we blame the founders of the Massachusetts Colony for banishing him [R. W.] from within their jurisdiction? In the annals of religious persecution, is there to be found a martyr more gently dealt with by those against whom he began the war of intolerance,—whose authority he persisted, even after professions of penitence and submission, in defying, till deserted even by the wife of his bosom,—and whose utmost severity of punishment upon him was only an order for his removal, as a nuisance, from among them?" [John Quincy Adams, *The N. Eng. Confed. of* 1643, in 3 *Mass. Hist. Coll.* ix: 209.]

340 Without intending in the slightest degree to cast any ridicule upon Roger Williams, I venture, in this

7. Once more, it may be suggested that the accurate investigation of this topic will duly note the pregnant fact that, in the course of his subsequent life, Mr. Williams was led to justify, in nearly every item, the treatment which he received from Massachusetts. This may be specifically seen in the following particulars.

(1) Less than two years after his flight from Salem we find him writing to Gov. Winthrop for advice.[341] The occasion was some discontent which had arisen among the first settlers of Providence in regard to the foundation on which they stood. They had no patent, and yet it was needful, somehow, as Williams said: "to be compact in a civill way & power."[342] Mr. Williams conceived the idea of propounding "a double subscription;" one for the masters of families, and another for the young men. And as to these he wanted Mr. Winthrop's judgment. The essence of the former was to be the pledge: "from time to time to subiect our selues in actiue or passiue obedience to such orders & agreements as shall be made by the greater number of the present howseholders, & such as shall be hereafter admitted by their consent into the same priviledge & covenant in our ordinarie meeting." The latter more briefly bound the young men, and others who might be inhabitants without being admitted to this company of householders, to subject themselves "in actiue or passiue obedience" to such laws as that company might think fit to make. This company of householders practically corresponded to the company of freemen in Massachusetts; and these young men, and others, occupied in Providence, almost identically, the position which Mr. Williams himself, and all others who had never taken the Freemen's Oath, occupied in the Bay. And had it occurred to Mr. Williams two years before, that persons so situated ought to yield "actiue or passiue obedience" to such "orders & agreements" as seemed wise to that majority with whom the responsibility of affairs rested; he would have been able to have remained comfortably at Salem, with the content of many, and the sufferance of all.

---

connection, to recall to the memory of those of my readers whose familiarity with "public characters" runs back a few years, two venerable persons, whose "gift" lay largely in the interruption of public meetings — especially those of a particular character; and who again and again, in a limp state, had to be lugged out by main force. I refer to "Aunt Nabby Folsom," and "Father Lamson." I think many persons felt — and had a right to feel — that those venerable and eccentric bores were guilty of rank persecution in the way in which they inflicted themselves upon certain assemblies; while they (good souls) fancied themselves to be martyrs to — I know not what!

341 The letter bears no date, but it addresses Winthrop as "Deputie Governor," which office he held from May 1636, to May 1637; while internal evidence indicates that it was written soon after the settlement of Providence, which is believed to have been in the summer of 1636, and just before Endecott's Expedition against the Pequots, which sailed late in August, or early in September of the same year. So that the letter was probably written late in July, or in the early part of August, 1636; or from eighteen to twenty months after its author exchanged his home at Salem for the courtesies — and discomforts — of the *Sowams* wigwams.

342 This letter is in 4 *Mass. Hist. Coll.* vi: 186.

It is a curious commentary, which deserves to be noted here, upon the actual position of Mr. Williams's mind at this time upon that question of "soul-liberty" of which so much is made in his case, that in this formula of civil government as thus proposed by him, nothing whatever is said upon that subject; the clause "only in civill thinges," which was appended to it when actually adopted as the basis of the Providence Plantation, having been subsequently added.[343]

(2) Not long after we find Mr. Williams asserting, and seeking to exercise, the right to refuse to persons considered undesirable, permission to become residents at Providence. Under date of 8–18 March 1640, he wrote to Mr. Winthrop concerning Samuel Gorton, as follows:[344]

Master Gorton having foully abused high and low at Aquednick is now bewitching and bemadding poore Providence, both with his uncleane and foule censures of all the Ministers of this Country, (for which my self have in Christs name withstood him) and also denying all visible and externall Ordinances [the very thing which Williams subsequently did himself] in depth of Familisme, against which I have a little disputed and written, and shall, (the most High assisting) to death: As Paul said of Asia, I of Providence (almost) All suck in his poyson, as at first they did at Aquednick. *Some few and my selfe withstande his Inhabitation, and Towne-priviledges, without confession and reformation of his uncivill and inhumane practises at Portsmouth:*[345] Yet the tyde is too strong against us, and I feare (if the framer of Hearts helpe not) it will force mee to little Patience, a little Isle next to your Prudence.[346]

Possibly Mr. Williams underrated his influence, as it seems to be clear that Gorton, and not he, was the man eventually compelled to remove.[347]

(3) It is evident, again, that Mr. Williams and his company claimed, and exercised, the right to disfranchise any person who had been admitted to their number, whose presence and co-action proved to be, in their judgment, incompatible with their prosperity. We happen to have the best possible evidence of this in the case of Joshua Verin. Of him Williams wrote to Winthrop, 22 May–1 June 1638, as follows:[348]

Sir, we haue beene long aflicted by a young man, boysterous & desperate, Philip Verins sonn

---

[343] Compare Staples's account in *Annals of the Town of Providence, etc.* [*Coll. R. I. Hist. Soc.* v: 39] with Williams's own draft, in his letter above cited.

[344] See the letter in Winslow's *Hypocrisie Unmasked, etc.* 55.

[345] It would appear from Morton [*N. Eng. Mem.* 108] that the difficulty at Portsmouth, to which reference is here made, was mutinous and seditious "carriage:" "there he and they carried so in outrage and riotously, as they were in danger to have caused Bloodshed, etc."

[346] Prudence is the island in Narragansett Bay over against the mouth of Bristol harbor, and the passage through to Mount Hope Bay taken by the Fall River steamers; and had been purchased for Winthrop, by Williams, of Canonicus, by deed dated 10–20 Nov. 1637.

[347] "Such was his [Gorton's] carriage at Plimouth and *Providence*, at his first settling, as neither of the Governments durst admit or receive him into cohabitation, but refused him as a pest to all societies." [Winslow, *Hypocrisie Unmasked, etc.* 68.] So he says again that Gorton: "was whipt and banished at Roade Island, for mutinie and sedition, in the open Court there: *also at Providence, as factious there, etc.*" [*Ibid*, 66.]

[348] 4 *Mass. Hist. Coll.* vi: 245.

of Salem, who, as he hath refused to heare the word with vs (which we molested him not for) this twelue month, so because he could not draw his wife, a gracious & modest woman, to the same vngodlines with him, he hath troden her vnder foote tyranically & brutishly: which she & we long bearing, though with his furious blows she went in danger of life, at the last *the maior vote of vs discard him from our civill freedome, or disfranchize*, &c.: he will haue justice (as he clamours) at other Courts, etc.

It is worthy of notice that the reason given for thus casting this young man out of their company, was not that he was cruel and inhuman in the treatment of her whom he had vowed to love and cherish; but that he restrained her liberty of conscience.[349] As if *his* conscience had no rights, which, *in that place*, were entitled to respect!

(4) Again, we discover Mr. Williams repeatedly assuming toward others, the very ground which, in Massachusetts, had been taken toward himself.

a. In the case of "one vnruly person," concerning whom—probably in the spring of 1637—he wrote to Mr. Winthrop thus:[350]

Deare sir, (notwithstanding our differences concerning the worship of God & the ordinances ministred by Antichrists power) you haue bene alwayes pleased lovingly to answer my boldnes in civill things: let me once more find favour in your eyes to gratifie my selfe, Mr. James, & many, or most, of the townesmen combined, in advising what to say, or doe, to one vnruly person who *openly in towne meeting more then once professeth to hope for & long for, a better government then the countrey hath yet*, & lets not to particularize, by a generall Governour, &c. The white[351] which such a speech, or person, levells at can be no other then *the rasing of the fundamentall liberties of the countrey, which ought to be dearer to vs then our right eyes.*

---

349 Gov. Winthrop [*Journal*, i: 282] a short time after, throws further light upon this case. He says, under date of 13 Dec. 1638: "at Providence, also, the devil was not idle. For whereas, at their first coming thither, Mr. Williams and the rest did make an order, that no man should be molested for his conscience, now men's wives, and children, and servants, claimed liberty hereby to go to all religious meetings, though never so often, or though private, upon the week-days; and because one Verin refused to let his wife go to Mr. Williams so oft as she was called for, they required to have him censured. But there stood up one Arnold, a witty man of their own company, and withstood it, telling them that, when he consented to that order, he never intended it should extend to the breach of any ordinance of God, such as the subjection of wives to their husbands, etc., and gave divers solid reasons against it. Then one Greene (who had married the wife of one Beggerly, whose husband is living and no divorce, etc., but only it was said, that he had lived in adultery, and had confessed it) he replied, that, if they should restrain their wives, etc., all the women in the country would cry out of them, etc. Arnold answered him thus: Did you pretend to leave the Massachusetts, because you would not offend God to please men, and would you now break an ordinance and commandment of God to please women? Some were of opinion that, if Verin would not suffer his wife to have her liberty, the church should dispose of her to some other man, who would use her better. Arnold told them, that it was not the woman's desire to go so oft from home, but only Mr. Williams's, and others. In conclusion, when they would have censured Verin, Arnold told them that it was against their own order, for Verin did that he did out of conscience; and their order was, that no man should be censured for his conscience." Staples's [*Annals of Providence, etc.* 23] gives, under date of 21–31 May 1638 (the day before the date of Mr. Williams's letter above), the following, as the vote passed in Verin's case: "Joshua Verin, for breach of covenant in restraining liberty of conscience, shall be witheld the liberty of voting, till he declare the contrary." This was, certainly, an ingenious way of putting it, and probably proved effective!

350 4 *Mass. Hist. Coll.* vi: 243.

351 Mr. Williams uses this metaphor more than once in those of his letters which have reached us. He evidently refers to the white spot in the center of a target at which arrows were shot.

Mr. Winthrop's answer to this has not come to light. If one could find it, surely it would prove the triumph of courtesy over impulse in the mind of its penman, did it not contain some not unclear allusion to that word of Paul: "Happy is he that condemneth not himself in that thing which he alloweth."[352]

b. In the case of William Harris. Harris was one of those who had joined Mr. Williams on his first leaving Salem,[353] and had taken a somewhat prominent part in the early affairs of Providence.[354] In, or about, 1657, he wrote a "booke," for which Roger Williams entered against him, at the General Court of Commissioners, which commenced to sit at Newport on the 19–29 May, 1657, the rather serious charge of High Treason.[355] When the Court met at Warwick on the 4–14 July following, by its order Harris read his "booke" in its presence, and Mr. Williams read his charge and his reply to the treatise. The following action then taken, will make it clear in what Harris had offended, and what the attitude of his accuser, who himself had had some experience in the same line, now was:[356]

Concerninge William Harris, his booke and speeches upon it; we find therein delivered as for doctrine, *havinge much bowd the Scriptures* to maintaine, that he can say *it is his conscience ought not to yield subjection to any human order amongst men.*

Whereas the sayd Harris hath been charged for the sayd booke, and words, with High Treason; and inasmuch as we being soe remote from England, cannot be soe well acquainted in the laws thereof in that behalfe provided, as the State now stands; though we cannot but conclude his behaviour therein to be both contemptuous and seditious; we thought best therefore, to send over his writinge with the charge and his reply, to Mr. John Clarke, desiringe him to commend the matter in our and the Commonwealth's behalfe, for further judgement as he shall see the cause require; and, in the meane time, to binde the sayd Harris in good bonds to the good behaviour untill their sentence be knowne.[357]

Whether the matter of this "booke" were any more treasonable, in itself, as an onslaught upon "human order amongst men;" or any more dangerous in its probable influence upon the Colony of Rhode Island and Providence Plantations in 1657, than Mr. Williams's own "treatise" against the Patent, and his other teachings, had been almost a quarter of a century before in the Bay — since neither of them have come down to us — must remain matter of conjecture. It will not be hard, I think, however, to conclude that in his treatment of Mr.

[352] Rom. xiv: 22.

[353] See note 217 *ante*, p. 56.

[354] See Staples's *Annals, etc.* 20, 33, 35, 40, 43, 78, 112; *R. I. Col. Rec.* i: 20, 24, 27, 31, 299, 361, 363, 364, 428, 431, etc.

[355] *R. I. Col. Rec.* i: 361.

[356] *Ibid*, 364. See, also, Staples's *Annals of Providence*, 148.

[357] The bonds were £500. Nothing seems to have come of this sending to England. Harris remained active in affairs, went to England four times, was captured on the last voyage by a Barbary corsair, sold at Algiers as a slave, after servitude of a year ransomed for $1200, and, broken down by his trials, died in three days after reaching London in the spring of 1681. [Arnold's *Hist. R. I.* i: 437.]

Harris, and in the temper which he manifested towards him, Mr. Williams badly blotted his own character, while making it forevermore impossible even for his special apologists to deny that he therein endorsed the treatment which had been meted to himself by Massachusetts.

Witness still further, as illustrating his spirit in this same thing, the following, written by Mr. Williams probably in the autumn of 1672 :[358]

He [W. Harris] was a Pretender in Old England, but in New, my experience hath told me, that he can be one with the Quakers, yea Jesuits or Mahumetans, for his own worldly ends and advantage. He is long known to haue put Scorns & Jeers upon the eminent Inhabitants of Town and Country. He hath been notorious for quarrelling, and challenging, and fighting, even when he pretended with the Quakers against Carnal Weapons ; so that there stands upon Record in the Town-book of Providence an Act of Disfranchisement upon him for fighting and shedding Blood in the street,[359] and for maintaining and allowing it (for ought I know) to this day. Then he turns Generallist, and writes against all Magist-ates, Laws, Courts, Charters, Prisons, Rates, &c., pretending himself and his Saints to be the Higher Powers (as now the Quakers do) and in publick writings he stir'd up the People (most seditiously and desperately threatening to begin with the Massachusetts) and to cry out "no Lords, no Masters," as is yet to be seen in his Writing : this cost my self and the Colony much trouble. Then (as the Wind favoured his ends) no man more cries up Magistrates : then not finding that pretence, nor the People called Baptists[360] (in whom he confided) serving his ends. He flies to Connecticut Colony (then and still in great Contest with us) in hopes to attain his gaping about Land from them, if they prevail over us : to this end he in publick Speech and Writing applauds Connecticut Charter and damns ours, and his Royal Majesties favour also for granting us favour (as to our Consciences) which he largely endeavours by writing to prove the K. Majesty by Laws could not do. My self (being in place) by Speech & Writing opposed him, & Mr. B. Arnold, then Governour, and Mr. Jo. Clark Deputy Governour, Capt. Cranstone and all the Magistrates, he was Committed for speaking & writing against his Majesties Honour, Prerogative, & Authority : He lay some time in Prison until the General Assembly, where the Quaker (by his wicked, ungodly, and disloyal plots) prevailing, he by their means gets loose, and leaves open a door for any man to challenge the Kings Majesty for being too Godly or Christian, in being too favourable to the Souls of his Subjects against his Laws &c.

c. In the case of the Quakers, also, there seems to be some evidence of the fact that Mr. Williams did not scruple to assume toward others an attitude resembling that which the Court of the Bay had taken toward himself. At any rate we find Richard Scott[361] affirming :[362]

Though he [R. W.] professed Liberty of Conscience, and was so zealous for it at the first Coming home of the Charter, that nothing in Government must be Acted, till that was granted;

---

358 *Geo. Fox Digg'd out of His Burrowes, etc.* 206.

359 See Staples's *Annals of Providence, etc.* 147.

360 A very strange way of speaking, if Mr. Williams considered himself a Baptist.

361 Richard Scott was the first householder to sign the first agreement concerning which Mr. Williams consulted Mr. Winthrop [note 342 *ante*]. He was assessed £3 6s. 8d. in 1650, when the highest tax was (B. Arnold) £5, and Mr. Williams paid £1 13s. 4d. ; was for a time a Baptist, and afterwards became a Quaker. [Staples's *Annals, etc.* 35, 39, 43, 78, 409.]

362 *New England Fire-brand Quenched, etc.* 247.

yet he could be the Forwardest in their Government to prosecute against those, that could not Join with him in it: as witness his Presenting of it to the Court at Newport.[363]

And when this would not take Effect, afterwards, when the Commissioners[364] were Two of them at Providence, being in the House of Thomas Olney, Senior, of the same Town; Roger Williams propounded this Question to them:

We have a People here amongst us, which will not Act in our Government with us: What course shall we take with them?

Then George Cartwright, one of the Commissioners, asked him: What manner of Persons they were? Do they live quietly and peaceably amongst you? This they could not deny; Then he made them this answer:

If they can Govern themselves, they have no need of your Government.

At which they were silent.

(5) Still further, it is evident that Mr. Williams's own subsequent statement of his doctrine of Liberty of Conscience is adequate to condemn himself, and justify the Massachusetts men in the course which they reluctantly took. This doctrine we find him explaining, in Jan. 1654–5 — almost twenty years after he left Salem — to his fellow-citizens of the town of Providence, as follows:[365]

That ever I should speak or write a tittle, that tends to such an infinite liberty of conscience, [as that it is blood-guiltiness, and contrary to the rule of the gospel, to execute judgment upon transgressors against the public or private weal] is a mistake, and which I have ever disclaimed and abhorred. To prevent such mistakes, I at present shall only propose this case:

There goes many a ship to sea, with many hundred souls in one ship, whose weal and woe is common; and is a true picture of a common-wealth, or an human combination, or society. It hath fallen out some times that both Papists and Protestants, Jews and Turks, may be embarked into one ship. Upon which supposal, I affirm that all the liberty of conscience that ever I pleaded for, turns upon these two hinges: That none of the Papists, Protestants, Jews or Turks, be forced to come to the ship's prayers or worship; nor compelled from their own particular prayers, or worship, if they practice any. I further add, that I never denied, that notwithstanding this liberty, the commander of this ship ought to command the ships course; yea, and also command that justice, peace and sobriety to be kept and practised, both among the seamen and all the passengers. If any of the seamen refuse to perform their service, or passenger to pay their freight: if any refuse to help in person or purse, towards the common charges or defence; if any *refuse to obey the common laws and orders of the ship, concerning their common peace or preservation;* if any *shall mutiny and rise up against their commanders and officers;* if any should *preach or write* that there ought to be no commanders nor officers, because all are equal in Christ, therefore no masters nor officers, no laws nor orders, no corrections nor punishments; I say: I never denied but in such cases, whatever is pretended, the commander, or commanders, may judge, resist, compel and punish such transgressors, according to their deserts and merits.

The clauses which I have italicised above, it seems to me in spirit, if not in

---

[363] I take it this refers to his accusing Harris of High Treason.

[364] This was the term then employed in Rhode Island, to designate those delegates of towns to the General Assembly, which were known as "Deputies," or "Representatives," in Massachusetts.

[365] Backus's *Hist. N. Eng.* i: 297. It is also upon the Providence *Records*.

letter, fully include the case of Mr. Williams himself when he was preaching and writing against the Patent and the Oath, and refusing to obey, and doing all he could to persuade others to rise up against, the usages and laws which, founded upon them, were felt by the magistrates to be for "the common peace" and "preservation."

(6) I find in the manner in which Mr. Williams repeatedly speaks of the men who banished him, and their associates, after years had added something to his own experience and wisdom, a change of tone and temper concerning them, with evidence of his recognition of their right to exercise some little selection in their company. For example, he says, probably in the autumn of 1672:[333]

> This [Separation] (as before I hinted) was the heavenly Principle of those many precious and gallant Worthies, the Leaders and Corner-Stones of these New England Colonies, viz.: they desired to worship God in purity according to those perswasions in their Consciences, which they believed God had lighted up.
>
> They desired such for their Fellow Worshippers as they (upon a Christian account) could have evidence that to be true and real Worshippers of God in Spirit and Truth also.

This does not sound much like the "abundant ignorance and negligence, and consequently grosse abominations and pollutions of Worship;"[367] the "spirituall guilt liable to God's sentence and plagues;" the "spirit and disposition of spiritual drunkennesse and whoredome, a soule-sleepe and a soule-sicknesse;"[368] the "Antichristian filthines and communions with dead works, dead worships, dead persons in Gods worship;"[369] the "immoderate worldlines" an "Ulcer or Gangrene of Obstinacy;"[370] a "form of a square house upon the Keele of a Ship, which will never prove a soul-saving true Arke, or Church of Christ Jesus, according to the Patterne;"[371] and the other fierce denunciations with which he fulmined against the churches of the Bay, when he himself in his youthful rashness lived among them.

Quite as little does the following, from the same curious volume, — penned "when nearing the sober limit of four-score"[372] — where he testifies to:[373]

> A large effusion of the Holy Spirit of God upon so many precious Leaders and Followers, who ventured their All to New England upon many Heavenly Grounds, three especially:
>
> *First*, the enjoyment of God according to their Consciences.
>
> *Secondly*, Of holding out Light to Americans.
>
> *Thirdly*, The advancing of the English Name and Plantations.
>
> These three ends the most High and Holy God hath graciously helpt his poor Protestants in a Wilderness to Endeavour to promote, etc.

---

366 *Geo. Fox Digg'd, etc. Apendix, etc.* 15.
367 *Mr. Cotton's Letter Examined, etc.* 18.
368 *Ibid*, 27.
369 *Ibid*, 35.
370 *Ibid*, 38.
371 *Ibid*, 46.
372 Prof. Diman, *Pub. Nar. Club*, v: iii.
373 *Geo. Fox Digg'd, etc. Apendix, etc.* 93.

(7) Again I find him a few years later, when he seems to have passed fourscore (and it is the last utterance but two which has been preserved from him) addressing a paper to the town clerk of Providence — of date 15–25 Jan. 1680–1, — in which he speaks solemnly and earnestly in regard to the conduct of those who hindered the welfare of the State by refusing the payment of taxes, on some excuse of conscience. From the twenty considerations which he enumerates, take the following as indicating the maturest temper of his mind:[374]

Government and order in families, towns, etc., is the ordinance of the Most High — Rom. xiii. — for the peace and good of mankind.

It is written in the hearts of all mankind, even in pagans, that mankind cannot keep together without some government.

No government is maintained without tribute, custom, rates, taxes, etc.

It is but folly to resist, (one or more, and if one, why not more ?) God hath stirred up the spirit of the Governor, magistrates and officers, driven to it by necessity, to be unanimously resolved to see the matter finished ; and *it is the duty of every man to maintain, encourage, and strengthen the hand of authority.*

Here he clearly urges one of two alternatives, either: (1) that the person who finds his conscience leading him to conclusions which would array him against the government under which he lives, should take that circumstance in conclusive proof that his conscience is acting wrongly, and ought not to be obeyed; or (2) that such a person, while accepting such decision of conscience in the abstract, should waive it in the concrete, so far as to submit himself to the ordinance concerning which he doubts, when the safety and welfare of the government appear to depend upon it.

This reasoning almost half a century before would have saved him from all those conflicts in the Bay, out of which his expulsion grew.

(8) And, finally, there was that in Mr. Williams's conduct in regard to the Patent — then and after, — which clearly condemned himself, and went so far, at least, toward justifying the Massachusetts men.

a. In the first place, he must have known before he sailed from England to ally his fortunes with those of this plantation, what, for substance, its Patent was; must have known the vital and all-pervasive quality of the relation of that instrument to the legal and commercial affairs of the colonists; and must have known that it was as impossible for them, in the situation which they occupied, essentially to modify its character; as it would be for the man suspended over the dizzy edge of Dover Cliff,

—— that gathers samphire ; dreadful trade !

unassisted, to exchange a bad rope for a good one, as he hangs!

---

[374] Knowles's *Memoir*, 351. Mr. Knowles, as in other | cases, fails to indicate where his authority may be found.

"Under these circumstances"—pertinently inquires one of the most intelligent and thoroughly informed writers who has contributed to the discussion of this subject[375]—"under these circumstances, it may not unreasonably be asked, why did he come at all within the jurisdiction of a government whose chartered privileges it were a sin to acknowledge, and purchase a house, and settle down as an inhabitant? And why did he finally regard a banishment from the place as a punishment grievous to be borne?"

b. In the second place, it is not easy to see how Mr. Williams could be free from serious blame for the representations which he made of the terms and spirit of the Patents of Kings James and Charles. The exact language which he employed in his "treatise" is not, to be sure, in our possession; but we have it for substance, reported by Winthrop and Cotton, both of whom had read the document; while its author's own admissions in his books which remain, endorse the general correctness of the representations which they make.

(i.) He charged King James with telling "a solemn public lye," in claiming in his Patent to have been the first Christian prince that discovered New England.[376] But the Patent does not undertake to state who discovered New England. What it says on that subject is the following:[377]

> Forasmuch as We have been certainly given to understand by divers of our good Subjects, that have for these many Yeares past frequented those Coasts and Territoryes, between the Degrees of Fourty and Fourty-eight, that *there is noe other the Subjects of any Christian King or State*, by any authoritie from their Soveraignes, Lords, or Princes, *actually in Possession of any of the said Lands or Precincts*, whereby any Right, Claim, Interest or Title, may, might, or ought by that meanes accrue, belong, or appertaine unto them, or any of them. [It then refers to the devastations of pestilence and war by which the territory in question had been left, for many leagues together, without inhabitant, or claimant; as suggesting that the time had come for settling the land so deserted, and proceeds:] In Contemplacion and serious Consideracion whereof, Wee have thougt it fitt according to our Kingly Duty, soe much as in Us lyeth, to second and followe God's sacred Will, rendering reverend Thanks to his Divine Majestie for His gracious favour *in laying open and revealing the same unto us, before any other Christian Prince or State*, by which Meanes without Offence, and as We trust to his Glory, Wee may with Boldness goe on to the settling of soe hopefull a Work, etc.
>
> [Further on,[378] this express proviso is inserted, viz.:] Provided always that any of the Premises herein before mentioned, and by these Presents intended and meant to be granted, *be not actually possessed or inhabited by any other Christian Prince, or Estate, etc.*

Surely every candid mind must admit that there is nothing here to justify the strong and offensive language employed by Mr. Williams.

---

[375] Mr. Charles Deane, LL. D., who is especially familiar with all our charter literature. See his discussion of this subject in *Proceedings of Mass. Hist. Soc.* 1871–1873, 353.

[376] *Ibid*, 343.

[377] See the Patent, in Hazard's *Historical Collections*, i: 103–118.

[378] *Ibid*, 111.

(ii.) He charged both kings "with blasphemye for callinge Europe Christendom, or the Christian world, etc."[379] Winthrop goes into an effective argument[380] to show that it could not be "Blasphemye" to "name thinges from the better parte," to call all baptized ones "Christians to distinguishe them from the Turks, etc," and to style "a nation that professethe the faith of Jesus Christ (be it in truethe or not) from other nations which professe him not, to saye they are Christians." But he might have gone further. The words "Christendom," or "Christian World," do not appear to be found in either Patent; the nearest approach to them being the innocuous descriptive term cited above: "Christian Prince, or State," which Charles expressly quotes from his father's grant, to incorporate it in his own.

To undertake to raise substantial mutiny in the plantation by working up so simple and harmless a thing as this into a fierce charge of "blasphemye," seems now to have been as uncandid, as it was absurd.

(iii.) He charged upon those Patents "a sinne of unjust usurpation upon others possessions."[381] This was his great point: that Kings James and Charles had made the pretence of giving to the colonists, land which really belonged to its own aboriginal inhabitants.[382]

There are two aspects in which this matter may be regarded; that of abstract right, and that of the existing law of nations.

First, as to abstract right. By abstract right a white man is as good as an Indian. Had the individuals composing the Massachusetts Company been driven hither by irresistible east winds, been shipwrecked upon Cape Ann, and found themselves upon the soil without previous intent; they would have had the natural right to occupy without purchase any land found free from occupation which their necessities required, — because no person existed who could claim prior right to hold or sell it. God made it for men. No men, as yet, held it from Him. Therefore whatsoever men might first desire, need and take possession of it, must have the abstract right to do so. And if they found savage neighbors roaming over adjacent soil, occupying and using territory which would be useful to them; such new comers would acquire, and succeed to, all that Indian right of occupation and of use, when they should have amicably purchased the same. And thenceforth these new comers, either primarily by their own occupation, or secondarily by succeeding to that exercised before

---

[379] *Proceedings, etc.* (as above) 343.

[380] *Ibid*, 344.

[381] *Ibid*, 343.

[382] He admitted that the following was a fair statement of his opinion, viz: "That we have not [*i. e.*, have no right to hold] our Land by Pattent from the King, but that the Natives are the true owners of it, and that we ought to repent of such a receiving it by Pattent." [*Mr. Cotton's Letter Examined, etc.* 4. See also his *Bloudy Tenent Yet more Bloudy, etc.* 277.]

them by the aborigines, would — so far as abstract justice goes — be in equitable possession of all territory so acquired. Nor could the fact that the Massachusetts Company actually came with a purpose, and a Patent from the King, vacate or impair the natural right which they would have possessed in the case supposed. So that since — notwithstanding their Patent — the New England men always did honorably pay all Indian claimants for the territory on which they sat down;[383] so far as abstract right went, Mr. Williams clearly had no ground for censuring the colonists.

Second, as to the law. This was perfectly well settled then, and it remains essentially unmodified, and in full force, to this day. Three principles were involved: (*a*) the King was the original proprietor of all the land of a kingdom, and the true and only source of all land titles; (*b*) the discovery of a new country vested the title of it in the King by whose subjects, and authority, it was made; and (*c*) this right of ultimate dominion over a newly discovered country, was subject to a right of occupancy on the part of the original savage inhabitants. With regard to this latter principle, which has been adopted by our own government, and applied to its relations to the American Indians, Chancellor Kent remarks:[384]

The rule that the Indian title was subordinate to the absolute, ultimate title of the government of the European colonists, and that the Indians were to be considered as occupants, and entitled to protection in peace in that character only, and incapable of transferring their right to others; was the best one that could be adopted with safety. The weak and helpless condition in which we found the Indians, and the immeasurable superiority of their civilized neighbors, would not admit of the application of any more liberal and equal doctrine to the case of Indian lands and contracts. It was founded on the pretension of converting the discovery of the country into a conquest; and it is now too late to draw into discussion the validity of that pretension, or the restriction which it imposes. It is established by numerous compacts, treaties, laws and ordinances, and founded on immemorial usage. The country has been colonized and settled, and is now held, by that title. It is the law of the land, and no court of justice can permit the right to be disturbed by speculative reasonings on abstract rights.[385]

---

[383] John Cotton says: "if we tooke any Lands from the Natives, it was by way of purchase, and free consent." [*Reply to Mr. Williams, etc.* 27.] This was in accordance with the original instructions given by the Company to Endecott, as follows: "If any of the saluages ptend right of inheritance to all or any pt. of the lands graunted in o^r pattent, wee pray yo^w endeavo^r to p^rchase their tytle, that wee may avoyde the least scruple of intrusion." [*Mass. Col. Rec.* i: 394.] And in 1676 Gov. Josias Winslow declared: "I think I can clearly say that before these present troubles [Philip's War] broke out, the English did not possess one foot of land in this Colony, but what was fairly obtained by honest purchase of the Indian proprietors." [Increase Mather's *Brief History, etc. Postscript*, p. 2.] Vattel bears the same testimony. [*Droit des Gens.* c. i. sec. 81, 209.] See also *Did the Pilgrims wrong the Indians?* [*Congregational Quarterly*, i: 129.]

[384] *Commentaries on American Law*, iii: 463.

[385] There have been several decisions of our Supreme Court on this general subject. In the case of *Johnson* v. *M'Intosh*, [8 *Wheaton Rep.* 543] the conclusion was substantially that above stated by Chancellor Kent. In the case of *Cherokee Nation* v. *State of Georgia*, [5 *Peters' U. S. Rep.* 1] and that of *Worcester* v. *State of Georgia*, [6 *Peters' U. S. Rep.* 515] the same principle was restated. In the latter it was held that royal grants, or charters, asserted a title to the country as

If now, Mr. Williams were cognizant of the law of nations, he knew that under it the king was quite right in granting, and the Massachusetts grantees in receiving, their Patent; so that no reason for complaint existed on that score. While, if he were familiar with the facts in the case, he knew that those grantees interpreted their Charter as only protecting them outwardly from France, or Spain, or some other European power, while giving them the right to acquire by amicable purchase from the Indian, that title of occupancy and use which remained in him, and was essential to their full ownership; and which, in point of fact, they did acquire in every instance in which they made a settlement. Both together satisfied the demands of law and equity. And when both are faithfully considered, it is very difficult to acquit Mr. Williams of ignorance, or unfairness, or both, in what he said about them.

c. In the third place, Mr. Williams afterwards accepted for the colony of Rhode Island and Providence Plantations, and was there active under, a Patent from the English crown, which made for it precisely the same assumptions with, and was open to precisely the same objections as, those for Massachusetts, which a quarter of a century earlier he had so unsparingly denounced.

It is only important, for the purpose which I have in view, that I should call attention here to two facts:

(i.) Roger Williams was a consenting party to this Charter. Of the twenty-three persons on whose behalf John Clarke petitioned the king for it, he was the tenth.[386] He was also the tenth of the twenty-six grantees named in the instrument. He was the third of the ten Assistants therein nominated. So much as this, indeed, might have happened without his knowledge or assent. But we find him at once uniting with others in carrying out the provisions of the new Patent on its arrival. He was present to give his "solemn engagement, by oath, or otherwyse, for the due and faythfull performeance" of his duty as an Assistant, at the first meeting of the General Assembly under its provisions, at Newport 1–11 March 1663–4.[387] His name was placed first on the list by that Assembly made of the freemen who were "accepted members of this Company, Corporation and Collony."[388] He was appointed to transcribe the Charter.[389] He was, at once, *ex-officio* as an Assistant, named as a magistrate under it.[390] He served under it as a Deputy in 1667, and as an Assistant in the

against Europeans only, leaving them blank paper so far as the rights of the natives were concerned. See the general question of the inherent propriety of the advance of civilization, notwithstanding the adverse claim of rude tribes to keep it out, argued with candor and ability by Chancellor Kent. [*Commentaries, etc.* iii: 469–473.]

386 See the Charter *in extenso*, in *R. I. Col. Rec.* ii: 3–21.

387 *Ibid*, 22.

388 *Ibid*, 24.

389 *Ibid*, 25.

390 *Ibid*, 28.

years 1664, 1665, 1670, 1671 and 1672,[301] and during all these years I find no trace of any the least complaint against this Patent, or objection to it, from his lip or pen.

(ii.) This Charter in that vital point of the assumption of the crown to own and grant the lands of the natives, against which Mr. Williams had so strenuously objected, was kindred in spirit to, and in fact identical in language with, the previous Patents to Massachusetts of Charles the First, and his father James the First. I will prove this by arranging that clause of each of the three Charters to which reference is made, in parallel columns:[302]

[*Two Massachusetts Charters.*]		[*Rhode Island Charter.*]
JAMES I. 1620.	CHARLES I. 1628–9.	CHARLES II. 1663.
do by these Presents *absolutely give, grant and confirm* unto the said Councill . . and unto their Successors for ever, all the aforesaid Lands and Grounds, etc. . . . *to be holden of Us* . . as of our Manor of East Greenwich in our County of Kent, in free and comon Soccage, and not in Capite, nor by Knights Service, yielding and paying therefore to Us, our Heires, our Successors, the fifth part of the Ore of Gold and Silver, which from time to time, and att all times heereafter, shall happen to be found, etc.	doe for vs, our heires and successors, *give and grant vnto* the said Sir Henry Rosewell, etc., all landes and groundes, place and places, soyles, woodes, etc., lyeing within the said boundes and lymytts, and every parte and parcell thereof . . *to be holden of us*, our heires and successors, as of our mannor of Eastgreenewich in our Countie of Kent, within our realme of England, in free and common soccage, etc. yeilding and paying therefore to vs, etc. the fifte parte onlie of all oare of gould and silver, etc.	for vs, our heires and successours, *doe give, graunt and confirme vnto* the sayd Governour and Company, etc. all that parte of *our dominiones* in New England, in America, conteyneing the Nahantick and Nanhyganset Bay, and countryes and partes adjacent . . . *to be holden of vs*, our heires and successours, as of the Mannor of East-Greenwich in our County of Kent, in free and comon soccage, etc. yeilding and paying therefor, to vs, etc. only the fifth part of all the oare of gold and silver, etc.

One glance is sufficient here to establish the fact that this second Patent of Rhode Island, in so far as it touches the immediate subject under consideration, is indistinguishable from the two Massachusetts Patents.

Mr. Williams clearly began at Providence with the endeavor to carry out faithfully his own radical ideas. When he went to England in 1643, he obtained, through the Commissioners of Plantations, a Charter which contained no grant of land, but simply empowered the Providence planters to rule themselves, conformably to the laws of England, "so far as the Nature and Constitution of the place will admit."[303] The colonists undertook as individuals to extinguish the

301 *Ibid*, 22, 96, 185, 302, 373, 431.

302 Find these clauses: King James's, in Hazard's *Hist. Coll.* i: 111; King Charles Ist's, in *Mass. Col. Rec.* i: 7, 9; King Charles IId's, in *R. I. Col. Rec.* ii: 18, 19.

303 See the First Patent, *R. I. Col. Rec.* i: 143–146.

Indian titles. It proved a difficult work.[304] The same Indian might sell the same land to different parties. Boundaries were elastic. And, in the absence of any supreme power to adjudge between contestants, confusion reigned. Under that Charter the Providence plantation was not a success.[305] And, having learned wisdom by experience, there seems to have been a general consent, on the part of all, to accept, if not to seek, a second Charter which should bring them into a closer fellowship with their sister colonies.

Surely, now, the circumstance that Mr. Williams, having tested his own theories on this subject through the greater part of a generation, found it wise quietly to abandon them in favor of the exact doctrine which he had written and preached against at Plymouth and Salem; is one calculated to shed light upon the question whether the Massachusetts men of 1635 were wholly unreasonable in thrusting him — such as he then was — out of their company; and deserves the serious consideration of all who wish to reach a full and fair judgment of Roger Williams as he really was.

And not until the student has patiently considered the points here presented — the peculiar character of the plantation; the idiosyncrasies of the man; the actual nature of a "banishment" often overestimated, as well as misunderstood; the temper of the times; the quality of the necessity which Mr. Williams's himself had created, and the nature of the alternative which he had forced upon the colonists; yet the thorough and inexhaustible kindness with which, nevertheless, they treated him; with the facts that — in nearly every particular — he subsequently confessed the substantial justice of their dealing with him,

---

[304] Judge Sullivan, in his *History of the District of Maine* (1795), discusses the whole subject of Indian titles. He says: "as the Savages had no ideas of a permanent use and improvement of the soil, or ever had a personal, or individual right in it, or ever, by annexing their labour to it, rendered it better, or more apt, for the use of man; I am led to conclude that they had no more property in the soil on which they hunted, than they had in the waters in which they fished." His further conclusion is that: "the Indian conveyances clearly amounted to nothing more than a contract, made by the Chief, on consent of his tribe, that the Savages should not make war on the white people for taking lands to a certain extent into possession. In this way we may account for one Sachem's selling the same tract to several different purchasers: for if the deed was only an agreement upon peace and friendship, there could, in the Indian's view, be no immorality in making the contract with as many as might appear to demand it. And a wish in some of the savages to trade with the white people, and to learn the art of agriculture, might be a principal motive." [p. 135.]

[305] As to this, I refer the reader to an authority before cited: "It would probably be no departure from the truth to say that the government of 'Providence Plantations,' under this [the first] charter, and indeed the government of Providence before the charter went into operation, was a failure. There seemed to be no authority for the settlement of disputes which constantly arose. Perhaps fit materials for a government were wanting. These disputes related largely to their lands. Williams is responsible for much of this disorder. The careless and indefinite manner in which the original conveyances of Providence and Pawtuxet were drawn, as well as those subsequently made by him to his companions, was the source of a bitter and prolonged controversy, not finally settled till the next century. It shows that Williams, however able a dialectician, was a poor man of business.

"These Indian deeds at best, and however carefully drawn, were often a source of perplexity and litigation in all the colonies." [*Mr. Charles Deane, LL. D. Proceedings Mass. Hist. Soc.* 1873. 356.]

and that in the important matter of the Patent, he abandoned his own opinion to revert to theirs — will he be in a position fitting him to speak wisely and conclusively upon this vexed passage of New England history.[306]

IT seems to be a very natural thing that a few words should here be added as to some of the essentials for a just judgment in regard to the Baptists, the Quakers, and the general subject of religious liberty, as related to the opinions, the policy, and the conduct of our fathers. I shall confine myself to three or four suggestions merely, without entering upon any full discussion of topics too fruitful for these narrow limits.

1. We are to remember that the founders of New England lived in the earlier half of the seventeenth, and not the later half of the nineteenth, century. So

[306] I scarcely think there has been so much honestly meant misrepresentation concerning any other person in modern history. Two strong yet entirely unlike motives have led different writers to draw from an imperfect acquaintance with the subject, mistaken inferences in regard to it. The Baptists, as I have already intimated, have done this on the one hand. The Unitarians, in earlier days when they were more drawn than at present to speak harshly of the founders of New England, fell into the same temptation, on the other. This seems to account for some, at least, of Dr. Bentley's frequent blunders. It may, perhaps, explain Dr. Parkman's averment: "at the present day, when just notions of religious liberty have extensively prevailed, they [*i. e.* the causes of Mr. Williams's banishment] will be deemed, of course, utterly insufficient; and nothing but a full consideration of the condition of our Puritan fathers, and the dangers of an infant colony, as well as of the general spirit of the times, will protect them from the charge of oppressive cruelty." [*Christian Examiner*, xvi: 81.] Possibly from the same source came the *dictum:* "if the Massachusetts colonists erected their civil and ecclesiascal organization on an illiberal basis, they, and not Roger Williams, must be held responsible for the bad consequences which might have resulted to it from his proclamation of a vital principle." [*North American Review*, lxi: 9.] That the (Baptist) *Christian Review* [x: 275] should say: "The first annunciation of this great principle [*i. e.* of religious freedom] by Roger Williams, awakened suspicion in the colony; his boldness in the cause of truth confirmed it; and the firmness with which he defended his opinions in every case, led to his final banishment," is not remarkable: especially when one finds that the pen so writing was the same which soon after gave to the world that *History of Rhode Island* which I have already had occasion to criticise as partly failing, through a lack of thoroughness, to do justice to the subject. From another quarter of the compass, still, come the fierce criticisms of that modern High-Churchman, the late Peter Oliver, who says: "Roger Williams was cast out into the wilderness, because he taught that it was unlawful even 'to hear the godly ministers' of the Church of England. Harmless enough, truly, was this fanaticism in Massachusetts, at the time he spoke, etc." [*The Puritan Commonwealth*, 192.] Dr. Hague perhaps capped the climax of absurdity, when [*Historical Discourse Delivered at the celebration of the Second Centennial of the First Baptist Church in Providence*, 7 *Nov.* 1839, 20, 91] he called him, as he escaped from Salem, a "*venerable* pilgrim," and declared that "however strong might have been his aversion to any class of sentiments, however pungent his invective, he never betrayed one wish to infringe on the freedom of an opponent, or to use any other than moral means in promoting his opinions.' Nearest of all to the truth of the matter, Prof. Masson says of Roger Williams: "Personally he was most likeable — sincere to the core, and of a rich, glowing, peculiarly affectionate nature, which yearned even towards those from whom he differed publicly, and won their esteem in return. But what were they [the colonists] to do? Mere religious whimsics they might have borne with so far in Williams, including even his Individualism, or excess of Separatism; but here were attacks on law, property, social order! For a time it was hoped that reasonings, moderate censures and moral pressure would bring him round. But, though he shifted from place to place — leaving Salem for a time for New Plymouth, where he tried to get on with the mild Brewster, and then returning to Salem, where the people were so attached to him that they would have him to be their 'pastor' on the death of Skelton (1634) — yet as he became more determined in his singularities, and maintained them by writings, harder measures were used." [*Life of John Milton, etc.* ii: 561.]

obvious a thought ought not to need even an allusion; but we find men continually referring to the beginnings of our colonial career in terms which imply absolute forgetfulness of its simplest postulates. Surely the stream of social life and feeling in this rude wilderness could not be reasonably expected to rise higher than its fountain in the affluent and cultured metropolis of the mother-country. And yet—to take a single illustration—while Parliament was (as late as 4–14 Dec. 1660) there ordering the disinterment of the decaying remains of Cromwell, Bradshaw, and Ireton, in order that what was left of their mortal part should be hanged at Tyburn, and their heads stuck on poles upon the top of Westminster Hall fronting the Palace Yard;[397] and while Evelyn, almost in the beginning of the eighteenth century, saw the quarters of Perkins and Friend—"a dismal sight!"—set up upon Temple Bar;"[398] there are writers, and among them those of whom one would expect a better learning and candor,[399] who speak of such New England facts as, that when "King Philip" had been shot in Bristol woods in 1676 (he being, from a legal point of view, considered a rebel against King Charles the 2d) his body was quartered, and his head exposed for years at Plymouth;[400] as of barbarities so shocking, and inhuman, as almost to compel us to look upon our fathers as monsters, and not as men!

We may as well blame the New England colonists for not using the telegraph and the fast mail train, when as yet they had neither a courier, nor so much as even any rude road along which a passenger wagon might jolt its way; as to find fault with them for not lifting themselves in all the domain of thought and feeling out of the intellectual and spiritual average of their days, up toward the broader culture of subsequent ages. Nor, unless we take special pains to force our minds back toward the low level of the acquisitions of their time, shall we find it easy to comprehend how comparatively little they knew, and could know, in many directions in which knowledge has so long been common and cheap with us, and our immediate fathers before us.

I date the era of the settlement of New England, here, with the advent of the Pilgrims of 1620, rather than with that of the Puritans of ten years later, because it synchronizes exactly with the birth-date of that revival of learning, which is commonly identified with the first issue of the *Instauratio Magna* of Lord Bacon, in that year.[401] And I now desire to call the reader's attention to the meager quality of the scientific and general erudition of that era, which is revealed in

---

397 Knight's *Pop. Hist. Eng.* iv: 248.

398 Evelyn's *Diary*, 10 Apr. 1696.

399 Even Mr. Drake, *Biog. and Hist. of Indians of N. A.* (11th ed.) 227, fails to remember—as might have been expected from his large information—the obvious principle here considered; and Mr. Savage in his annotation of Gov. Winthrop's *Journal* more than once transgresses it. [*E. g.* i: 53, 167; ii: 174, etc.

400 Increase Mather, *Brief Hist.* 47; Niles's *Hist. Ind. and Fr. Wars*, in 3 *Mass. Hist. Coll.* vi: 190; *Thacher's Hist. Plymouth*, 389.

401 Hallam's *Introduc. to Lit. of Europe, etc.* ii: 391.

the periods by which it was separated from the advent of various discoveries, and inventions, which long, long ago, have taken their places with us among familiar things. When the Mayflower dropped her anchor in Plymouth harbor, wise men were still in doubt whether the Copernican, ought to supplant the Ptolemaic, world-theory.[402] It was two years after that date before Asellius discovered the fact, and the philosophy, of the *chyle*, and its relation to the digestive process; and two years, before England saw her first newspaper.[403] It was five years, before hackney-coaches began to be kept for hire in London.[404] It was eight years, before William Harvey, in his *Exercitatio Anatomica de Motu Cordis et Sanguinis*, promulgated the doctrine of the circulation of the blood.[405] It was eighteen years, before Galileo announced the first true law of motion.[406] It was twenty years, before Gascoigne, by fixing a cross of fine wires in the focus of the telescope, raised it from an instructive curiosity to the dignity of a far-seeing eye that can accurately note celestial phenomena; and twenty-eight, before the barometer began to be available as an indicator of the hight of mountains, or the coming on of storms.[407] It was thirty-six years, before Huyghens, applying Galileo's oscillating pendulum to a simple registry of wheels and pinions, furnished the world with a measure of time more accurate than the sun itself.[408] It was forty-four years, before Willis described the nerve-center, and laid the foundation of that knowledge of the nervous system which we now possess.[409] It was forty-six years, before Newton, sitting in his garden, was led on to the development of the law of universal gravitation, "the greatest scientific discovery ever made."[410] It was forty-seven years, before the erection of the observatory of Paris, followed eight years after by that at Greenwich, opened the way for the modern progress of astronomy.[411] It was fifty-two years, before the same great mind which had developed the law of gravitation, enabled men to explain the rainbow, by demonstrating that light is composed of rays of different colors and varying refrangibility.[412] It was fifty-three years, before the first almanac, in present shape, was published at Oxford, Eng.[413] It was fifty-six years, before Römer discovered the fact that light travels along its course in a measurable time.[414] It was seventy-five years, before Dr. Woodward began to comprehend,

---

[402] Dr. Whewell shews that Lord Bacon was not a Copernican, and Milton undecided; and thinks that Salusbury, who, in 1661, published a translation of some of Galileo's works, perhaps did as much as any one else to convince England. [*Hist. Induct. Sciences*, i: 295-299.]

[403] *Ibid*, iii: 338; Powers's *Handy-Book about Books, etc.* 97.

[404] Appleton's *Cyclopedia*, sub voce "Coach."

[405] Whewell's *Hist. Induct. Sciences*, iii: 331.

[406] *Ibid*, ii: 20.

[407] *Ibid*, ii: 208; Appleton's *Cyclopedia*, sub voce.

[408] Whewell's *Hist. Induct. Sciences*, ii: 210.

[409] *Ibid*, iii: 351.

[410] *Ibid*, ii: 117, 121.

[411] *Ibid*, ii: 215, 216.

[412] *Ibid*, ii: 281.

[413] Powers's *Handy-Book, etc.* 39.

[414] Whewell's *Hist. Induct. Sciences*, ii: 199.

and announce, the fact that the surface of the earth exists in geological strata.[415] It was eighty-nine years, before a daily newspaper was started in England.[416] It was one hundred years, before the thermometer was made available for its uses of observation.[417] It was one hundred and thirteen years, before Dufay expounded the laws of electricity.[418] It was one hundred and twenty-six years, before Cunæus invented the Leyden jar, and produced the electric shock.[419] It was one hundred and thirty-eight years, before Cronstedt settled the first principles of the science of mineralogy.[420] It was one hundred and forty years, before the establishment of street lamps in London.[421] It was one hundred and forty-eight years, before Watt produced, and patented, the steam-engine.[422] It was one hundred and fifty-one years, before Arkwright was manufacturing cotton cloth by means of spindles and looms driven by water.[423] It was one hundred and sixty-four years, before Cavendish found out that water is compounded of oxygen and hydrogen gas.[424] It was one hundred and seventy-one years, before Galvani announced the science which took his name, and which has made the telegraph possible in our own time.[425] It was one hundred and ninety-eight years, before the first ship crossed the Atlantic under steam;[426] and two hundred and nine years, before Stevenson's "Rocket" led the long succession of locomotives of the nineteenth century.[427]

Separated from the present in point of science by this far remove, we are to take note also that in many departments of feeling as well as thought, the English people in the days of which we speak were in a condition so unlike that of their children, as to make it difficult for us to do them justice; as witness one further fact — that more than two hundred persons were hanged in England, and thousands were burned in Scotland, during the seventeenth century, for witchcraft alone.[428]

2. We need to refer again[429] to the fact that the theory of the toleration of various and variant ideas in religion, had not then established itself in the world among reputable doctrines. The ancient idea was of one all-embracing, infallible and unchangeable church. And in England the Reformation had

---

415 *Ibid*, iii: 411.

416 Powers's *Handy-Book, etc.* 40.

417 Appleton's *Cyclopedia*, sub voce.

418 Whewell's *Hist. Induct. Sciences*, iii: 8.

419 *Ibid*, iii: 11.

420 *Ibid*, iii: 198.

421 *Old England*, ii: 359.

422 Appleton's *Cyclopedia*, sub voce.

423 *Ibid*, sub voce "Arkwright."

424 Whewell's *Hist. Induct. Sciences*, iii: 111.

425 *Ibid*, iii: 62.

426 Appletons's *Cyclopedia*, sub voce "Steam navigation."

427 *Ibid*, sub voce "Steam carriage."

428 Upham's *Salem Witchcraft, etc.* i: 347. Not only was there this palliation for the witchcraft delusion at Salem, but it is a fact also that even William Penn presided, in his judicial character, at the trial of two Swedish women for witchcraft; so that nothing saved Pennsylvania from a like blot upon her annals, but the accident of a flaw in the indictment. [*Ibid*, 414.]

429 See p. 86, and note 317, *ante*.

scarcely more than transferred that idea from the Pope's church to that of Henry VIII. And when our fathers dared to differ with that State church in matters of polity, they did so with the sincere belief that the government was right in its fundamental principles, only mistaken in their application; right in rigidly ruling with reference to spiritual things, only wrong in the data by which that rule was determined; right in compelling men as to their church polity, only wrong as to the kind of polity which was the object of such compulsion. It would be the hight of absurdity, therefore, to expect that, when landed after a voyage of three thousand miles in the North American wilderness, such Englishmen should launch themselves at once into a subsequent century. The only course natural to them was — *mutatis mutandis* — to reproduce as well as they could on the western side of the Atlantic the mother-country, as they thought she ought to be, and as, if they had had the power, they would have made her to be, at home.

The notion of toleration had had existence for more than a century, as a purely speculative conception. But as a practical working-day principle, it was almost inevitable that it should only be the birth of a considerable and painful experience. As new sects were evolved, and each took its turn of bearing persecution, each necessarily claimed for itself the right to be; and so, each adding one new demand in that direction, the way was gradually prepared for the idea of general, and equal, liberty for all. There can be no doubt that Mr. Williams, though far from being the discoverer, or first promulgator, of the doctrine, and though holding it originally in a crude form, was in his maturer years one of its most zealous and successful advocates, and that he did much in his connection with civil affairs in Rhode Island to favor and further it. But it cannot be held to be in any sense a just matter of reproach to the Massachusetts men that they shared the training, and so the prepossessions and prejudices, of their time, and dreaded the advent of those new ideas in religion which they honestly conceived must, almost of necessity, be pernicious — as men dread the malarias and miasmas of an unknown low country.

3. We ought not, further, to forget that new sects in those days were apt to be associated with the ideas of fanaticism, and civil license, in their most offensive and dangerous form; so that for this reason good men, and the lovers of good order, were prejudiced against them in advance. I think, indeed, our fathers strongly doubted whether *any* religion were tolerable for the English State, except the Established Church, and their own form of dissent from it. John Cotton early taught the Church in Boston (New England) that the pouring out of the third vial [*Rev.* xvi: 4–7] should be so interpreted as to endorse the Statute of 27th Elizabeth, which put to death Priests and Jesuits; "because

they had bloudy intendments in their comming, intending to kill the Queene, or corrupt the State with unwholsome and pernicious Doctrine, to draw the people from their allegeance, to the obedience of the Sea of Rome."[430]

Nor, be it remembered here, is the question strictly so much what these new sects really did hold and teach, as what they were then commonly reported and believed to hold and teach. Ephraim Pagitt, in his *Heresiography*,[431] and a few kindred writers, were responsible for the creation of a serious popular distrust of novelties in religious faith. He represents the *Familists* as teaching that Henry Nicholas could no more err than Christ; that his books are of equal authority with the Bible; that all days are alike; that they attained perfection, and needed not to pray for the forgiveness of sins; while he declares that they indulged in a lewd and shameless life.[432] He says the *Antinomians* held that it is sufficient for a wicked man to believe, and not to doubt of his salvation; that the child of God cannot sin, and need not ask forgiveness for any of his acts — it being nothing less than blasphemy for him to do so; that, if a man knows himself to be in a state of grace, though he get drunk or commit murder God sees no sin in him.[433] The following extract will convey some notion of the spirit in which Pagitt wrote, and will make it easy to see how a community leavened with such ideas should regard the advent of men of novel sentiments with apprehension. After describing fifteen or twenty such sects, — he names more than forty — and giving some details of the heresies and excesses of each, he goes on:[434]

> They preach, print and practice their heretical opinions openly: for books, *vide* the bloudy Tenet, witnesse a Tractate of divorce, in which the bonds are let loose to inordinate lust: a pamphlet also in which the soul is laid a sleep from the hour of death unto the hour of judgement, with many others.
>
> Yea, since the suspension of our Church-government, every one that listeth turneth Preacher, as Shoe-makers, Coblers, Button-makers, Hostlers and such like, take upon them to expound the holy Scriptures, intrude into our Pulpits, and vent strange doctrine, tending to faction, sedition and blasphemy.
>
> What mischiefe these Sectaries have already done, wee that have cure of souls in London finde and see with great griefe of heart: viz., Our congregations forsaking their Pastors; our people becomming of the Tribe of Gad, running after seducers as if they were mad; Infants not to be brought to the Sacrament of Baptisme; men refusing to receive the holy Communion,

---

430 *The Powring ovt of the Seven Vials, etc.* (ed. 1642) 3d Vial, 4; (ed. 1645) 34.

431 This was first published in 1645. I have seen in the British Museum, and the libraries at Cambridge, [Eng.] other editions; of 1645 (again), 1646, 1647, 1647 (again), 1654, and 1661; while Lowndes mentions another of 1662; showing a very large circulation for the book.

432 *Heresiography*, (ed. 1654) 80–87. W. Wilkinson quite sustains most of these charges of Pagitt, in his *Confutation of Certaine Articles delivered vnto the Familye of Loue, (with Certaine profitable Notes to know an Heretique, especially an Anabaptist), etc.* 1579.

433 *Ibid*, 91–102.

434 *Ibid*, ix.

and the Lords Prayer accounted abominable, etc. A Volumn will hardly contain the hurt that these Sectaries have in a very short time done to this poor Church; and doth not the Commonwealth suffer with the Church? Whence are all these distractions? Who are the Incendiaries that have kindled and blown this fire among us, but these?

Quite in the same vein is Mr. Thomas Edwards, who says in his famous *Gangræna*:[435]

This Land is become already in many places a Chaos, a Babel, another Amsterdam, yea, worse; we are beyond that, and in the highway to Munster (if God prevent it not) but if a general Toleration should be granted, so much written and stood for, England would quickly become a Sodom, an Egypt, Babylon, yea, worse then all these: Certainly, as it would be the most provoking sin against God that ever Parliament was guilty of in this Kingdome, like to that of Ieroboam, to cut it off and to destroy it from the face of the earth; so it would prove the cause and fountain of all kind of damnable heresies and blasphemies, loose and ungodly practises, bitter and unnatural divisions in families and Churches; it would destroy all Religion, and as Polutheisme among the Heathen brought in Atheisme, so would many Religions bring in none among us; let but the Reader well review and consider of all the Heresies, blasphemies, practises laid down in this Book, all broached and acted in England within these four last yeers, yea more especially within this last yeer; and if one man hath observed and gathered so much, what Armies of blasphemies and monstrous heresies are there thinke we, if all that have been vented were drawn into one Synopsis? . . . Should any man seven yeers ago have said that of many in England (which now all men see) that many of the Professors and people in England shall be Arrians, Anti-trinitarians, Anti-Scripturists, nay blaspheme, deride the Scriptures, give over all prayer, hearing Sermons, and other holy duties; be for Toleration of all Religions, Poperie, Blasphemie, Atheisme, it would have bin said, It cannot be; and the persons who now are fallen, would have said as Hazael, Are we dogs that we should doe such things? and yet we see it is so; and what may we thanke for this, but liberty, impunity, and want of government? We have the plague of Egypt upon us, frogs out of the bottomlesse pit covering our land, comming into our Houses, Bed-chambers, Beds, Churches; a man can hardly come into any place, but some croaking frog or other will be comming up upon him.

And in much the same way mourns Robert Baillie:[436]

It is marvailed by many whence these new Monsters of Sects have arisen: Some spare not, from this ground, liberally to blasphem the Reformation in hand, and to magnifie the Bishops as if they had kept down, and this did set up, the Sects which now praedominate. But these murmurers would do well in their calm and sober times, to remember that none of the named Sects are births of one day; but all of them were bred and born under the wings of no other Dame than Episcopacy: the tyranny and superstition of this Step-mother, was the seed and spawn of Brownisme, the great root of the most of our Sects; all which were many yeers ago brought forth, however kept within doors so long as any Church-Disciplin was on foot: Now, indeed, every Monster walks in the street without controlement, while all Ecclesiastick Government is cast asleep; this too too long inter-reign and meer Anarchy hath invited every

---

[435] *Gangræna, or a Catalogue and Discovery of many of the Errours, Heresies, Blasphemies and pernicious practices of the Sectaries of this time, etc.* (1646), 120.

[436] *A Dissvasive from the Errours of the Time: Wherein the Tenets of the principall Sects, etc., are drawn together, etc.* (1645), 6.

unclean creature to creep out of its cave, and shew in publike its mishapen face to all, who like to behold.

There can be no manner of doubt that—strong as this language seems to our time, it fairly expressed the predominant feeling of the majority of the good men of the seventeenth century. They dreaded these new sects from afar, as they dreaded conflagration, or the plague. In fact *Pagitt* makes use of these exact comparisons:[437]

How dangerous the fostering of Hereticks hath been, Histories declare, *viz.:* Almighty God sent downe fire from heaven, and consum'd Antioch, being a nursery of Hereticks [*Paulus Diacon.* lib. 15.] And also how the earth opened, and swallowed Nicomedia, the meeting place of the blasphemous Arians [*Theod.* lib. 2, cap. xxvi]: also in the Commentaries of Sleiden, how the Anabaptists meeting first in Conventicles, surprised Munster, and how hardly Amsterdam escaped them, *Lambertus Hortensius* writeth.

The plague is of all diseases most infectious: I have lived among you [this extract is from the Dedication to the Lord Mayor and Aldermen of the city of London] almost a Jubile, and seen your great care and provision to keep the City from infection, in the shutting up the sick, and in carrying them to your Pest-house; in setting Warders to keep the whole from the sick; in making of fires and perfuming the streets; in resorting to your Churches; in pouring out your prayers to Almighty God with fasting and almes to be propitious to you. *The plague of Heresie is greater, and you are now in more danger then when you buried five thousand a week!* You have power to keep these Hereticks & Sectaries from Conventicles, and sholing together to infect one another.

Fire is dangerous, many great Cities in Europe have been almost ruinated by it: I have seen your diligence and dexterity in quenching it in the beginning; your breaking open your Pipes for water, making flouds in your streets; your Engines to cast the water upon the houses: your industry and paines is admirable. *Heresie is as dangerous as fire; use your best endeavours to quench it, before it consumes us!*

And even a man of so good and gracious a spirit as Samuel Rutherford of St. Andrews, whose "Letters" are so fragrant with the sweetest manifestations of the Divine life in the soul of man, as to have won for themselves a permanent place in the closet-literature of the Church, in his *Survey of The Spiritual Antichrist* (1648)—I quote from a copy in my possession bearing the autographs both of John Cotton, and John Norton—could speak of:[438]

the lawlesse Spirit of Enthysiasts, *the murthering spirit of Anabaptists, Libertines, Familists,* who *kill all, as Antichristian, that are not of their way.*

4. Still further, it is obvious that the Anabaptists and the Quakers presented themselves to the early settlers of New England in a guise eminently calculated to excite prejudice and hostility against themselves; the more especially as our fathers were—as we have seen—far from being prepossessed in their favor.

---

437 *Heresiography, etc.* xiii.

438 Part ii: 239.

It is not necessary to take space here to recount the painful and bloody history of those monomaniacs of Munster, who, just one hundred years before the settlement of New England, had made the name of Anabaptist one to excite loathing and horror. It is sufficient to note that our fathers supposed they had the most undoubted authority for the conclusion that these persons not only believed Christ not to be true God, being only a gifted man; that there is no original sin, and that infants ought not to be baptized; but believed that they themselves acted by a divine inspiration; that they were the righteous, and that the righteous had the right to wash their feet in the blood of the wicked; that property ought to be held in common; that it is unlawful for a Christian man to be a magistrate, or to obey a magistrate; that an oath is not to be used in processes of justice; and that a believer should not be tied to one wife, but may marry as many as he likes.[439] The New England men supposed they had abundant warrant for the truth of statements involving the name of Anabaptist with the most indecent, as well as painful, frenzies;[440] and they found the prom-

[439] The authorities on which they especially relied, appear to have been these, viz.: Sleidanus *De Statu Religionis, etc. Commentarii*, Libri. 5, (1555); Lambertus Hortensius *Tvmvltvvm Anabaptistarvm*, (1548, but there is in the British Museum a reprint, of date 1637); Bullinger's *An Holsum Antidotus, or Counterpoysen, agaynst the pestilent heresye and Secte of Anabaptistes, etc.* (1548), and his *Three Dialogues betweene the seditious libertine, or rebell Anabaptist, and the true obedient Christian: wherein Obedience to Magistrates is handled*, (1551 — this is in the Bodleian Library at Oxford); Martinus Duncanus's *Anabaptisticæ Hereseos Confutatio, et vere Christiani Baptismi, ac potissimum Pedobaptismatis Assertio, etc.* 1549, [a copy of which is in the Bodleian Library, Oxford]; Guy de Brez's *De Wortel, de Oorspronck, en het Fondament der Weder-dooperen van onsen tijde, etc.* [first published in 1565, and again in 1570 — of which edition a copy is in the Mennonite Library in Amsterdam. It was published also in French, from which portions, translated by "J. S." — the Catalogue of the Antiquarian Society at Worcester, says "Joshua Scottow" — were printed at Cambridge, N. E. in 1668; of which copies are in the Antiquarian, and Mass. Hist. Soc. Libraries, under the title of *The Rise, Spring and Foundation of the Anabaptists, or Rebaptized, of our Time, etc.* 4° pp. 52]; Cartwright's *Two Letters written ouer into England: the one to a godly Ladie, wherein the Anabaptistes errours are confuted, etc.* (1589); Calvin's *A Short Instruction for to arme all good Christian people agaynst the pestiferous errours of the common Secte of Anabaptistes, etc.* (1544 — this is in the Bodleian. It was printed again at London in 1549); and the work of Pagitt, above quoted. The godly Henry Ainsworth — one of the gentlest, loveliest and most learned of the English Brownists — had published in 1623, *A Seasonable Discourse; or a Censure upon a Dialogue of the Anabaptists, etc.*, which came to a second edition in 1642, and a third in 1644. [Among other books that one would do well to consult who wishes to complete his knowledge of the subject, may be named: Catrou's *Histoire des Anabatistes tant en Allemagne, Hollande qu'Angleterre, etc.* Paris, 1615; J. Gastius's *De Anabaptismi exordio, erroribus, historiis abominandis, confutationibus adjectis, etc.* Basileæ, 1544; Melancthon's *Adversus Anabaptistas judicium, etc.*; J. H. Ottius's *Annales Anabaptistici, hoc est, Historia universalis de Anabaptistarum origine, progressu, factionibus et schismatis, etc.* Basileæ, 1672; and Kerssenbrock's *Geschichte der Wiedertäuffer zu Münster, etc.* 1771.]

[440] I cite here, under the veil of the original Latin, one scene which appears to possess abundant authentication as having occurred at Amsterdam in 1535: "In uico Salinario *Ioannes Sibertus* habitabat, pannicida. Aberat is per hos dies procul à domo in orientalib. urbibus, ubi nogotiabant. Huc septem uiri et quinque fœmines convenerant: inter quos unus, cui *Theodorito* sartori nomen erat, se prophetam dixerat. Manè paulo post tertiam horam, in secretiori ædium parte pronum se in terram ad orandum propheta in conspectu omnium porrexit. Dum orat, tantus omnibus horror incessit, ut locus ipsis moueri, & omnia tremere uiderentur. . . Quatuor horis docendo & precando absumptis, propheta galeam capiti detractam, & thoracem ferreum exutum, ensem & alia bellica instrumenta excussa, in ignem congessit. His spoliatus, totus stetit nudus, ut non esset quo ea quæ ab oculis hominum sunt remouenda, & natura tegi haberi

inent good men, whose opinions they had been accustomed to receive on other subjects with the greatest deference, referring to such Anabaptists with a degree of reprobation[441] which was surely calculated to impair the welcome with which they might receive any new comers avowing that peculiar faith.

The first mention of Anabaptism in the history of the New England colonies appears to be in connection with Mr. Williams, and his new settlement at Providence; where early in 1638, becoming convinced that he had not been himself baptized, and seeing no other way to obtain the pure ordinance, he submitted to it at the hands of one Ezekiel Hollyman; after which he turned round and himself rebaptized Hollyman and some ten others.[442] This course of procedure was not, in itself, calculated to increase the respect felt by the Massachusetts men for this ism. Nor was the matter much mended, when, a few months after —on the logical ground that Hollyman had been, on this theory, unbaptized (and therefore unauthorized to administer the rite) when rebaptizing him—Mr.

---

que occulta uoluit, conderentur. Mandat sub hæc imperiose sex cæteris, ut suo exemplo se totos exuant. Paruerunt iussui. Inde & foeminæ uirorum exemplum secutæ, adeò omnem uestitum posuerunt, ut non esset funiculus reliquus, quo capitis comas substringerent, nulla naturali uericundia ductæ. Sic enim censuerat propheta, uniuersum id quod è terra natum factumque esset, in ignem conjici oportere, holocaustum Deo id futurum arbitratus. Grauis dirusque fœtor uestium igne correptarum, totam iam domum ita oppleuerat, ut mulier domus hospita, quæ harum rerum ignara ominum erat, eo experrecta, lecto exiliret, focos exploratura, ecquod incendium usquam esset. In tabulatum sursum progressa, nudos undecim promiscuos ibi offendit. Cui illicò pro imperio mandat, ut & ipsa ad præscriptum se ostenderet. Obtemperauit nulla mora, uestes in focum super aceruum aliarum cumulauit. Ita nudatis duodecim, nondum liquebat, quid rerum inceptarent. Ibi omnibus imperat propheta, ut currendo, clamandoque se imitarentur. Mox in publicum domo egressi horribili clamore per urbem sursum deorsum dimidiatam peruagantur. Clamor consentiens omnium hic erat: *Vae, uae, uae; diuina uindicta; diuina uindicta; diuina uindicta.* Nunquam in uita mortalium mugitus horrendior fuit auditus, nec existimabant horribiliorem ullo æuo exaudiri posse. Ciues armati in publicum prosiliunt, & forum inuadunt, rati ab hostibus urbem captam fuisse. Capti omnes in uincula ducuntur, extra unam mulierem. Hæc quò fuerit delapsa, inter nullos constare uideo. In curia dum nudi sedent, nulla uerecundia tacti, uestitum oblatum reiecerunt; tegi pertinaciter recusantes, *se nudam ueritatem esse* dictitarunt. [Lamb. Hortens. *Tvmvlt. Anabaptist. etc.* (ed. 1548) 59-61.] In a little book, now marked as "rarissime" by the dealers, printed at Leyden in the year before John Robinson and his company went thither from Amsterdam, entitled *Apocalypsis Insignium Aliquot Hæresiarcharvm, etc.* is given [p. 59] a disgusting portrait of this "prophet" tailor; which is surely ugly enough to take some possibility of genuineness. [See additional details in Pontanus *Rerum et urbis Am. Hist.* (1611) 35; Wagenaar's *Amsterdam*, i: 239-247; and Brandt's *Hist. Ref.* (London, 1720) i: 66.]

[441] I have never examined Calvin's work above referred to [note 439]; but I find him in his preface to his *Psychopannychia*, calling the Anabaptists a "nefarious herd," and adding: "against whom nothing I have said, equals their deserts." [Calvin's Tracts, (ed. Edinburgh, M.DCCC.LI) iii: 416.] Bullinger calls them the "very messengers of Sathan himselfe." [*Fiftie Godly and Learned Sermons, etc.* (ed. 1587) p. 569.] Ainsworth said of the Anabaptists: "very ignorantly and erroneously have they propounded their opinion; with some truth mixing much error, that the blind may lead the blind into the ditch." [*Seasonable Discourse*, ed. 1644, 13.] In the *Apocalypsis* above cited [note 440] occurs the following: "Anabaptistarum doctrina, Lector candide, simpliciter mendacium est, & fucus. Tu eos Divinipotes ac Prophetas censes? Falleris. Pseudoprophetæ sunt & falsi doctores. Quorum colluvione ac peste nego ab orbe condito quidquam nocentius ex Averni faucibus prodijsse." [iii.] Even Jeremy Taylor declared (and this was as late as 1647) that Anabaptism is "as much to be rooted out as anything that is the greatest pest and nuisance to the public interest." [*Liberty of Prophesying*, sec. 19.]

[442] Winthrop's *Journal*, i: 293. Winthrop says that Mr. Williams was seduced into Anabaptist views by the influence of Mrs. Scott, a sister of that famous disturber, Mistress Anne Hutchinson.

Williams renounced the rebaptism, and remained for the rest of his days—under the name of "Seeker"—a "Come-outer" from all religious rites and organisms.[443] A little before this time certain English clergymen had sent over a list of thirty-two questions in regard to religious affairs in New England, one of which (the 30th) was to the point whether all the New England churches were agreed in their faith and procedures. In 1643 an answer, drawn up by Richard Mather[444] was printed, in which, in reply to this question, it is affirmed that all the churches in the plantations of Plymouth, the Massachusetts and Connecticut agreed together; but that Anabaptism existed at Providence, and Familism at Rhode Island.[445]

The next we hear is in July 1641, when Winthrop says of the Rhode Island people:[446]

> Divers of them turned professed Anabaptists, and *would not wear any arms*, and *denied all magistracy among Christians*, and maintained that there were no churches since those founded by the Apostles and Evangelists, nor could any be, nor any pastors ordained, nor seals administered, but by such; and that the church was to want these all the time she continued in the wilderness, as yet she was.

The words which I have here italicised, indicate that these Anabaptists who were thus introducing the doctrine into New England, were infected with some, at least, of the loose and offensive notions which had characterized the sect in Europe, and in its earlier days.

In July 1644, one Thomas Painter, then of Hingham, who seems to have been an idle, obstinate and rather worthless person,[447] suddenly turned Anabaptist, and, "having a child born, he would not suffer his wife to bring it to the ordinance of baptism." The matter was aggravated by the fact that he was not himself a member of any church, although his wife was; and by his "obstinacy" and "very loose behaviour." They thought they exercised much patience with him, but finally:[448]

> because he was very poor, so as no other but corporal punishment could be fastened upon him, he was ordered to be whipped; *not for his opinion, but for reproaching the Lord's ordinance*, and for his bold and evil behaviour, both at home and in the court.

---

443 *Ibid*, i: 307.

444 "There is a book which bears the title of *An Answer of the Elders, etc.* printed in the year 1643: Of which Book my father Mather was the Sole author." [Increase Mather's *Order of the Gospel, etc.* 73.]

445 "Conformity to the Lyturgie and Ceremonies in some places to the Northward, *Anabaptisme at Providence*, and Familisme at Aquidneck, hinders that we cannot say the same of them." [*Answer of the Elders*, 82.]

446 Winthrop's *Journal*, ii: 38.

447 Winthrop says he had "been scandalous and burdensome by his idle and troublesome behaviour," in the three places (New Haven, Rowley and Charlestown) where he had lived before coming to his present abode. Savage [note to Winthrop] says he probably was complained of by Rowley, or Charlestown. [*Journal*, ii: 174.]

448 *Ibid*, ii: 175.

Whether this unwise — yet, under all the circumstances, by no means extraordinary — procedure had anything to do with it, or not, so many symptoms of approaching Anabaptism about this time manifested themselves, as to lead the General Court after much consideration and conference to enact a statute, which is worth quoting here in full for the revelation which it makes of the exact aspect in which the subject then presented itself to the most intelligent civilians and divines of Massachusetts. It was put upon the statute-book, 13–23 November 1644:[449]

> Forasmuch as experience hath plentifully & often pved yt since ye first arising of ye Anabaptists, about a hundred years since, they have bene ye incendiaries of comon wealths, & ye infectors of persons in maine mattrs of religion, & ye troublers of churches in all places where they have bene; & yt they who have held ye baptizing of infants unlawfull have usually held othr errors or heresies togethr therewith, though they have (as othr hereticks use to do) concealed ye same, till they spied out a fit advantage & oportunity to vent ym by way of question or scruple; & whereas divers of this kind have, since or comeg into New England, appeared amongst orselves, some whereof have (as othrs before ym) denied ye ordinance of magistracy, & ye lawfulnes of making warr, & othrs ye lawfulnes of matrats, & their inspection into any breach of ye first table; wch opinions, if they should be connived at by us, are like to be increased amongst us, & so must necessarily bring guilt upon us, infection & trouble to ye churches, & hazard to ye whole comon wealth, —
>
> It is ordered & agreed yt if any pson or psons wthin ys iurisdiction shall eithr openly condemne or oppose ye baptizg of infants, or go about secretly to seduce othrs from ye appbation or use thereof, or shall purposely depart ye congregation at ye administration of ye ordinance, or shall deny ye ordinance of magistracy, or their lawfull right or authority to make warr, or to punish ye outward breaches of ye first table, & shall appear to ye Cort wilfully & obstinately to continue therein after due time & meanes of conviction, every such pson or psons shalbe sentenced to banishmt.

There are two or three entries following upon the records, which are rather remarkable, and which find explanation in an elaborate document bearing date two years afterward, for the preservation of which we are indebted to the care of Gov. Hutchinson. In the autumn of 1645 divers persons made request for some alteration in this law, but the Court "voted yt ye lawe mentioned should not be altered at all, nor explained."[450] In the following spring seventy-eight persons, chiefly residents of Dorchester and Roxbury, petitioned that the statute should not be altered, but continued "wthout abrogation or weakening;" which was granted.[451] A few months later the General Court adopted a Declaration, called out by a Petition and Remonstrance which had been addressed to them by seven persons, chief of whom were Samuel Maverick, and Dr. Robert Child,

---

449 *Mass. Col. Rec.* ii: 85.

450 *Ibid*, ii: 141; iii: 51.

451 *Ibid*, ii: 149; iii: 64. "The Courte gratefully accepts of their acknowledgement, graunting their request."

making complaint of the government for various reasons, and threatening to appeal to Parliament. In that Declaration they say:[452]

They are offended also at our lawe against Anabaptists. The truth is, the great trouble we have beene putt unto and hazard also, by familisticall and anabaptisticall spirits, *whose conscience and religion hath been only to sett forth themselves and raise contentions in the country*, did provoke us to provide for our safety by a lawe, that all such should take notice, how unwelcome they should be unto us, either comeing or staying. But *for such as differ from us only in judgment*, in point of baptism, or some other points of lesse consequence, *and live peaceably amongst us*, without occasioning disturbance, &c., *such have no cause to complaine;* for *it hath never beene as yet putt in execution against any of them*, although such are knowne to live amongst us.

An explanation was also given in England by Mr. Winslow, which was by authority,[453] and which was, as follows:[454]

You have a severe law against Anabaptists, yea one was whipt at Massachusets for his Religion? And your law banisheth them?

Ans. 'Tis true, the Massachusets Governement have such a law as to banish, but not to whip in that kinde. And certaine men desiring some mitigation of it; It was answered in my hearing: 'Tis true, we have a severe law, but wee never did, or will, execute the rigour of it upon any, and have men living amongst us, nay some in our Churches of that judgment, and as long as they carry themselves peaceably as hitherto they doe, wee will leave them to God, our selves having performed the duty of brethren to them. And whereas there was one whipt amongst us; 'tis true wee knew his judgment what it was: but had hee not carried himselfe so contemptuously towards the Authority God hath betrusted us with in an high exemplary measure, wee had never so censured him: and therefore he may thank himself who suffered as an evill doer in that respect.[455] But *the reason wherefore wee are loath either to repeale or alter the law, is, Because wee would have it remaine in force to beare witnesse against their judgement and practice, which we conceive them to be erroneous.*[456]

At the very time when this law had been passed, a minister who denied the lawfulness of Pedo-Baptism was President of the infant Harvard College; while the divine who was elected, in 1654, to be his successor, believed immersion

---

[452] *Hutchinson Papers*, 216.

[453] "Our honored Govrnr, Deputy Govrnr, Rich: Bellingham, Esq., & Mr. Auditor Genrall are appointed a comittee to puse & examine all the answrs yt are brought into this Corte to yo petition of Doctor Child & Mr. Fowle, &c., & out of all to draw up such an answr thereto as they thinke most meete, & psent yo same to this Corte. & *furthr to treate wth Mr. Winslow & to agree wth him as an agent for us, to answer to what shalbe obiected against us in England*, & giveing engagement to ye said Mr Winslow accordingly." [*Mass. Col. Rec.* ii: 162.]

[454] *Hypocrisie Unmasked, etc.* 101.

[455] I take it the reference here is to the case of Painter before mentioned, [p. 115.]

[456] Gov. Leverett, and others, in the letter to Hon. Robert Boyle to which I have already referred [see note 313 *ante*] give much the same account of this matter. It will be remembered that they wrote in 1673. They say: "Hence, [on account of the general alarm felt at the dangers threatened, by Anabaptism, etc.] from our first times, laws have been made to secure us from that danger; which have, at some times, upon just occasions, been executed, upon some of that sort of people, who have exceeded the rules of moderation in matters of practice: but this we may say truly, that some peaceable Anabaptists, and some of other sects, who have deported themselves quietly, have and do live here, under the protection of this government, undisturbedly." [Letter, etc. Appendix to *Life of Hon. Rob. Boyle*, 456.]

essential to the validity of the rite;[457] so that there certainly seems to be some evidence, at least, that the case was as stated above.

In the autumn of 1648, a little excitement was temporarily caused in consequence of some "great misdemeanor," committed by Edward Starbuck, of Dover, one of the Assistants, "with profession of Anabaptistry;[458] but nothing is set down as having come of it.

Five years after the statute took its place on the records, we find traces of uneasiness in Massachusetts over the fact that the older Plymouth Colony—*par excellence*, the "Old" Colony—was exercising towards the Anabaptists a toleration which it was feared would grow to a common danger. One Obadiah Holmes, a native of Preston, England, who had been excommunicated from the church in Salem, and had removed to Rehoboth and, in some way, joined himself to Mr. Newman's church; in 1649 seceded from the same with eight others and organized an Anabaptist church.[459] He was excommunicated again and his companions also, while the Plymouth Court was petitioned to take action in the premises. That Court responded by enjoining these schismatics "to refrain from practices disagreeable to their brethren," and citing them to appear before it; on which appearance, Holmes and two others were merely bound over in £10, one for another.[460] Whereupon the General Court of Massachusetts wrote a letter to the General Court of Plymouth, complaining of their lenity, and urging a greater stringency; asking them to consider that "the infeccon of such diseases, being so neere vs, are likely to spread into our jurisdiccon, etc."[461] It does not appear that any Plymouth action followed this intercession, but Holmes, with a few of his followers, soon removed to Newport, where he joined himself to the Anabaptist church, which some five years before had been formed there by Dr. John Clarke, and his friends.[462]

Some months before this, William Coddington, sick of the unsettled state of civil affairs, which proved to be the result of the unorganized individualism which was then the key-note of the Rhode Island plantations, exaggerated by

---

[457] Quincy's *Hist. Har. Univ.* i: 18, 25.

[458] *Mass. Col. Rec.* ii: 253.

[459] Bliss's *Hist. Rehoboth*, 205.

[460] Baylies's *Hist. Mem. Plym. Col.* ii: 210; *Plym. Col. Rec.* ii: 147, 156, 162.

[461] *Mass. Col. Rec.* iii: 173. The letter begins: "Wee have heard heeretofore of diuerse Annabaptists, arisen vp in your jurisdiccon, and connived at; but being but few, wee well hoped that it might have pleased God, by the endeavo^rs of yourselves and the faithfull elders wth yow, to have reduced such erring men againe into the right way. But now, to our great greife, wee are credibly informed that your patient bearing wth such men hath p.duced another effect, namely, the multiplying and encreasing of the same errors, and wee feare maybe of other errors also, if timely care be not taken to suppresse the same. Perticulerly wee vnderstand that w^thin this few weekes there have binn at *Sea Cuncke* thirteene or fowerteene p'sons rebaptized (a swifte progresse in one toune;) yett wee heare not of any effectuall restriccon is entended thereabouts, etc." Seekonk had been the original Indian name of Rehoboth.

[462] Backus's *Hist. N. Eng.* i: 149. He thinks the Church must have been formed in 1644, or earlier.

the normal fact of the eccentric and impracticable character of many of the individuals who were then naturally attracted, or driven, thither ;[463] had gone to England to see if something could not be done in the way of remedy. He there obtained leave from the Council of State to institute a separate government for the islands of Rhode Island and Conanicut ;[464] he to be Governor, with a Council of not more than six Assistants.[465] In the autumn of 1650, it was understood that he was on his way home with this new instrument, and it was further understood that it was Mr. Coddington's desire, and intention, to bring about under it, if possible, the introduction of Rhode Island into the Confederacy then existing of the other Colonies, if not absolutely to procure its annexation to Massachusetts. Clarke and Coddington had not been on the best of terms since the disturbance occasioned by Nicholas Easton,[466] and, with many of his Newport adherents, the Anabaptist pastor was bitterly opposed to the new-coming order of things. When the crisis approached, he seems to have felt that a little persecution of the Anabaptists — if such a thing could be managed — by Massachusetts, might serve an important purpose, in prejudicing the Rhode Island mind against Coddington's scheme.[467] An occasion appears accordingly to have been made by which the red flag of the Anabaptistical fanaticism could be flouted full in the face of the Bay bull.

Among the early settlers of Lynn was one William Witter, a farmer residing at Swampscott, who, as early as 1643, had become so inspired with the genius of Anabaptism as to call infant baptism "a badge of the whore."[468] By 1646 he had progressed in this lovely spirit so far as to declare "y^{t} they who stayed whiles a child is baptized, doe worshipp ye Dyvell," and "broake ye Saboath."[469] Knowledge of his case reaching Mr. Clarke, a pilgrimage was determined upon for the purpose of public sympathy with this person, if not his open rebaptism, and reception into the Newport fellowship.[470] Such an expedition had in itself

---

463 Dr. Palfrey does not hesitate to intimate that the Rhode Island colonies then took the social sewerage of their neighbors — to the benefit of the latter: "It was an advantage to have, near by, a sufficient receptacle for the overflow of communities which would be the more wholesome for being drained." [*Hist. N. Eng.* ii: 343.]

464 Conanicut was the island lying between Rhode Island and what is Kingstown — now incorporated as the town of Jamestown.

465 *Journal of the Council of State*, State Paper Office, cited by *Palfrey*, ii: 344.

466 Winthrop's *Journal*, ii: 40.

467 "If Massachusetts was intolerant of Baptists, and if the execution of Coddington's scheme would place the Rhode Island Baptists more or less under her control, the necessity of self-defence admonished them that, if possible, that scheme should be defeated. . . . He judged well, that, at this moment, some striking practical evidence of the hostility of Massachusetts to Baptists would be efficacious to excite his Rhode Island friends to oppose the ascendency of Coddington." [Palfrey's *Hist. N. Eng.* ii: 350.]

468 Lewis and Newhall's *Annals of Lynn*, 209.

469 *Mass. Col. Rec.* iii: 67. The tolerant spirit of the Court comes out here in the record: "ye Court expst their patience tow^{r}ds him, only admonishing him till they see if he continew obstinate, etc." See also *Lewis & Newhall*, 219.

470 Gov. Arnold [*Hist. R. I.* i: 234] says the church "deputed" Clarke, and his two companions, "to visit

a promising look. It would lead through Boston, yet not far enough beyond it, to imperil the desired publicity. Yet nothing was neglected which should reasonably avail for fullest success. Clarke himself had left Boston fourteen years before to avoid being sent away, and he knew that his presence in the Massachusetts must bring him at once under the operation of the Anabaptist law of 1644; while, as an Assistant under the Rhode Island government,[471] and as pastor of the Newport Anabaptists, he doubtless felt himself to be sufficiently a man of mark to be tolerably sure of being "persecuted." But, for further security against failure, he took along with him John Crandall, son-in-law of Samuel Gorton; and also — to make assurance doubly sure — that very Obadiah Holmes who, a short time before, had been the occasion of the complaining letter of the Massachusetts Court to that at Plymouth.

The scheme succeeded perfectly. Saturday, 19–29 July 1651, saw this missionary company, after a three days' progress through the enemy's territory,[472] at their journey's end. Possibly it had been their original intent to attend Messrs. Whiting and Cobbett's "meeting" on Sunday morning and interrupt the same;[473] but when the time came, not seeing their way clear to that, Mr. Clarke preached at Witter's house to his two companions, their host and a few others who gathered

---

an aged member, residing near Lynn, etc." But Witter was not so *very* "aged" — being only then about 67 [Savage's *Gen. Dict.* iv: 620;] nor does it appear to be by any means certain that he was a member of the Newport Church, or of any other. Backus, indeed, professes to quote [i: 215] from the "Newport Church Papers," the statement that Witter was "a brother in the church, who, by reason of his advanced age, could not undertake so great a journey as to visit the church." But one cannot help thinking that those "Papers" must have been written long after the date of the occurrence (as is the obvious fact with some of the "Papers" of the First Baptist Church of Providence — which are not in accord with the truth of history,) and that their author confused the order of events. It is certain that neither Clarke nor Holmes, in the minutely circumstantial account which immediately after both gave [*Ill Newes, etc.*] say anything about being sent by the church; nor about Witter's being a church-member. They say they went "upon occasion of businesse." They speak (a year after) of him, as a Baptist with themselves; but in no way do they intimate that he had previously been such, except in desire. Furthermore Lewis and Newhall [*Annals, etc.* 230] say that Clarke rebaptized Witter on this occasion. This view receives strong support: (1) from the language of the *mittimus* [4 *Mass. Hist. Col.* ii: 31] which consigned the three men to Boston jail: "for suspition of having their hands in the rebaptizing of one, etc." (nobody suggesting that any person other than Witter was now rebaptized;) (2) from the language of the sentence, [*Ibid*, 32] which declared that Clarke had "administered the sacrament of the Supper to one excommunicate person [Holmes,] to another under admonition, and to another that was an inhabitant of Lin, and not in fellowship with any church" [who was this, if it were not Witter?]; (3) from the fact that Witter was presented at the Salem Court, in the November following, "*for beinge rebaptized*," [*Salem Court Rec.* 25, 9 mo. 1651]: which is a very remarkable fact if he had been, as Backus and Arnold claim, a member of the Newport Anabaptist Church for years; but which was a perfectly natural occurrence, if, after having been inclined for a long period to Anabaptist views, he had now been rebaptized by Clarke on this visit, — ostensibly on "business," but really for this purpose. The preponderance of evidence seems to me very clearly against the statement which has been common among Baptists, and which I see that my friend the learned professor of Ecclesiastical History in the Baptist Theological Seminary at Newton, is repeating in "Centennial Notes" in a prominent journal of that denomination, while these pages are going through the press.

[471] *R. I. Col. Rec.* i: 216, 220.

[472] Clarke's *Ill Newes from New England, etc.* 1–4.

[473] "Not having freedom in our Spirits for want of a clear Call from God to goe unto the Publike Assemblie to declare there what was the mind, and counsell of God concerning them." [*Ibid.*]

with them.[474] They were interrupted by two constables with a warrant, and taken to the "ordinary" for safe keeping. In the afternoon the officers carried them to "the meeting," where they deliberately put on their hats in time of prayer, (and kept them on until the constables "plucked" them off,) while Clarke went to reading a book, and, as soon as there was a pause, sprang to his feet and desired "to propose a few things." The pastor wanted to know whether he were a member of any church, and the magistrate, who had issued the warrant (Robert Bridges) said that if the congregation were willing to hear him he might speak, otherwise not; and Clarke beginning at once to attack the church as "not constituted according to the order of our Lord, &c.," the congregation concluded not to be willing, and he was soon silenced. On Monday they were examined by this magistrate, who decided to send them to Boston jail until the next Court; but, in some way giving him the slip, they managed to get back to Witter's, where they completed their interrupted service, and Clarke administered the Lord's Supper, having, it would seem, previously rebaptized Witter. On Tuesday Bridges made out his *mittimus*, and they were lodged in prison in Boston. The next week on Thursday — 31 July–10 Aug. 1651 — they had their trial. Being charged with Anabaptism Clarke disowned the name, and denied that he had ever rebaptized any; on the trickish plea that, since one's first child-baptism was no baptism, he had never *re*-baptized. He further "testified" against the Court; as did his companions. All ended in their being fined — as was usual in those days, to be whipped if they could not pay — and imprisoned until the matter be adjusted, the one way or the other. Endecott, as he was so apt to do, lost his temper while talking with Clarke, and said as much as that, while the Newport Anabaptist might have some success in dealing with weak-minded persons, he could do nothing whatever in an argument with the ministers; which Clarke insisted was tantamount to a promise to grant him a public disputation, and began to petition for that. The project seems to have been entertained by the magistrates, but before anything came of it somebody paid Clarke's fine, and he was very willing to leave for home.[475] The same thing was done with Crandall. Holmes seems to have had sterner stuff. Although "there were who would have paid the money[476] if he would accept it," he "durst not accept of deliverance in such a way."[477] He accordingly received thirty stripes.[478] When, in the following year, Clarke published

[474] "And to 4 or 5 Strangers, that came in unexpected after I had begun." [*Ibid.*]

[475] *Ibid*, 13.

[476] His fine was £30. [*Ibid.*]

[477] See his letter to London, detailing the entire transaction, in Clarke's *Ill Newes, etc*, 19.

[478] Arnold thinks he was "cruelly whipped." [*Hist. R. I.* i: 235]. But Clarke says "it was so easie to me, that I could well bear it, yea and in a manner felt it not;" and that he told the magistrates after it was over: "you have struck me as with Roses" [*Ill Newes, etc.* 22.] Dr. Palfrey suspects the executioner had orders

his version of all this in England, he was careful to declare that one purpose which he had in view in it all, was to make known "how that spirit by which they [the Massachusetts authorities] are led, would order the whole World, if either brought under them, or should come in unto them ;[479]—that is, how they would treat Rhode Island Baptists, were they to be annexed to their Colony.

The careful reader of New England history for that year will be apt to find, in the state of mind toward Massachusetts produced at Newport by this episode, and the relation of that state of mind to the reception of Coddington's plans after his return—the exact date of which is not given, but which appears to have been a few days subsequent to the whipping of Holmes[480]—the ground of what at the least will be a strong suspicion that there was a wheel within a wheel here revolving, and that the Massachusetts men in this thing, if sinning, were also adroitly made to serve a purpose in Rhode Island politics by their sin.

A few years passed in comparative quiet, when trouble arose in Charlestown. One Thomas Gould, a member of the church then under the care of Zachariah Symmes and Thomas Shepard, withheld his child from baptism. The church labored with and admonished him, but seem to have had long patience with him, in the face of unbecoming, if not contemptuous, conduct on his part. In the autumn of 1656 and the spring of 1657, he was dealt with by the County Court for his error. The next year, as he constantly neglected the Lord's Day meetings, he "was admonished for his breaking away from the church in weighty schism, and never having used any means to convince the church of any irregular proceeding, but continueing peremptiously and contumaceously to justifie his schisme."[481] He gradually found sympathizers, and on Sunday 8–18 Nov. 1663 a private meeting was organized at his house which—28 May–7 June 1665—grew into the first Baptist church of the Colony.[482] The church under Mr. Symmes, not being able to secure any tokens of repentance, on the 30th July–9 Aug. following, excommunicated them, "for their impertinency in their schismatical withdrawing from the church, and neglecting to hear the church.[483] The Court then took action. Gould and his companions were solemnly charged "not to persist in such pernicious practises." All ended in their adherence to their course, and their being disfranchised and fined, and—as they would not pay their fines—in their temporary imprisonment.

"to vindicate what they thought the majesty of the law, at little cost to the delinquent." [*Hist. N. Eng.* ii: 353.]

479 *Ill Newes, etc.* 1.

480 Clarke [4 *Mass. Hist. Coll.* ii: 44,] gives the date of Holmes's sentence as 31 July–10 Aug. 1651; while Arnold [*Hist. R. I.* i: 238] places "August, 1651" in the margin of his reference to Coddington's reaching Rhode Island on his return.

481 Charlestown *Church Records*, 6th 4th mo. 1658.

482 Now the First Baptist Church of Boston.

483 *Ibid, sub die* 30 July, 1665.

After a time something led the General Court to try another course, and a great debate as to the matters at issue began by appointment, on the 14–24 April 1668, between Revs. John Allin of Dedham, Thomas Cobbett of Ipswich, John Higginson of Salem, Samuel Danforth of Roxbury, Jonathan Mitchell of Cambridge and Thomas Shepard of Charlestown; and Gould, with seven sympathizers, three of whom were from Newport. Two days were spent in close discussion, "wth a great concourse of people," the effect of which — as might have been anticipated — was not as "prevalent wth" these Baptists, as the Court "could haue desired;" so that, neither party yielding, the chief offenders — Gould, Turner and Farnum — were banished, and refusing to leave, were again imprisoned. Strong sympathy was called out in their behalf. A petition with sixty-six signers interceded for them. But Gould was not set at liberty until in 1670. The society retreating to Noddles Island, a warrant was issued against them there.[484]

Various petty persecutions followed, and although in March 1681–2 the messengers of the colony were instructed to inform the king that "as for the Annabaptists, they are now subject to no other pœnal statutes then those of the Congregational way;" it cannot be denied that as compared with the "Standing Order," the Baptists, in one way or another, did have more or less cause of complaint; until, so lately as 1834, the amendment to the third article of the Bill of Rights put a final end to the policy inherited from the mother country, and cherished for more than two hundred years, under which all "dissenters" had to a greater or less extent suffered.

It seems fair, notwithstanding all here set down, to claim for our fathers a course of procedure toward the Baptists which was liberal for that time; as it surely was far more humane than that which the professors of the same faith received in the father-land.[485]

---

[484] This story of Gould (or Gold, as his name was then spelled) is told at considerable length by Mr. Frothingham [*History of Charlestown*, 163–172] and is much dwelt upon also by *Backus* [i: 355–415.] See further, *Mass. Col. Rec.* v: 271, 272, 347; and S. Willard's *Ne Sutor Ultra Crepidam*, etc. 1681. 4to. pp. 27.

[485] A glance at the facts will show that the Baptists were more persecuted, and longer persecuted, in England than here. Edward Wightman had been burned at Burton-upon-Trent, 11–21 April 1611, for being a Baptist. [Crosby's *Hist. Eng. Bap.* i: 108; Ivimey's *Hist. Eng. Bap.* i: 123; Evans's *Early Eng. Bap.* i: 233.] Edward Barber, minister to a small Baptist congregation in London, was thrown into prison in 1641, and kept there eleven months "for denying the baptism of infants." [*Crosby*, i: 219; *Ivimey*, i: 163.] Hanserd Knollys was more than once imprisoned for the same cause. [*Crosby*, i: 226–232.] Samuel Oates in 1646 lay for some time in irons, and was tried for his life for immersing a female, and was nearly drowned by a mob after his acquittal. [*Crosby*, i: 236; *Ivimey*, i: 197.] John Bunyan lay in Bedford jail twelve years, because he had been guilty of holding a Baptist "conventicle," in defiance of the law. [*Crosby*, ii: 92; *Ivimey*, i: 301; *Evans*, ii: 267.] Thomas Grantham — the author, in 1678, of *Christianismus Primitivus* — was ten times thrown into the common jail; often being kept there for months at a time. [Taylor's *Hist. Eng. Gen. Baptists*, i: 211; *Crosby*, ii: 149.] In 1661 Baptist meetings in London were again and again broken up by violence;

It was almost twenty years after the foundations of the Massachusetts Colony had been laid, before the sect of Quakers began to arise in England. George Fox of Drayton in Leicestershire, an ignorant but zealous shoemaker, conceiving himself raised up to disapprove of the existing institutions of religion, spent a long time in solitude, in roaming up and down the land, in fasting and meditation. He was a stern ascetic, clad in leather, and with his mind predisposed toward impressions of severe and outlandish duty. He fancied it was revealed to him that "the Lord forbad him to put off his Hat to any Men, high or low; and he was required to *Thou* and *Thee* every Man and Woman without Distinction, and not to bid People *Good Morrow* or *Good Evening;* neither might he bow or scrape with his Leg to any one."[486] It was furthermore "opened to him" that "Physicians, Lawyers, and Priests are generally void of that True Knowledge and Wisdom they ought to be guided by,"[487] that "Steeple-houses" are not "Churches," but are to be cried against as "idol-temples;" and that it was his calling to go about "to declare openly against all sorts of Sins," interrupting courts, market-gatherings, and especially church-services; which latter function he carried out in such a way as to make himself, to the popular thought, a common nuisance in the northern counties. As a matter of course he saw the inside of several prisons. Equally as a matter of course, he gained disciples. They called themselves "Friends," sometimes "Children of the Light," because they professed that they had in their conscience the light of Christ shining within. But the nickname of *Quakers* was soon applied to them, and has never become outworn.[488]

---

and Baptist ministers were thrust into close confinement without the ceremony of a warrant. [*Crosby*, ii: 161–164.] John James, preacher to a London congregation of Seventh-day Baptists, was imprisoned, on pretence of treason, and hanged at Tyburn 26 Nov.–6 Dec. 1661. [*Crosby*, ii: 165–171; *Ivimey*, i: 320–327; *Taylor*, i: 256–260.] From a *Narrative of the Apprehending etc. of John James, etc. 4to.* 1662, it appears that the poor man was treated with infamous barbarity. No sooner was the sentence of death passed than the tipstaff seized his cloak, and demanded payment for the use of it until the day of execution; and the day before his death the hangman came and demanded of him £20 (finally offering to take £.10) to give him an easy death, declaring he would torture him exceedingly unless he were paid; to whom James replied: "I must leave that to your mercy, for I have nothing to give you." In 1664 twelve Baptists, ten men and two women, taken at their meeting near Ailsbury, were tried and sentenced either to conform to the Church of England, or abjure the realm, and refusing to to do either, they were sentenced to death — but the king finally pardoned them. [*Crosby*, ii: 181.] As late as 1685, Elizabeth Gaunt — an Anabaptist who spent most of her time in visiting and succoring poor people — was arrested at London on a charge of treason, was condemned, and *burned* at Tyburn (23 Oct.–2 Nov.) [*Crosby*, iii: 185; *Ivimey*, i: 455; Bishop Burnet's *Hist. of his own Time*, 648.] Crosby says that, about 1670, the popular enmity rose against the Baptists so in England, that they were denied the use of the common [unconsecrated] burial places, and some, he says, "have been taken out of their graves, drawn upon a sledge to their own gates, and there left unburied!" [*Hist. Eng. Bap.* ii: 239.] And to this day no Baptist however saintly in England, alive or dead, has the same religious rights, social position, or privileges of sepulture, as he might have were he a Conformist of the most worthless character.

486 Sewel's *History of the People called Quakers, etc.* 18.

487 *Ibid*, 17.

488 "Gervas Bennet," — a Justice of the Peace, and an Independent, — "hearing that G. Fox bad him and those

The times favored rank growths in morals and religion; and, by 1654, as many as sixty of these ranting reformers were roaming up and down England, while emissaries of this "New Light" had crossed the border into Scotland, the channel to Ireland,[489] and the North Sea to Zealand and Holland, whence — ignorance of the language of the country interfering with their capacity for abusively enlightening steeple-house congregations — those who had undertaken the Dutch contract returned home, having found "but slight Entertainment there."[490] As the Quakers grew in numbers they grew also in heat, and in the capacity of making themselves intensely disagreeable to the average of decent people. Abundance of books were published by them, and against them. And some of the more extravagant — or insane — of their number, broke out into excesses, which sometimes only failed of the guilt of blasphemy by virtue of the infinite silliness that was in them. James Nayler, in 1656, entered Bristol riding on a horse led by a woman, while other attending women cast scarfs and handkerchiefs on the ground before him, the company shouting "Holy, Holy, Hosannah in the Highest,[491] etc."! One Isaac Furnier, having whittled a Doctor's title from the post of his door, "because the Spirit did testify so unto him," being asked whether, if the Spirit moved him to stab the Doctor with his knife, he should do it, answered "yes."[492] One Perrot, getting into prison at Rome, wrote letters, in which the Quakers themselves thought "some Sparks of Spiritual Pride" might be seen, which he signed "John," in "Imitation (as it seems) of the Apostle John."[493] Edward Burrough, coming into London on the 23 Nov.–3 Dec. 1658, meeting the funeral procession of Oliver Cromwell at Charing Cross, "felt such a Fire kindled in him, that he was, as it were, filled with the Indignation of the Lord, whose Fury ran through him, to cry: 'Plagues! Plagues! and Vengeance against the Authors of this Abomination!'"[494] Even the gentler sex felt the fierce frenzy, and a woman rushed past the guards one day into the Parliament House, with a pitcher in her hand, which she smashed to fragments before the Commons, shrieking: "So shall ye be broken in Pieces!"[495]

---

about him; *Tremble at the Word of the Lord!* took hold of this weighty Saying with such an airy Mind, that from thence he took Occasion to call him, and his Friends, scornfully QUAKERS. This new and unusual Denomination was taken up so eagerly, and spread so among the People, that not only the Priests there from that Time gave no other name to the Professors of the Light, but sounded it so gladly abroad that it soon ran over all England . . neighboring Countries and adjacent Kingdoms, etc." [*Ibid*, 24. See also *New England Fire Brand Quenched, etc.* i: 26.]

[489] *Ibid*, 78, 91.

[490] *Ibid*, 102.

[491] *Ibid*, 136. Fox and other Quakers considered Nayler "clouded in his understanding;" — he himself, later, became of that opinion — others thought they all were so; and, necessarily, with the masses of the people, Quakerism took the credit of the whole.

[492] *Ibid*, 133.

[493] *Ibid*, 282.

[494] *Ibid*, 187.

[495] *Ibid*, 180.

Some people fancied that these strange fanatics were Franciscan friars, in disguise;[496] and, altogether, many of the English people became stirred quite to alarm by them.

As a matter of course tidings of these things in due time crossed the Atlantic to these remote shores. They lost nothing in crossing. The colonists made up their minds that those turners of the world upside down would be coming hither also, and that such coming ought to be resisted. Franciscans in disguise or madmen without disguise, in any event, their presence would be unsavory and their influence pestilential—and, if possible, New England must be kept clear of them. By the autumn of 1654 some of the tracts of Lodowick Muggleton and John Reeves, who had acted somewhat as forerunners of Fox, and had boldly claimed to be the "last two witnesses and prophets of Jesus Christ,"[497] were found to have been shipped to Boston; and the General Court ordered them to be put to what it thought to be their best light-giving use, after the lecture, in the market place, by the executioner.[498] Twenty years had hardly yet effaced from the Massachusetts mind the grievous troubles which had been connected with Mrs. Anne Hutchinson's teachings and career; and the burned child dreaded the fire.

I have said that these tidings suffered no diminution in reaching New England. It is to be remembered, by every one who wishes fairly to weigh the conduct of our fathers, that the real question is what kind of people they thought the Quakers to be when they began to thrust themselves into the colony; even more than what kind of people these Quakers actually were. And it would be easy to show that there had come out of England stories, supposed to be authentic, which were calculated to make any community having the ordinary instincts of propriety, shrink with loathing from all threatening of Quaker contact?[499]

---

[496] Information to that effect was lodged under oath with the authorities of Bristol, Eng., 25 Jan.–5 Feb. 1654–5: "that certain Persons of the Franciscan Order in Rome, have of late come over into England, and under the Notion of Quakers, drawn together several Multitudes of People in London, etc. [*Ibid*, 85.]

[497] Spoken of in *Rev.* xi: 3. [See *Sewel*, 386; Palfrey's *Hist. N. E.* ii: 453.]

[498] *Mass. Col. Rec.* iv (1): 204.

[499] See Thomas Underhill's *Hell Broke Loose; or an History of the Quakers both Old and New*, 1660; [*passim*, but especially 6, 33, 36;] and John Wiggan's *Antichrist's strongest Hold Overturned; or, the Foundation of the Religion of the People called Quakers, Bared and Razed*, 1665; Baxter's *Quaker's Catechism, etc.*, 1656; John Faldo's *Quakerism no Christianity, etc.*, 1675; John Brown's *Quakerism the Pathway to Paganism, etc.*, 1678. Lesser known—many of them later—authorities are Schwarmgeister-Brut's *Neue, oder Hist. Erzehlung von d. Quakern, denen der Ränter, etc., etc.*, 1661; Croese's *Quaker-Historie, von deren Ursprung bis auf jüngsthin entstandene Trennung*, 1696; Feustking's *Gynaeceum Haeretico-Fanaticum, oder Historie u. Beschreib, d. falschen Prophetinnen, Quäckerinnen, etc*, 1704; and *Quäcker-Greuel; das ist, Abscheuliche Irthum der Quäcker*, 1702 [in the Boston Public Library]; *A Warning to Souls to beware of Quakers and Quakerism, etc.*, 1677; *A Brief Discovery of some of the Blasphemous and Seditious Principles and Practices of the People called*

In the spring of 1656 the General Court appointed a Fast Day, among other things, "to seeke the face of God in behalf of our native countrje in referenc to the abounding of errors, *especially those of the Raunters and Quakers, etc.*"[500] Within a month a Barbadoes vessel arrived, bringing two Quaker women. Under the alien law, which had been passed in the old Antinomian times,[501] these were sent back as soon as possible, and some books which they had brought were burned. In four or five weeks (7–17 August) another vessel arrived from England with four men and four women of this sect on board, and the matter was made more impressive by the fact that some stray idler getting on board the ship in the harbor, by the time her anchor was down, had been enrolled as a convert! On their examination before the magistrates, they used their tongues freely in "testimony;" one of the women informing two of the elders that she considered them as "hirelings, Baals, and seed of the serpent." They were kept in jail until the ship sailed on her return, when they were sent home in her.[502]

The next meeting of the Commissioners of the United Colonies was held at Plymouth, commencing on the 4–14 of the following September. The Massachusetts authorities, by a communication to them dated 2–12 of that month, among other suggestions which seemed to them to require notice, say:[503]

heere hath arived amongst vs seuerall p.sons proffessing themselues quakers, fitt Instruments to propagate the kingdome of Sathan; for the Securing of ourselues and our Naighbours from such pests wee haue Imprisoned them till they bee dispatched away to the place from whence they came, etc. [going on to urge that] some generall rules may bee alsoe comended to each Generall court to prevent the coming in amongst vs from foraigne places such Notorious heretiques as quakers, Ranters, etc.

The Commissioners, after due consideration, responded by the recommendation following, viz.:[504]

Wee doe further propose to the seuerall generall Courts that all quakers, Ranters, and other notorious heretiques bee prohibited coming into the vnited Collonies, and if any shall heerafter come or arise amongst vs, that they bee forth with cecured, or remoued out of all the Jurisdictions.

The public sentiment of the Bay Colony then fully justifying the step here proposed, at the meeting of the General Court on the 14–24 October next

---

Quakers, etc., 1699; and *Some Few of the Quaker's Many Horrid Blasphemies, Heresies, and their Bloody, Treasonable Principles, Destructive to Government, etc.*, 1699. [The last three are in the Library of the American Antiquarian Society, at Worcester.]

[500] *Mass. Col. Rec.* iv (1): 276.

[501] *Ibid*, i: 196; Winthrop's *Journal*, i: 224.

[502] Palfrey's *Hist. N. Eng.* ii: 464.

[503] *Acts of the Commissioners of the United Colonies*, ii: 156.

[504] *Ibid*, 158. Both these citations may be found also in Hazard's *Hist. Coll.* ii: 347, 349.

ensuing, a law was passed, whose terms are worth considering, for the indication which they give of the honest convictions then entertained in Massachusetts, as to the character of these persons:[505]

Whereas there is a cursed sect of hæreticks lately risen vp in the world, wch are comonly called Quakers, *who take vppon them to be imediately sent of God*, and *infallibly asisted by the Spirit* to speake & write blasphemouth opinions, *despising gouernment & the order of God in church & comonwealth*, speaking evill of dignitjes, *reproaching and revjling magistrates and ministers*, seeking to turne the people from the faith & gaine proseljtes to theire pernicious wajes, this Court, taking into serious consideration the p.mises, and *to prevent the like mischiefe as by theire meanes is wrought in our native land*, doth heereby order, etc., etc.

The provisions of this law were severe. The ship-master who should bring them was liable in £100, and to carry them back, if he could not prove his ignorance of their character. The Quaker was to be whipped, and imprisoned until his re-shipment; which was to be as speedy as possible, and he restrained from all chance of making converts during the interval. Any person importing Quaker books was liable for them in £5 apiece; and any person defending Quaker opinions, was finable — for the first offence £2, for the second £4; and, if obdurate, was to be banished. The law was intended to be so severe as to furnish an absolute preventive against the dreaded immigration. It was quite in accord, however, with the best wisdom, and the most humane temper of those times; and, as we shall see hereafter, its working was child's play compared with treatment which was meted out to the same offenders in England. The New Haven plantation passed a similar law in the following spring;[506] and even the tolerant Old Colony was moved from its usual mildness to take temporary measures against the common enemy.[507]

The great hobby of the Quakers of those days was to "testify;" which was usually accomplished by rude intrusion upon sacred places and services, with violent speech. And they seemed almost to suspect their own fidelity if they could not succeed by such "testimony" in so exasperating somebody as to receive harsh treatment in consequence. The *similia similibus curantur* principle did not prove to work well in their case, and the sterner the statutes which were made against them, the more they were stirred up to test their severity.[508]

---

505 *Mass. Col. Rec.* iv (1): 277.

506 *Rec. Col. New Haven*, ii: 217.

507 See Volume of Laws — *Rec. Plym. Col.* xi: 100. The law passed in 1657 was repealed 13 June, 1660. [*Ibid*, 101.]

508 "The Turk's method of dealing with the Quaker emissaries was the happiest. Prompted by that superstitious reverence which he was educated to pay to lunatics, as persons inspired; he received these visitors with deferential and ceremonious observance, and with a prodigious activity of genuflections and salams bowed them out of his country. They could make nothing of it, and in that quarter gave up their enterprise in despair." [Palfrey's *Hist. N. Eng.* ii: 473 (note).]

Being banished, they had "a religious concern"[509] to thrust themselves back upon the forbidden ground. Provoked by this persistent pertinacity the Colonies at last, after exhausting all milder statutes in vain,[510] on recommendation of their Commissioners[511] — of date 23 Sept.–3 Oct. 1658 — applied to the case of the Quakers that provision which since the days of Nicholas Frost (Oct. 1632) in Massachusetts,[512] and John Dawes in Connecticut,[513] had been resorted to to enforce the law of banishment; and which eleven years before had been applied to the case of Jesuits and other emissaries of Rome;[514] namely: that such banishment be "upon pajne of death," should the subject of it venture to return within the jurisdiction.[515] In every preceding case this provision had been found effectual, and not a doubt seems to have been entertained that the experience of the past would be again repeated, and that, under cover of this most emphatic testimony to the point that the New England Colonies did not desire, and did not intend to tolerate, upon the premises which with great self-denial they had secured, and settled, and which they had every legal and moral right to control, the presence of these wild enthusiasts, they would be able to live without molestation from them. The view generally taken was ably stated in a treatise prepared at the request of the Court, by John Norton, and designed "to manifest the evill of theire [the Quaker] tenets and dainger of theire practises as tending to the subvertion of religion, of church-order, & civill government, and the necessitje that this gouernment is put vpon (for the preservation of religion & theire oune peace & safety) to exclude such persons from amongst them, who, after due meanes of conviction, shall remaine obstinate & pertinatious, etc."[516]

The book was published at Cambridge in 1659, and the tenor of it may be inferred from a single sentence:[517]

> The wolf which ventures over the wide sea, out of a ravening desire to prey upon the sheep; when landed, discovered and taken, hath no cause to complain, though, for the security of the flock, he be penned up with that door opening upon the fold fast shut, but having another door purposely left open whereby he may depart at his pleasure, either returning from whence he came, or otherwise quitting the place.[518]

---

[509] Besse's *Collection of the Sufferings of the People called Quakers, etc.* ii: 181.

[510] See Statutes of Oct, 1657 and May, 1658. [*Mass. Col. Rec.* iv (1:) 308, 321.]

[511] *Acts of Com. of Unit. Col., etc.* ii: 212.

[512] See p. 16 *ante*, and *Mass. Col. Rec.* i: 100.

[513] *Pub. Rec. of Col. of Conn.* i: 242.

[514] *Mass. Col. Rec.* ii: 193; iii: 112.

[515] *Ibid*, iv (1): 346.

[516] *Ibid*, iv (1): 348.

[517] *Heart of New England Rent, etc.* 56.

[518] Francis Howgil replied to this treatise with *The Heart of New England Hardened through Wickedness;* in a characteristic spirit saying to Norton therein: "thou must not think that this poor Tract of thine, which is full of Deceit and Confusion, Error, Blasphemy and Madness; though thou publish it by the Appointment of the General Court, that it will cover your Wickedness, or hide you from being discovered to moderate People, neither will shelter you in the Day of the Lord

For a time all went well under this law. The first six Quakers apprehended under it, were Laurence and Cassandra Southwick, Josiah, their son, Samuel Shattuck, Nicholas Phelps and Joshua Buffum, all of Salem;[519] and being banished they came not again. Then followed others who imagined themselves "moved of the Lord" to enter the Massachusetts Colony, and "constrained in the Love and Power of the Lord, not to depart, but to stay in the Jurisdiction, and to try the bloody Law unto Death."[520] William Robinson, Marmaduke Stevenson, and Mary Dyer were first tried, convicted, and sentenced, "for rebelljon, sedition & presumtuous obtruding themselves vpon vs, not wthstanding theire being sentenced to banishment on pajne of death, etc.,"[521] and neither party flinching, the two men were hanged; the woman being persuaded at the last moment — "finding nothing from the Lord to the contrary"[522] — to accept of the deliverance offered, if she would depart to Rhode Island from whence she came. When the worst thus came to the worst, the people scarcely sustained the government; which felt itself called upon to make appeal to its constituency, in which — insisting that it desired the Quakers' "life absent rather then theire death present" — it recapitulated with succinct force the legal aspects of the matter, fully demonstrating the lawfulness of what had been done, and making out a strong case in defence of the position that "Christ and his saints were led by one spirit, and those people by another; for rather then they would not shew theire contempt of authoritje, and make disturbance amongst his people, they choose to goe contrary to the expresse directions of Jesus Christ, & the approoved examples of his saints, although it be to the hazard & perrill of their oune liues;"[523] yet, withal, conspicuously failing to demonstrate also either the wisdom, or the humanity, of their course.

Mary Dyer could not be easy. Where she spent the winter is not known, except that she was not in her proper place with her husband and children, at Newport.[524] Could she have felt "a motion of the Lord upon her spirit" to attend to His Word as it is revealed in such passages of the Scripture, as that which commands believers to study to be quiet and to do their own business;[525] and especially that which ordains that women be discreet, chaste, keepers at home, good, obedient to their own husbands;[526] in place of mistaking the crude

. . . neither all this Covering which thou hast made will not vindicate your wicked Practices, nor shelter you from the Storms, and Thunders, and Plagues, and Terror, and Wrath, which is to be poured out, etc." [*Works*, 321, 323.]

[519] Bishop's *New England Judged, etc.* (1661), 79; [ed. 1703, 100.]

[520] *Ibid*, 95. [ed. 1703, 114.] See also Besse's *Collection, etc.* ii: 198–220, and *Sewel*, 219–227, 263–269.

[521] *Mass. Col. Rec.* iv (1): 383.

[522] Mary Dyer's Letter to the Court. Besse's *Collection, etc.* ii: 205.

[523] *Mass. Col. Rec.* iv (1): 386, 390.

[524] "I have not seen her above this half-year." *Letter* of William Dyer to Gov. Endecott, 27 May, 1660; cited by Palfrey. [*Hist. N. Eng.* ii: 479.]

[525] 1 Thess. iv: 11.

[526] Tit. ii: 5.

fancies of her own heated imagination for the voice from heaven, she might have filled out a useful life, and slept in peace by the side of her kindred. But when the May flowers bloomed again, her restless spirit led her stealthily by forest by-paths back to Boston, and to a fate which with as just, as somber, a pathos her husband characterized as one: "for I know not what end, or to what purpose."[527] If her own interior intent had been, however, to make an unpopular enactment still more unpopular by illustrating the terrors of its severity, there can be no doubt that she succeeded in the same. For a time various expedients were resorted to, to get round the terrible law without more blood.[528]

But there was to be another sufferer. William Leddra, who had been banished, "was under such necessity of Conscience that he could not forbear returning thither."[529] He was tried, and, as there was no conceivable reason under the law as it was, why he should not be, he was found guilty. He was offered life and freedom if he would go away; but his answer was: "to make you a promise I cannot."[530] The issue was too square to be evaded, and this fourth poor enthusiast was hanged. But it was the last of these deplorable executions. Winlock Christison was at the same time awaiting his fate in Boston jail, but his courage failed, and he wrote to the Court his promise: "that, if I may have my libarty, I have freedome to depart this Jurisdiction; and I know not y^t^ ever I shall com into it any more."[531] So great was, by this time, the division of feeling in the government itself, and so decided the popular disapproval of their course, that, in any event, his life would have been spared, and his submission was useful only to break the fall of the magistrates. The General Court which was in session; "being desirous to try all meanes wth as much lenity as may consist with our safety, to prevent the intrusions of the Quakers, etc," hastened to make large alteration in the law, with the purpose of substituting milder penalties for that of death; only nominally retaining that, if, after three trials, the court should "judge not meete to release them."[532] But no enforcement of the severities of the new statute ever took place. This mildness was the sober second thought of the Government, and its cheerful concession to the will of the

---

527 William Dyer's *Letter*, as above.

528 *Mass. Col. Rec.* iv (1): 419, 433.

529 Sewel's *History, etc.* 263.

530 *Ibid*, 266. See also concerning his case, Besse's *Collection, etc.* ii: 213–220; Bishop's *New England Judged, etc.* 154, ii: 11, [ed. 1703,] 64, 313, 326.

531 *Mass. Archives*, x: 273. Hutchinson recognizes this paper. [*Hist. Mass.* (ed. 1795) i: 186.] The Quaker historians were evidently unaware that the archives of the enemy contained this proof positive, in his own hand-writing, that Christison showed the white feather; for they unite in representing him as "resting in sweet peace and quietness," in view of his approaching doom — as continuing "in Faith and Patience, ready to abide the good Pleasure of God concerning him, and to suffer Death for a good Conscience, as his Brethren had done before him," with more which is even more violently inconsistent with the actual facts. His release they attribute to "some Intelligence from London." [Bishop's *New England Judged*, ii: 35 (ed. 1703, 340); Sewel's *History, etc.* 271; Besse's *Coll. etc.* ii: 223.]

532 *Mass. Col. Rec.* iv (2): 2, 3.

people; and not its sullen submission to the *mandamus* of Charles the Second — as it has been the fashion to allege.[533] The document so called was not given at Whitehall until 9–19 September, 1661, and was not served upon the Governor at Boston until more than six weeks after that date[534] — or more than six months subsequent to the enactment of the new law, and the clear adoption of the more humane policy.

If it were a trial to some of the best men of the Colony to be driven to this letting-down, in which they did not — with their light — believe;[535] it must have been, on the other hand, both a chagrin and a solicitude to the prominent advocates of the new policy, that the Quakers seemed for some time after to be more than ever filled with the spirit of disorder. Every person who fancied that it might be a fine thing to be a disciple of the terrible "man in leathern breeches,"[536] seems, all at once, to have put on airs and "testified." These new lights were particularly hard on the ministers of religion. They always called them "Priests," generally with one or more unfriendly or scurrilous adjectives. "Dark Priests," "Wicked Priests," "Blockish Priests," "Blasphemous Priests," "Oppressive Priests," "Priest-tories," "Hireling Priests," "Notorious Thieves and Robbers," "Savage Brutes," "Develish Priests" — are a few of the elegant and charitable references which one finds thickly scattered through the pages of Bishop, Fox, Howgil and Burnyeat, and their compeers, and applied to those humble and self-denying men who had brought the old truths of God dear to the church in every age, into this wilderness, and were patiently trying to prepare here the way of the Lord. They thrust themselves into private houses, and "warned" their tenants.[537] They wrote vituperative letters to people.[538] They had "a burden of the Lord" to post up wrathful,

---

[533] "procured a *Mandamus* from that Monarch, by which an effectual Stop was put to the Proceedings in New England of putting Men to Death for Religion, by which their blind Zeal and Fury would otherwise probably have destroyed many innocent People." [*Besse*, i: xxxii.]

[534] Sewel's *History, etc.* 273. Bishop's *New Eng. Judged, etc.* ii: 38 [ed. 1703, 344.] *Palfrey*, ii: 520.

[535] Bishop says: "Then said your Governour [Endecott] after they [the Court] had voted once [in Christison's case] and some of them would not consent, 'I could find in my heart' (such a thirst had he after the blood of the Innocent) 'to go home,' being in a great rage; and so misbehaved himself on the Seat of Judgement, that he furiously flung something on the Table, etc." [*Ibid*, ii: 34 (ed. 1703, 339).]

[536] Geo. Fox's *Journal*, 55. "It was a dreadful thing to them [the Priests] when it was told them 'The man in leathern breeches [Geo. Fox himself] is come.'"

[537] Two Quaker women did this to Roger Williams. "They bid me," he says, "Repent and Hearken to the Light within me. [As if Roger had ever been noticeably lacking in that grace!] I prayd them to sit down, that we might quietly reason together; they would not; then standing, I askt them the ground of their such Travel and Employment; they alledged *Ioels Prophesie*; I answered, that was fulfilled, that was not everydayes work; besides their business was not Prophetical but Apostolical, &c. They regarded not my Answers nor Admonitions, but powred the Curses and Judgements of God against me, and hurried away." [*Geo. Fox Digg'd, etc. Apendix, etc.* 27.]

[538] See one of John Smith's to Gov. Endecott, [*Bishop*, ii: 124; (ed. 1703) 445]; another of Mary Trask and

scolding, and impudent documents in the market-places.[539] And, not satisfied with anything short of actual disturbance of the public peace, in many, even of the remote country towns, these people on the Lord's Day, and in time of religious worship, invaded the "steeple-houses" — few of which, to be sure, then afforded steeples — and, with immovable hats on their infatuated heads, broke up the service by clamorously announcing that such exercises were an abomination to the Lord.[540] Some of them devoted themselves to travelling from town to town, "being moved" to "visit the Seed of God in those parts."[541] George Wilson rushed through the streets of Boston shouting: "The Lord is coming with fire and sword!"[542] Thomas Newhouse "gave a sign" in the Boston meeting-house, carrying two glass bottles in his hands; which, doubtless in imitation of the London woman in the Parliament House,[543] he dashed together, by way of emphasizing his bawl: "So shall ye be broken in Pieces!"[544] Edward Wharton was "pressed in spirit" to repair to Dover and proclaim "Wo, Vengeance and the Indignation of the Lord" upon the Court in session there.[545] John Liddal wandered as far as Flatbush, with his half insane cry: "Turn; turn; from your evil wayes."[546]

In this thing the women quite outdid the men. Elizabeth Hooton promenaded the streets of Cambridge, and subsequently those of Boston, shrieking: "Repentance! Repentance! A day of Howling, and Sad Lamentation is coming upon you all from the Lord!"[547] Mary Tompkins, on the First Day of the week at Oyster River, broke up the service of God's house by "declaring the Truth [that is to say, freeing her mind] to the People;" the scene ending in deplorable confusion.[548] Hannah Wright, a mere girl of less than fifteen summers, toiled "in the motion of the Lord" from Oyster Bay, L. I., through all the long hard journey to Boston, that she might pipe in the ears of the Court: "a Warning in the Name of the Lord."[549] Catherine Chatham exhibited herself in the streets of Boston "under a great Exercise and Concern of Mind" clad in sackcloth, "as a sign of the Indignation of the Lord against that oppressing and tyrannical Spirit which bore Rule in the Magistracy of that Place."[550]

Margaret Smith to the same [*Ibid*, ii: 130, (ed. 1703) 453]; and one of George Keith to the Ministers of Boston. [*Pres. & Ind. Vis. Churches in N. Eng. and Elsewhere, Brought to the Test, etc.* 204.]

539 See Geo. Keith's "Call and Warning from the Lord, to the People of Boston, and New England, to Repent, etc.," which was "set up in the most publick place in the Town of Boston, the 21st of the 4th Month [21 June–1 July] 1688." [*Ibid*, 195.]

540 Hutchinson's *Hist. Mass.* (ed. 1795) i: 187; *Bishop*, ii: 50, 144; (ed. 1703) 354, 471.

541 *Bishop*, ii: 87; (ed. 1703) 400. Besse's *Collection, etc.* ii: 227.

542 *Bishop*, ii: 46; (ed. 1703) 351.

543 See p. 125 *ante*.

544 *Bishop*, ii: 113; (ed. 1703) 431.

545 *Ibid*, ii: 108; (ed. 1703) 425.

546 *Ibid*, ii: 107; (ed. 1703) 424.

547 *Ibid*, ii: 98, 103; (ed. 1703) 414, 418, A, 191.

548 *Ibid*, ii: 76; (ed. 1703) 386.

549 *Ibid*, ii: 136; (ed. 1703) 461.

550 *Ibid*, ii: 104; (ed. 1703) 420; *Besse*, ii: 231.

Margaret Brewster improved upon this. She went, in 1677, in time of public service into "Thatcher's meeting" [the Old South] in Boston on Sunday, "in Sackcloth, with Ashes upon her Head, and barefoot, and her Face blacked," and, with three other women and a man, made "a horrible Disturbance," so affrighting some delicate females who were present as to endanger their serious illness; her call to do so being that "she was constrained in a prophetick Manner" to warn the people that she "had a Foresight given her of that grievous Calamity called the Black-Pox."[551]

This was bad enough. But there was a lower depth. About five years after the last Quaker execution, and the adoption of a humaner policy, Mrs. Lydia Wardell found herself "under a Duty and Concern" of marching stark naked up and down the aisles of the church in Newbury, in time of public Sabbath service, in consideration of their miserable condition — as "a sign." The Quaker historian, with sweet simplicity, describes the result, as follows: "This she performed, but they, instead of religiously reflecting on their own Condition, which she came in that Manner to represent to them, fell into a Rage, and presently laid Hands on her, and hurried her away to the Court at Ipswich, which was held at a Tavern in that Town."[552] Not long after, Deborah Wilson, "being a young woman of a very modest and retired Life, and of sober Conversation," imagined herself inspired of the Lord to perambulate the streets of Salem in utter nakedness, as symbolizing the "naked truth" to a wicked and corrupt generation.[553] Having, "in part, performed some part thereof as aforesaid, she was soon laid hands on," and dealt with by the magistrates for her indecent exposure.[554]

It is a remarkable fact that not a word of censure — not even so much as any hint of concession that these crack-brained zealots might possibly have been mistaken in their apprehensions of duty — escapes the principal Quaker writers in their reference to these sickening exhibitions; while it seems difficult for them to find language strong enough to express their horror of the "cruelty" which, in the interest of public decency, sought to repress such excesses.[555] Indeed,

[551] *Ibid* (ed. 1703) 491; A, 103; *Besse*, ii: 260.

[552] *Ibid*, ii: 69; (ed. 1703) 376; *Besse*, ii: 235.

[553] The careful reader will be struck at several points with the remarkable resemblance between these Quaker outrages upon decency and propriety, and those of the Anabaptists of the century before. These wretched females copied the frenzy of the followers of the tailor of Amsterdam [see p. 114 *ante*]; while the shouts of many, in the churches and the streets, almost literally reproduced the *Vae! vae! vae! divina Vindicta! divina Vindicta! divina Vindicta!* of those miserable dupes.

[554] *Bishop*, ii: 74; (ed. 1703) 383; *Besse*, ii: 236.

[555] It will be noticed that I have cited Quaker witnesses altogether, in proof of the above shameful occurrences. Bishop calls the authorities who dealt with Lydia Wardell "unreasonable bruit beasts, whose name shall rot, and their memory perish" [ii: 69; (ed. 1703) 377]; and says the treatment of Deborah Wilson was "a savage cruelty seldom heard of, as it was most barbarous injustice," done by "Wicked Rulers." [*Ibid*, ii: 74 (ed. 1703) 383]. Besse says: "this cruel sentence was publickly executed on a Woman of exemplary Virtue and unspotted Chastity, *for her Obedience to what she believed the Spirit of the Lord had enjoined her to do.*" [ii: 235.]

when, in the great debate at Newport in August 1672, between Roger Williams and the Quakers, he made a strong and telling point against them of "their stripping stark naked their Men, and Women, and Maidens, and passing along in publick places and Streets unto the Assemblyes of Men and Youths, and so were beheld and gazed upon by them! And this under a pretence of being stirred up by God as a Service or Worship unto God, as an act of Christian Religion proceeding from the immediate moving of the most holy Spirit of God, most glorious in purity, and purity and holiness it self;" they undertook first to deny that any of their women had ever thus transgressed, and when confuted as to this by Mr. Williams's citing out of their own *Bishop* the two cases above referred to, they finally settled down upon the conclusion that: "if the Lord God so commanded his Sons and Daughters, it must be obeyed!"[556]

Perhaps the most revolting occurrence connected with this passage in New England history, is one related by Increase Mather. He says:[557]

> I think myself bound to acquaint the world, that not many moneths ago, [his book was published in 1684] a man, passing under the name of Jonathan Dunen [Dunham] (*alias* Singleterry) a singing Quaker, drew away the wife of one of Marshfield to follow him; also one Mary Ross, falling into their company, was quickly possessed with the devil, playing such frentick and diabolical tricks as the like hath seldom been known or heard of; for she made herself naked, burning all her clothes, and, with infinite blasphemy, said she was Christ, and gave names to her Apostles, calling Dunen by the name of Peter, another by the name of Thomas; declaring that she would be dead for three dayes, and then rise again; and, accordingly, seemed to die. And while she was pretendedly dead, her Apostle Dunen gave out that they should see glorious things after her resurrection; but that which she then did was, she commanded Dunen to sacrifice a dog. The man and the two women Quakers danced naked together, having nothing but their shirts on. The constable brought them before the magistrates in Plimouth, where Ross uttered such prodigious blasphemy as is not fit to be mentioned; Dunen fell down like a dead man upon the floor, and so lay for about an hour, and then came to himself. The magistrates demanding the reason of his strange actings, his answer was, that Mary Ross bid him, and he had no power to resist.[558]

It is to be conceded that the better sort of the new sect by this time had begun to repudiate excesses like these last of Dunham and his crew;[559] but it was inevitable that the sober portion of the population of New England should find

---

556 *Geo. Fox Digg'd, etc.* 38–40.

557 *An Essay for the Recording of Illustrious Providences, etc.* [Russell Smith's reprint, 1856] 244.

558 Plymouth Records endorse the general fidelity of the above narration. The hearing before the magistrates was in July 1683. The dog belonged to John Irish, of Little Compton, R. I., and was slaughtered and thrown upon "a fier in the said house, against the declared will of the said Irish." Jonathan Dunen [Dunham] was "centanced to be publickly whipt att the post," and ordered out of the jurisdiction, and was further condemned to be "soe serued as oft as hee shall vnessesaryly returne into it to deseminate his corupt principles." [*Plym. Col. Rec.* vi: 113.]

559 See especially George Keith's *The Presbyterian and Independent Visible Churches in New England, and else-where, Brought to the Test, etc., With a Call and Warning, etc., to Repent, etc.* (1691), 215.

it difficult to draw the line between "Old" and "New Quakers," and should be slow to see in any who passed under that name, the qualities which create and adorn reputable and estimable citizenship.

Three thoughts suggest themselves after this glance at such facts.

1. It is easier to find fault with our fathers in this, as in some other matters, than to put ourselves in their place, and declare, with confidence, how we should have improved upon their methods. To have thrown open the plantation to free Quaker ingress, with England in the condition in which it then was, would have been to have invited the influx of an unmanageable, overwhelming and disastrous host, and must have been tantamount to the surrender at once of all those peculiar ideas and cherished purposes, the attempt to attain and develop which for themselves, and their offspring, had inspired, sustained and sweetened their difficult enterprise. To keep it shut against such immigrants was what they undertook, by processes which would have availed with reasonable men, and with any unreasonable men short of the exceptional zealots with whom they were compelled to deal. They surely had the right to put Quakers outside their jurisdiction, and to do their best to keep them there.[560] They had found the sentence of banishment " on pajne of death " if violated, effectual in all previous cases; and the government had no reason to suppose it would not prove effectual in this case, until it found itself confronting William Robinson and Marmaduke Stevenson with halters round their necks. Doubtless it should then have relented — since they would not. But that had not been the New England way; nor was it any where the temper of those times. Barrow and Greenwood and Penry had been hanged in England, avowing their loyalty to the Queen with their last breath, purely and simply for their religious faith;[561] while these men added to the most serious offence in doctrine, most flat defiance of the State. Doubtless in that supreme moment when Mary Dyer was spared, "vpon an inconsiderable intercession,"[562] it would have been the wisest policy to have spared the others also; but if in this enlightened day there be any son of those Puritans who in the most exigent crises of his own affairs, has never failed to adopt that course which his own afterthought, not merely, but the afterthought of seven generations, could endorse as the best possible — let *him* cast the first stone at the memory of the fathers for their offence.[563]

---

[560] See the discussion of the right of the Colony to control its membership, with reference to the case of Roger Williams, p. 17 *ante*. See further the suggestions on pp. 80, 81 *ante*.

[561] Waddington's *Congregational History*, ii: 79, 91.

[562] *Mass. Col. Rec.* iv (1): 386.

[563] Dr. Palfrey sums up his clear and candid account of the matter thus: "No householder has a more unqualified title to declare who shall have the shelter of his roof, than had the Governor and Company of Massachusetts Bay to decide who should be sojourners or visitors within their precincts. Their danger was real, though the experiment proved it to be far less than was at first supposed. The provocations which were offered

2. As it was, the Quakers suffered lightly in New England as compared with their experience in the mother-country. Joseph Besse, in 1753, published in two folio volumes an elaborate account, apparently founded upon most patient and extended research, of the sufferings which "the People called Quakers" had been called to undergo "for the testimony of a good conscience."[564] His statistics, and his detailed narratives, cover all the countries into which Quakers had wandered.

He has gathered together *one hundred and seventy* (170) instances of what he conceives to have been various hard usage of the Quakers in New England; *four* having been hanged, *twenty-two* banished on pain of death, and *twenty-five* banished on pain of lesser penalties.[565]

At the same time he gives — to a greater or less extent — the particulars of *thirteen thousand two hundred and fifty-eight* (13,258) instances of the contemporaneous persecution of Quakers in England, Scotland and Ireland.[566] *Two hundred and nineteen* (219), were sentenced to banishment in one lot from Bristol.[567] *Three hundred and sixty* (360) suffered death — not by hanging, but by prison hardships, and in other ways bitterly known to all who for any reason in those days came under the ban of the State.[568] Many were carried off by prison fevers,[569] and the like distempers. Some almost literally rotted in jail, in a confinement extending to eight and ten years, before death brought relief."[570]

Hundreds of those who did not absolutely perish in close confinement, came near to death in consequence of the shocking privations which they were compelled to endure.[571] Some who were in extreme old age, and even totally blind, were mercilessly imprisoned, simply for being found in attendance at a Quaker meeting.[572] Some were cast into the midst of convicted felons, who robbed and abused them.[573] Seven were, on one occasion, in Merionethshire, kept confined ten weeks in an uncleansed hog-sty, with the normal occupants all that time noisily seeking repossession, and the frequent rain drenching them through the shabby roof.[574]

---

were exceedingly offensive. It is hard to say what should have been done with disturbers so unmanageable. But that one thing should not have been done till they had become more mischievous, is plain enough. They should not have been put to death. Sooner than put them to death, it were devoutly to be wished that the annoyed dwellers in Massachusetts had opened their hospitable drawing-rooms to naked women, and suffered their ministers to ascend the pulpits by steps paved with fragments of glass bottles." [*History New England*, ii: 485.]

564 *A Collection of the Sufferings of the People called Quakers, etc.*, from 1650 to 1689. London. 2 vols. fol. (pp. lv, 767, 648).

565 *Ibid*, i: xxx; ii: 624–626.

566 *Ibid*, ii: 539–624.

567 *Ibid*, i: 51; ii: 637.

568 *Ibid*, ii: 634–636.

569 *Ibid*, i: 533, 690; ii: 108.

570 *Ibid*, i: 609, 642, 644.

571 *Ibid*, i: 682, 745.

572 *Ibid*, i: 686.

573 *Ibid*, i: 690, 692.

574 *Ibid*, i: 746.

One cannot wonder that Francis Howgil should have spoken to the English nation a "Warning" even sharper than those which he dispensed to New England; saying of the Quakers:[575]

They have been as for a Prey, and for a Spoil unto all, and unreasonable Men have plowed long Furrows upon their Backs, and they have had no Helper in the Earth; but, on the contrary, every one hath lent his Hand to bow them down, and tread upon them as Ashes under the Soles of their Feet, and yet no Evil to lay to their Charge. . . Therefore O Nation, consider and take this one Warning more, that thou proceed not further to thy Hurt, and thou repent when it is too late.

I repeat the expression of my conviction that it is not a reasonable demand from any man, that the first settlers of New England be condemned as lacking in all that was fairly to be expected of them, if they did not at once out-measure the mother-country in the scope of their charity, or the breadth and largeness of their public spirit. And I am quite willing that their treatment of both Baptists and Quakers be compared, in all the details which history has preserved, with that received by those persons in England, and in London itself; confident that the more extended the investigation, the more triumphant will the vindication of the Puritans be made.

3. Nor is it possible to forget that there is a constant exposure to erroneous conclusions on such a subject as this, by means of the almost inevitable coloring which is thrown back upon the past from the associations of the present. The Baptists of our day are quiet and well-behaved persons, comparing favorably in spiritual attainments and usefulness, in general culture, and in special cases of scholastic eminence, with any other denomination of Christians known to the nineteenth century. While the broad-brimmed, and drab-clad Quaker of our time has such marked preëminence in all the peaceful and thrifty virtues, as to make it almost impossible for us to think that any person bearing his distinguishing name, could ever have been other than a benediction among his fellows.

But the simple, inexorable, fact of history remains, that the Quaker of the seventeenth century — and it is a very curious study to mark in how many points the Baptists of that day resembled the Quakers[576] (and it might be one still more curious to philosophize upon it) — was essentially a coarse, blustering, conceited, disagreeable, impudent fanatic; whose religion gained subjective

[575] *The Dawnings of the Gospel-Day, etc.* (1676) 342. Howgil had published, in 1659, *The Popish Inquisition Newly Erected in New England, etc.*, and also *The Heart of New England Hardned, etc.*, in answer to John Norton's "Heart of New England Rent," etc.

[576] See this subject briefly, but very suggestively, handled by Prof. Diman in his Introduction to the edition published in 1872, by the Narragansett Club, of Williams's *Geo. Fox Digg'd out of his Burrowes, etc.* [*Pub. Nar. Club*, v: viii, ix.]

comfort in exact proportion to the objective comfort of which it was able to deprive others; and which broke out into its choicest exhibitions in acts which were not only at that time in the nature of a public scandal and nuisance, but which even in the brightest light of this nineteenth century, and in those lands where freedom of conscience has gained its most illustrious triumphs, would subject those who should be guilty of them to the immediate and stringent attention of the Police Court. The disturbance of public Sabbath worship, and the indecent exposure of the person — whether conscience be pleaded for them, or not — are punished, and rightly punished, as crimes by every civilized government.

Those men, whom Roger Williams knew as "Pragmatical and Insulting Souls," "Bundles of Ignorance and Boisterousness," with "a Face of Brass, and a Tongue set on fire from the Hell of Lyes and Fury;" and to argue against whom — at the age, it would seem, of more than three-score and ten — he rowed "with his old bones" from Providence to Newport[577] up to midnight before the appointed morning of discussion; were as unlike the sleek, benignant Friends, whom all people now take pleasure in knowing, as the wild Texas steer, maddened by the fever-torture of thirst and the goading torment of the jolt and clatter of a cattle-train; broken loose and tearing terribly through crowded city streets — tossing children, trampling women, and making dangerous confusion thrice confounded everywhere, until calmed by some policeman's rifle — is unlike the meek-eyed and patient ox which leans obedient to the yoke, as with steadfast step he draws the straight dark furrow behind him, along which, by and by, the harvest of autumn is sweetly to smile.

This, then, is the conclusion of the whole matter. Our fathers, if they were better in many things than Englishmen of their day who did not help to colonize New England; made no pretence to be such — surely made none to excel their generation in their theory of liberty of conscience. They came here to secure that freedom for themselves, which they would much have preferred to enjoy at home, but could not there attain. They never dreamed that they were settling the Bay in order to afford harbor for all sorts of persons who could not live comfortably elsewhere. They were settling it for themselves; for those who thought essentially as they did; and for their children after them. Having bought and paid for it; and exiled themselves and variously suffered for it; and knowing that before the bar of God and the tribunals of man, they had indefeasible right to it; they wanted that territory to themselves, for their own use. The world was all before others where to choose. There was land enough

---

[577] *Geo. Fox Digg'd, etc.* 24, 63, etc.; see also *Pub.* | *Nar. Club*, v: xxix–xxxviii.

lying waste in the outreaching wilderness, for a hundred Baptist and Quaker colonies. And surely it was not an unnatural, nor, under the circumstances, an inhospitable, desire, that these alien elements should go elsewhere. The Puritans did what they could to make them go. They failed. Probably they submitted to the inevitable with as good a grace as any of their children — or any of this generation who are the children of wiser, or weaker, men — could have taught them to do. They did not at once outgrow their past, or their present; but they never undertook, nor claimed, to do so. And if Massachusetts as Colony, and Commonwealth, failed to abolish all lingering union between Church and State until within the memory of the middle-aged men of to-day; there is this to be said about it, that it is by no means sure that any middle-aged man of to-day will live long enough to see the mother-country — to say nothing of the rest of the world — stand, on this question, where the Bay State has been standing for more than the last forty years.

They held no abstract theory about liberty of conscience. Few men of their generation really did that in the modern sense; being quite contented with a doctrine on that subject which would assure their own personal liberty of thought and action.[578] And they never "persecuted" either Baptists or Quakers, for differing with them. This point was made clear by an eminent New England jurist, when he said:[579]

> A man persecutes nobody, by defending his own from encroachment. The lands within their chartered limits were theirs. The government was theirs. The faith and modes of worship were theirs. Under their grant from the Council at Plymouth, and their Charter from the Crown, they secured to themselves, as we have seen, substantially a fee-simple in their lands, which they could protect against all encroachments. They endeavored to secure to themselves, also, a theologic fee-simple so to speak, or at least a life-estate, and they were exceedingly tenacious of this, and more sensitive to trespasses upon it than to trespasses upon property, in the proportion that the concerns of religion held a higher place in their estimation than mere temporal affairs. There was little temptation to commit trespasses upon their temporal fee. But there were other zealots besides themselves, who were quite desirous of becoming tenants in common, at least, if not disseizors, of their ecclesiastical fee. The attempt was promptly met, first by warning off; and when that failed, by an ecclesiastical action of trespass, resulting in a fine; and when that failed, by a process of ejectment, called a sentence of banishment.

The New England men while they lived, only asked fair and just treatment.

---

[578] This is the way the Romanists pleaded for Liberty of Conscience in England: "Since there must be Heresies, and our judgments are as different as our Faces; since breeding and education doth so much sway, and hath so great influence on many Religions; and that Sectaries are grown numerous; we ought to have a Latitude of Charity for those that dissent, *if they be not Impostors or turbulent Incendiaries.*" [*The Advocate of Conscience Liberty, or an Apology for Toleration Rightly Stated, etc.* (1673.) 52.]

[579] Hon. Joel Parker, *Lowell Lectures by Members Mass. Hist. Soc.* 418. The extract on the next page [141] is from Rev. Dr. Ray Palmer's Poem entitled "Home." [*Poetical Works*, 138.]

They ought to have it now that they are dead. And they ought to have it from their own. The man who to-day rejoices in this rich heritage of their bequeathment, owes it to common honesty to form upon the facts of the case an intelligent and candid opinion, as to the real character of the first settlers of Massachusetts. It is a much less difficult task to abuse them on hearsay, than it is to imitate their virtues. As sings one of their sons:

Not faultless were they, else were they not men;
Yet less their own the faults than of their time;
Of times long past, when many an error reigned
As yet unchallenged, blinding all alike
To truths since seen as in the midday blaze.
Beyond their fellows, keenly had they pierced
Error's thick-veiling mists, and Truth discerned
In her diviner forms; aside had flung
Falsehoods long honored, maxims cherished long,
That mighty ills had wrought; the good, the right,
In their great hearts they worshiped; these they sought,
As misers search for gold, with deathless love;
Clung to them found, as with the grasp of fate!
What if perchance from ardor so intense
Of quenchless earnestness, their zeal o'erglowed
At times, and they — their vision not yet clear —
There erred where all the world had erred till then?
Ah! ye who meanly seek to tear away
The honors thickly clustered round their brows,
Yours, yours the lack of heavenly charity
Ye charge on them; yours with far less defence!
On you returned at last shall rest the shame;
And as the sun from the clear mirror wipes
The envious vapor that its luster dimmed,
Just Time their names to honor shall restore.

CHRONOLOGICAL TABLE OF EVENTS.

[*Dates not exactly identified are marked with a dash.*]

Day of wk.	Month. Old Style.	Month. New Style.	Year.	Event.	Page.
—	—	—	1599 } 1603 }	Roger Williams born, probably in Wales	3
Th.	11 Apr.	21 Apr.	1611	Edward Wightman burned as an Anabaptist in England . .	123
F.	3 Nov.	13 Nov.	1620	King James's Patent to Council for New England	9
M.	25 June	5 July	1621	R. W. elected Scholar at Sutton's Hospital	2
W.	1 Jan.	11 Jan.	1623–4	Patent sold by Ld. Sheffield to Cushman, Winslow, etc. . .	9
F.	9 July	19 July	1624	R. W. obtained an exhibition at Charter House	2
Th.	7 July	17 July	1625	R. W. matriculated at Pembroke Coll. Cambridge	2
—	— Jan.	—	1626–7	R. W. took degree of B. A. there	2
—	—	—	1627	R. W. probably beneficed in Lincolnshire	3
T.	4 Mar.	14 Mar.	1628–9	New grant and confirmation of Charter by Charles I. . . .	9
Th.	30 April	10 May	1629	Act of Company authorizing Endecott to form a gov^{t}. at Salem	12
—	Summer.	—	"	Endecott sends home the Brownes	14
W.	26 Aug.	5 Sept.	"	"Agreement" signed by Winthrop and others	12
T.	10 Feb.	20 Feb.	1629–30	Gen. Court of Company in London approves Endecott's course	16
M.	23 Aug.	2 Sept.	1630	First meeting of Company on N. E. soil, at Charlestown. Process issued against T. Morton	13
T.	7 Sept.	17 Sept.	"	Court-order in case of T. Morton	14
T.	28 Sept.	8 Oct.	"	Order to T. Gray to remove beyond the jurisdiction	14
T.	19 Oct.	29 Oct.	"	*Another* Roger Williams (of Dorchester) applies to be freeman	28
Th.	11 Nov.	21 Nov.	"	Two gentlemen refused permission to settle without "testimony"	17
W.	1 Dec.	11 Dec.	"	R. W. and wife sail in the Lyon from Bristol for Boston	3
F.	5 Feb.	15 Feb.	1630–1	Lyon arrives off Nantasket	3
M.	1 Mar.	11 Mar.	"	Seven common folks, with Sir Chris. Gardiner, "banished"	14
—	—	—	"	R. W. invited to be Teacher to the Boston Church, and declines	4
T.	12 April	22 Apr.	1631	Letter from Winthrop and others to Endecott at Salem about R. W.	4
T.	3 May	13 May	"	T. Walford and wife ordered beyond the jurisdiction . . .	14
W.	18 May	28 May	"	The *other* Roger Williams takes the Freeman's oath . . .	28
T.	14 June	24 June	"	Ratcliffe ordered beyond the jurisdiction	14
T.	6 Sept.	16 Sept.	"	Lynn ordered beyond the jurisdiction	14
T.	27 Sept.	7 Oct.	"	Court-order in case of Plaistow	19
—	—	—	"	R. W. goes from Salem to Plymouth	5
M.	3 Oct.	13 Oct.	1632	Nich. Frost ordered away on pain of death, should he return	16
—	— Oct.	—	"	Visit of Winthrop and Wilson to Plymouth over Sabbath .	6
—	—	—	"	R. W. studies Algonkin, and fraternizes with the Indians .	6
—	—	—	—	His eldest child born at Plymouth	7
—	— Jan.	—	1632–3	Sir Christopher Gardiner, and others, petition the king against the Colony	21

Day of wk.	Month. Old Style.	Month. New Style.	Year.	EVENT.	Page.
——	Summer.	——	1633	R. W. removes to Salem, assisting Mr. Skelton, "but not in office"	7
T.	3 Sept.	13 Sept.	"	Capt. Stone ordered off under penalty of death	16
——	— Nov.	——	1633	R. W. and Mr. Skelton object to ministers' meetings	26
F.	27 Dec.	6 Jan.	1633–4	Court takes action about R. W.'s "treatise"	27
Th.	3 Jan.	13 Jan.	"	Winthrop writes to Endecott about R. W.	27
Th.	24 Jan.	3 Feb.	"	Court met about R. W.'s "treatise," and he promises submission	29
——	— Feb.	——	"	Order in Council detaining ships for N. E. and demanding the Charter	21
Th.	21 Feb.	3 Mar.	"	Cradock replies to Council that the Charter is gone to Mass.	13
Th.	7 Mar.	17 Mar.	"	Troubles about women's veils at Boston, etc.	31
M.	28 Apr.	8 May	1634	Commission granted to regulate Plantations, etc.	22
——	— July	——	"	Magistrates decline to surrender Charter till Court meets	22
S.	2 Aug.	12 Aug.	"	Mr. Skelton dies at Salem	36
M.	4 Aug.	14 Aug.	"	Jeffery shows Gov. Winthrop T. Morton's exultant letter	22
W.	3 Sept.	13 Sept.	"	Court meets, keeps quiet about Charter, and begins fortifying	22
W.	17 Sept.	27 Sept.	"	Fast Day (special) R. W. preaches at Salem—faithfully	31
Th.	18 Sept.	28 Sept.	"	Griffin arrives with copy of Commission of 28 Apr.–8 May	22
W.	5 Nov.	15 Nov.	"	Complaint that the flag has been mutilated at Salem	31
Th.	27 Nov.	7 Dec.	"	R. W. summoned to the Court	32
——	— Dec.	——	"	Cudworth writes that R. W. is at Salem, but not pastor	36
W.	19 Feb.	1 Mar.	1634–5	Court convenes the Elders for advice	23
M.	3 Mar.	13 Mar.	"	Court meets and orders continued military preparations	32
W.	1 Apr.	10 Apr.	1635	Resident's Oath enacted — which R. W. preaches against	33
Th.	30 Apr.	10 May	"	Court sends for R. W. in regard to that attack	33
Th.	14 May	24 May	"	Court modifies existing form of Freeman's Oath	33
——	——	——	"	R. W. ordained by Salem Church, its pastor	36
T.	16 June	26 June	"	Ship arrives with news that the old N. E. Council is dissolved	23
W.	8 July	18 July	"	R. W. cited to next Court to answer for his teaching against the Oaths, etc.	37
——	——	——	"	Salem people petition Court for some Marblehead land	38
——	——	——	"	The Court lays the petition on the table for the time	38
——	——	——	"	R. W. sends letters of complaint to the other churches	39
W.	22 July	1 Aug.	"	Boston Church replies to Salem Church letter	42
——	——	——	"	R. W. and Elder Sharpe reply to this Boston letter	42
S.	15 Aug.	25 Aug.	"	The Great Storm	43
S.	16 Aug.	26 Aug.	"	R. W. sick. Sends letter to his church withdrawing communion	44
W.	2 Sept.	12 Sept.	"	Court meets. Sends Salem Deputies home to ask questions	46
——	——	——	"	Writ of *Quo warranto* granted in England against Colony	23
T.	6 Oct.	16 Oct.	"	Particular Court meets at New Town	49
Th.	8 Oct.	18 Oct.	"	Gen. Court meets, and, among other things, tries R. W.	49
——	——	——	"	List of members. List of ministers, etc.	51
——	——	——	"	Court orders John Smyth beyond the jurisdiction	56
F.	9 Oct.	19 Oct.	"	R. W. "banished"	58
——	——	——	"	R. W. taken sick	60
F.	20 Nov.	30 Nov.	"	R. W.'s six weeks of leave expire, Court permits him to stay till spring, if he will not teach his views	60
——	——	——	"	Judgment given on the *Quo warranto* in London	23
——	——	——	"	R. W. recovers, breaks his pledge, and begins to preach again	61

Day of wk.	Month. Old Style.	Month. New Style.	Year.	Event.	Page.
—	— Jan.	—	1635–6	Court meet and take action in R. W.'s case	61
—	—	—	"	They send James Penn, their Marshal, to cite R. W. . . .	61
—	—	—	"	A committee from Salem insist that he is still too sick . . .	62
—	—	—	"	R. W. starts through the woods for *Sowams*	62
—	—	—	"	The Court direct Underhill to put R. W. on board ship . .	62
—	—	—	"	He goes to Salem for that purpose, but finds the bird flown.	62
—	— Aug.	—	1636	R. W. writes to Mr. Winthrop asking advice	91
F.	10 Nov.	20 Nov.	1637	R. W. buys Prudence of *Canonicus* for Gov. Winthrop . .	92
—	Early	in	1638	R. W. is rebaptized	114
M.	21 May	31 May	"	Providence disfranchises Verin	93
T.	22 May	1 June	"	R. W. writes Gov. Winthrop about Verin	92
M.	1 July	11 July	1639	Hugh Peter notifies the Dorchester Church that Salem Church has excommunicated R. W.	64
𝔖.	8 Mar.	18 Mar.	1640	R. W. writes Gov. Winthrop about Samuel Gorton	92
—	— July	—	1641	Anabaptists first mentioned in New England	115
—	—	—	1643	Wm. Witter at Swampscot calls Infant Baptism hard names	119
Th.	14 Mar.	24 Mar.	1643–4	R. W. gets first Charter of Rhode Island	103
—	— July	—	1644	T. Painter refuses to have his child baptized at Hingham .	115
W.	13 Nov.	23 Nov.	"	General Court pass a law against the Anabaptists	116
—	Autumn	—	1645	Divers persons request an alteration in this law	116
W.	18 Feb.	28 Feb.	1645–6	Witter is presented at Salem Court for violent speech on Baptism	119
—	Spring	—	1646	Seventy-eight persons petition for alteration in Anabaptist law	116
W.	4 Nov.	14 Nov.	"	General Court adopt declaration about Anabaptists, etc. . .	116
—	Autumn	—	1648	Ed. Starbuck commits some Anabaptistical offence	118
—	—	—	1649	Obadiah Holmes *et al.* secede from Rehoboth Church and form an Anabaptist Church	118
—	Summer	—	"	Complaint made to Plymouth Court of Holmes, *et al.* . . .	118
Th.	18 Oct.	28 Oct.	"	Mass. General Court write letter to Plymouth Court about Holmes *et al.*, remonstrating against its mild way of treating them	118
M.	29 Oct.	8 Nov.	"	Plymouth Court acts mildly towards them, notwithstanding,	118
—	—	—	1650	Holmes goes to Newport and joins Clarke's Anabaptist Church there	118
—	Summer	—	"	Coddington obtains in England New Charter for R. I. . .	119
W.	30 Oct.	9 Nov.	"	Geo. Fox first imprisoned in England as a Quaker, and that new Sect begins to make a noise in the world	124
W.	16 July	26 July	1651	Clarke and party leave Newport to obtain a little persecution in Massachusetts	120
S.	19 July	29 July	"	They reach Witter's house at Swampscot	120
𝔖.	20 July	30 July	"	Clarke preaches there, and the party is arrested	120
M.	21 July	31 July	"	They get back clandestinely to Witter's house and finish service, having rebaptized Witter	121
T.	22 July	1 Aug.	"	Are sent to Boston jail	121
Th.	31 July	10 Aug.	"	Have their trial	121
F.	5 Sept.	15 Sept.	"	Holmes whipped — having insisted upon it	121
T.	25 Nov.	5 Dec.	"	Witter presented at Salem Court for having been rebaptized	120
—	—	—	1654	As many as 60 Quaker Missionaries at work in Europe . .	125
W.	18 Oct.	28 Oct.	" "	First Quaker books arrive in Mass., and are made light of in the market-place, by Court-order	126
—	— Jan.	—	1654–5	R. W. explains to his fellow citizens of Providence what he means by liberty of conscience	96

Day of wk.	MONTH. Old Style.	MONTH. New Style.	YEAR.	EVENT.	Page.
W.	14 May	24 May	1656	Fast Day ordered in Mass. with special reference to Quakers, and other calamities	127
F.	11 July	21 July	"	First detachment of Quakers arrive in Boston from Barbadoes, and the magistrates — under law of 1637 — order them sent back	127
Th.	7 Aug.	17 Aug.	"	Second lot come	127
T.	2 Sept.	12 Sept.	"	Gen. Court addresses Commissioners of the United Colonies on the subject	127
Th.	4 Sept.	14 Sept.	"	Commissioners advise Courts to pass laws against Quakers	
T.	14 Oct.	24 Oct.	"	Mass. Gen. Court enacts such a law	127
——	——	——	"	Thomas Gould of Charlestown presented for Anabaptism .	122
T.	19 May	29 May	1657	R. W. charges W. Harris with high treason	94
S.	4 July	14 July	"	That charge heard and acted upon	94
F.	6 June	16 June	1658	Charlestown Church labors with Thomas Gould	122
Th.	23 Sept.	3 Oct.	"	Quaker law amended so that return after banishment should be "on pajne of death"	129
T.	19 Oct.	29 Oct.	"	Court banish first six Quakers under new law, and direct John Norton to write a book against the Sect	130
T.	23 Nov.	3 Dec.	"	The Quaker Ed. Burrough attacks Cromwell's funeral . .	125
Th.	27 Oct.	6 Nov.	1659	Robinson and Stevenson hanged	130
F.	1 June	11 June	1660	Mary Dyer hanged	131
T.	4 Dec.	14 Dec.	"	Parliament orders the disinterment of Cromwell, Bradshaw and Ireton, and that their remains be hanged, and their heads stuck up on Westminster Hall	106
Th.	14 Mar.	24 Mar.	1660–1	William Leddra hanged	131
F.	7 June	17 June	1661	Winlock Christison begs off	131
M.	9 Sept.	19 Sept.	"	So-called "*Mandamus*" issued by Charles II. at Whitehall	132
——	— Nov.	——	"	Served on the Massachusetts authorities	132
T.	26 Nov.	6 Dec.	"	A Baptist preacher hanged at Tyburn	124
S.	8 Nov.	18 Nov.	1663	Thos. Gould starts a private Anabaptist meeting in his house at Charlestown	122
T.	1 Mar.	11 Mar.	1663–4	R. W. active under a Charter in R. I., identical with that which he had denounced in Mass.	102
S.	28 May	7 June	1665	Gould's meeting grows into what is now 1st Bapt. Ch., Boston	122
S.	30 July	9 Aug.	"	Gould excommunicated by Charlestown Church	122
——	——	——	"	Deborah Wilson promenades Salem in extreme undress . .	134
S.	——	——	"	Lydia Wardell marches naked into Newbury meeeting . .	134
T.	14 Apr.	24 Apr.	1668	Great debate with Baptists at Boston commences	123
Th.	7 May	17 May	"	Gould *et al.* banished and imprisoned	123
W.	14 Oct.	24 Oct.	"	Gould *et al.* petition for release, being reënforced by the petition of 66 others	123
——	——	——	1670	Gould set at liberty	123
F.	9 Aug.	19 Aug.	1672	R. W's. great debate with the Quakers begins at Newport	135
S.	8 July	18 July	1677	Margaret Brewster disturbs the Old South meeting	134
S.	15 Jan.	25 Jan.	1680–1	R. W. to Town Clerk of Providence, urges the duty of every man's upholding the civil authority	98
——	— Mar.	——	1681–2	Colony reports to the king that the Anabaptists are no longer discriminated against in its laws	123
——	— July	——	1683	Dunham tried at Plymouth for sacrificing a dog, in his Quaker orgies at Little Compton	135
F.	23 Oct.	2 Nov.	1685	Elizabeth Gaunt, an Anabaptist, burned at Tyburn, Eng. .	124
Th.	21 June	1 July	1688	Geo. Keith posts his fierce Quaker "warning" in the Market-place at Boston	133

www.ingramcontent.com/pod-product-compliance
Lightning Source LLC
LaVergne TN
LVHW021407110826

845150LV00007B/1821

* 9 7 8 1 4 2 5 5 1 1 7 9 1 *